Trauma and
FULFILLMENT THERAPY

SERIES IN TRAUMA AND LOSS

CONSULTING EDITORS

Charles R. Figley and Therese A. Rando

TRAUMA AND FULFILLMENT THERAPY
A Wholist Framework

By
Paul Valent,
MBBS, DPM (ENG), FRANZCP

USA	Publishing Office:	BRUNNER/MAZEL
		A member of the Taylor & Francis Group
		325 Chestnut Street
		Philadelphia, PA 19106
		Tel: (215) 625-8900
		Fax: (215) 625-2940
	Distribution Center:	BRUNNER/MAZEL
		A member of the Taylor & Francis Group
		47 Runway Road
		Levittown, PA 19057
		Tel: (215) 269-0400
		Fax: (215) 269-0363
UK		BRUNNER/MAZEL
		A member of the Taylor & Francis Group
		1 Gunpowder Square
		London EC4A 3DE
		Tel: +44 171 583 0490
		Fax: +44 171 583 0581

TRAUMA AND FULFILLMENT THERAPY: A Wholist Framework

1 2 3 4 5 6 7 8 9 0

Printed by Braun-Brumfield, Ann Arbor, MI, 1998.
Cover design by Carolyn O'Brien.

A CIP catalog record for this book is available from the British Library.

∞ The paper in this publication meets the requirements of the ANSI Standard Z39.48-1984 (Permanence of Paper)

Library of Congress Cataloging-in-Publication Data

Valent, Paul.
   Trauma and fulfillment therapy: a wholist framework / Paul
Valent.
     p. cm.—(Series in trauma and loss, ISSN 1090-9575)
    Includes bibliographical references (p. 195).

    1. Psychic trauma—Treatment—Philosophy. 2. Self-realization—
Therapeutic use. I. Title. II. Series.
RC552-T7V34 1998
616.85'2106—dc21   98-30412
                                                                  CIP

ISBN 0-87630-938-4 (alk. paper)
ISBN 0-87630-939-2 (pbk. : alk. paper)

Contents

Preface

People have always been vitally interested in the forces which disrupted, and those which fulfilled their lives. Whether called the forces of chaos and order, light and dark, good and evil, life and death, a dialectic has been implied in which opposing divine or semidivine protagonists determine human destiny. As well as the ephemeral nature of these forces, their apparently opposing features may blur. For instance, killing may be seen as good or evil at different times, and death can be experienced as a meaningful part of life.

The title of this book, *Trauma and Fulfillment Therapy,* implies replacement of the above dialectics with a new one. It also implies that the new protagonists in this dialectic, trauma and fulfillment (of life), can be studied scientifically, and further, that this science can help to tip the balance toward the fulfillment part of the dialectic.

The new scientific discipline which encompasses this dialectic is traumatology. That is, traumatology is the study of serious threats to the survival and fulfillment of life. It aims to mitigate effects of trauma and enhance life's fulfillment—hence the term trauma and fulfillment therapy.

Trauma can disrupt every aspect of human fulfillment. It may produce biological, psychological, and social turmoil, make the nightmares of mankind tangible, and disrupt the sense of a coherent, moral, principled, spiritual, meaningful, and purposeful sense of self and the universe. To grapple with this range of human issues requires a philosophical approach which encompasses the whole range of human fulfillments and traumas.

Such a philosophical view is offered in this book under the name of the wholist view or philosophy. Wholist implies whole, encompasses holist from holistic (a combination of biological, psychological, and social), and also hol of holonic (Koestler, 1983). Holonic includes the range from w(hol)e down to the smallest parts, the "on" signifying electr(on), prot(on), et cetera.

The simultaneously unifying and specifying view presented resembles quantum mechanics where views of the cosmos and atoms also mutually enlighten each other. Yet, in everyday life too, visual and metaphorical views capture complex nonlinear physical and mental situations. For instance, in the physical world such a view of trees (comprising roots, trunk, branches, leaves, bark, sap, circulation, physiology, place in forest) rather than restricted partial views, may form practical bases to view health and damage. The same may be said of the metaphorical tree of life of humans.

In traumatology a pebble hitting a pond is often used to symbolize trauma, and the subsequent ripples its effects. In the wholist view many reasons may influence different types of pebbles to hit different ponds, and the different facets of pebbles at the time of impact and properties of ponds determine the three-dimensional nature of ripples. The wholist perspective facilitates both total views of ponds and pebbles, as well as point, line, and volume sectors of it.

While the wholist philosophy is governed by an overarching life-trauma dialectic, its view here is called the wholist perspective. Described in detail in a previous volume (Valent, 1998a) and summarized in this one, the wholist perspective is noted to comprise the triaxial framework and survival strategies.

The triaxial framework contains three dimensions of trauma and life which may be likened to matter, space, and time freezing out from the big bang's soup of energy. The triaxial framework provides dimensions or coordinates by which traumatic stress and fulfillment phenomena can be orientated. Its three dimensions or axes are the process, parameters, and depth axes. The process axis describes the process from stressors through traumas to illnesses, or alternatively to adaptive satisfactions. The parameter axis describes parameters of situations, including type of traumatic situation, disaster phases, phase in life cycle of victims, and their social system level (individual, group, and so on). The depth axis defines the level of human function, ranging from physiological/instinctive through morality, values, identity, to spiritual and existential purpose levels.

Survival strategies are like primary colors or notes of an octave, which provide the tapestries or symphonies of life and its disruptions over the dimensions of the triaxial framework. The eight survival strategies are rescue-caretaking, attachment, assertiveness/goal achievement, adaptation/goal surrender, fight, flight, competition, and cooperation. Their adaptive and maladaptive, biological, psychological, and social components, and defenses against them, provide the different qualities which provide particular multiplicities of clinical pictures.

The wholist perspective then is like a dictionary which translates nature's arrangements of trauma and fulfillment (arranged in what may be called wholist language) into ordinary language. Wholist perspective components are then like metaphors and equations, which indicate the patterns of nature's linguistic associations, and help to give structure to apparent chaos. In other words, the wholist perspective and its language help to make sense of, and can meaningfully categorize, the great variety of fluctuating, often contradictory traumatic stress and fulfillment manifestations.

Attempts to repair human disruptions have been almost as varied as their manifestations. The wholist perspective does not invent new therapies or techniques, but it is suggested that its language can clarify, classify, give perspective, enrich, and extend current ones.

This is made somewhat easier by the discovery of overarching treatment principles (also called treatment elements or ingredients), which are shown to be ubiquitously present in different proportions in all trauma therapies. The elements are recognition and diagnosis of trauma and its ramifications, non-specific (counter-trauma) therapy, symptomatic treatment, and specific trauma and fulfillment therapy. These elements are detailed in the book.

Applied to each treatment element, the wholist perspective hones, defines, unifies, and specifies it and its components. The perspective thus facilitates rich yet efficiently tailored treatment. For instance, as part of specific trauma therapy it facilitates dual focus of attention on past maladaptive and current adaptive survival strategies. Doing so at many points and intersections of the triaxial framework enhances new meanings and significances over the different human dimensions.

The book consists of four parts. Part 1 introduces the apparent chaos of both traumatic stress and fulfillment manifestations and their treatments. Chapter 1 does so through three clinical examples, but also introduces the life-trauma dialectic and the wholist perspective. Chapter 2 highlights different treatments which have been developed in various traumatic situations such as war, psychosomatic medicine, bereavement, and sexual abuse, and sees how Janet and Freud conceptualized trauma therapy. Next, different forms of therapy such as drugs, "power therapies," cognitive behavior, and psychodynamic therapies are presented. Finally, the four treatment principles of trauma therapy are abstracted.

Part 2 presents the wholist perspective. Chapter 3 describes the triaxial framework and chapter 4 describes the eight survival strategies across the triaxial framework.

Part 3 describes how the wholist perspective is applied to the four treatment elements. Chapter 5 deals with recognition and reading the modes and means of communication in the wholist language. It gives examples of honing and categorization of traumatic stress and fulfillment manifestations. Categorizations of anxieties, guilts, angers, meanings, values, and religious views are presented. Chapter 6 applies the wholist perspective to the other treatment elements—nonspecific, symptomatic, and specific therapies. Planning and tailoring of treatment and research issues are addressed.

Part 4 provides clinical examples of trauma and fulfillment therapy. Chapter 7 examines general issues such as length of therapies and the nature of the fulfillment part of therapy. It gives clinical examples which highlight use of triaxial framework, survival strategy, and defense concepts. Chapter 8 indicates treatment issues at the time or soon after traumatic events. Chapter 9 takes up treatment in early stages but when symptoms may already become entrenched, and categories of symptoms and illnesses are suggested as heuristically and practically useful. Chapter 10 examines therapies in adults who had suffered severe childhood traumas. Aspects of recognition, reading the wholist language, and memories are addressed. Chapter 11 examines conceptualization of helper symptoms and illnesses parallel to those of victims, and examines transgenerational trauma transmission. Chapter 12 concludes the book.

Though the book concentrates on trauma and fulfillment therapy, of necessity it touches many important issues and helps to clarify them. They include the nature and validity of memory; the nature of defenses (a taxonomy of defenses is presented); the nature of morals, principles, values, dignity, identity, meanings, the sacred, and purpose. Hence this book is of interest not only to traumatologists and medical, psychiatric, and social health professionals, but to lawyers, ethicists (a code of traumatology ethics is suggested), students of humanist philosophies, and the public in general.

As noted at the beginning of the preface, views and treatments of human ills are influenced by philosophies of the day, and they are often expressed in contemporaneous myths. For instance, in keeping with human disasters being explained as punishment for sins, the sin of eating of the tree of the knowledge of good and evil was used to explain human travails.

Traumatology may offer a reinterpretation of this myth. Eating from the tree of the knowledge of good and evil is gaining knowledge of fulfillment and trauma. Expulsion from paradise means relinquishing the fantasy that supernatural forces protect us. Being made in the image of God, and now having achieved Godlike knowledge means that there is only mankind which can work for its own salvation. The need for knowledge tips from that of knowing God to knowing nature and mankind itself. One of Adam's first tasks was to name and categorize nature. The toil continues in traumatology. Integrating knowledge of trauma and fulfillment helps tip the balance in the favor of the latter.

Acknowledgments

One of the most pleasant tasks in writing this book is to be able to express gratitude to those who contributed to me being able to write it.

In one way it has been a very long journey from the murky, unexpressed traumas of the past to the secure and happy present in which words can now express experiences. First and foremost, I thank my parents who provided for me as much as possible a counter-trauma environment and opportunities to learn.

I have been lucky to have had many further opportunities to learn in medicine, psychiatry, psychotherapy, liaison psychiatry, and varied trauma work. I have had many good teachers and supervisors to whom I am grateful.

Thanks go to physicians Drs. Ian Jones (deceased), Graeme Schmidt, and Peter Williams who encouraged me to pursue my interests in biopsychosocial medicine, and introduced me to the rich world of dying patients. Thanks go to Dr. Bill Orchard who encouraged me in liaison psychiatry, and special thanks go to Dr. Allen Yuen, who as Director of the Emergency Department at Prince Henry's Hospital and Monash Medical Center encouraged me in liaison work there. Our friendship continues. Thanks go to the staff in those departments who supported me. Their names are too many to mention but Drs. Graeme Thomson and Craig Castle, Sisters Irene Kinsella and Helen Ryan, and Berenice Neumann come immediately to mind. I am grateful to our liaison and traumatology team members, especially Tony Catanese and Ellen Berah, as well as my many registrars, interns, and students who helped me develop my thoughts.

In the making of this book I am grateful to Prof. Charles Figley, Dr. Ian Thomas, and my wife Julie for reading my chapters. I am thankful to Sue Wind for her library help and to Fred Hocking for lending me his precious books. And I am particularly grateful to my publisher Taylor & Francis, and editors Bernadette Capelle and Erik Shveima for their patience, understanding, and execution of the book into print. I acknowledge Brunner/Mazel for allowing me to reprint the figures and Table 2 in this book from previous publications. I am grateful to the Australasian Society of Traumatic Stress Studies for allowing me to share my submission to them for a code of ethics (which has since been accepted by the Society).

Very special gratitude goes to Prof. Charles Figley, who originally suggested that I write these two volumes. It has taken more time than either of us thought to have produced them, and I am grateful for the unswerving continual support and loyalty Charles offered me throughout this time. I thank him also for his friendship which developed and cemented itself over this time.

Without my family this book could not have been written. Dani helped me with the references, Ariel with the figures, Amy with her cheer. But the support, understanding, tolerance, and above all, the image of happiness provided by all of my children was an inspiration. I thank my mother-in-law Jo for her continued support and for listening to me over cups of coffee.

My wife Julie has been the cornerstone of support throughout the writing of these books. Her normality, cheer, love, help, devotion, and faith when things were uncertain or tense were such that, without them, the book could not have been written. My family gave me the safety and security, happiness and hope which were necessary to balance the immersion in trauma in this book. I thank them and hope the book will be some little reward for their efforts.

Last but not least, I thank the many patients who taught me so much through sharing with me their traumas and strengths, and who have permitted me to use the material from their treatments for this book. I dedicate this book to them, and the others who may benefit from this book.

Part One

Introduction to Traumatic Stress and Its Treatment

This section introduces the wide range of traumatic situations, disaster phases, and traumatic sequelae which trauma and fulfillment treatment need to address. Such situations, it will be shown, span biological, psychological, and social arenas, and human levels from physiology to the soul.

Chapter 1 introduces the life-trauma dialectic, the basic philosophy which underlies this breadth and depth of trauma and fulfillment. This is followed by three case vignettes which illustrate the range of traumatology and challenges to conceptualization and effecting trauma and fulfillment treatment within it. In the latter part of the chapter the wholist model with its triaxial framework and survival strategy constituents is introduced. This model, presented more fully in a previous book (Valent, 1998a), will be used to conceptualize traumatology phenomena and treatment principles in later chapters.

Chapter 2 presents a historical overview. First, the views of Janet and Freud, the pioneers of trauma therapy, are presented. Next, treatments in a variety of traumatic situations are reviewed. This is followed by a review of the major forms of therapy which have evolved. Finally, four important and ubiquitous treatment principles are abstracted from the literature.

Chapter 1

Introduction

The concept of trauma and fulfillment treatment reflects the view taken in this book, that trauma is the other pole of life, forming with it a *life-trauma* dialectic.

Philosophers have thought that death was the opposite dialectical partner to life, represented by ultimate terror and the gnawing fear affecting everything (Becker, 1973). And yet death may also be seen as the final fulfillment of a ripe life, a chosen option to help others, or a way out of a life with no meaning. It may be that ultimate (traumatic) threat is not to life, but to a meaningful life, to purposeful survival and fulfillment. Death is terrifying and absurd (Lifton, 1980) only when it threatens to terminate the hope of a purposeful life. People struggle to survive as long as they have the hope of a fulfilling life.

Within the life-trauma dialectic the purpose of life then may be said to be **to survive and fulfill oneself according to the life cycle, and to help others do the same. Trauma is a threat to purposeful survival and fulfillment according to the life cycle of self and others**.

Trauma and fulfillment treatment then entails treating trauma and its sequelae while at the same time enhancing hope and fulfillment.

Just as trauma affects every part of life, dealing with it has been extremely varied. The range has spanned from blaming victims for having been sinful and adding to their punishments, to helping them at the cost of helpers' lives and health. The young science of traumatology (Donovan, 1991; 1993) is still evolving concepts to understand both stress and trauma and their treatment. However, it is clear that treatment requires not only easing discomforts but also restoration of a fulfilling life.

> A woman whose husband had been murdered said, "I can put up with my PTSD symptoms which make sense. What I can't put up with is that my life has no meaning. Perhaps you can help me share what I know with others whose families were murdered."

The woman also demonstrates two broad approaches of treatment in traumatology. The first relies on a phenomenological illness model (Chapter 3), where clusters of symptoms form particular illnesses such as Post-Traumatic Stress Disorder (PTSD) (American Psychiatric Association, 1980; 1994) and for which specific treatments are sought. The other approach is dynamic, which ameliorates various stress responses through understanding their variable sources—for instance, the woman's guilt for not saving her husband. In practice the two approaches overlap. The wholist approach subsumes and extends both approaches, for instance, by attempting to realign disrupted morality, meanings, and purpose. The life-trauma dialectic applied to the woman may indicate that her survival and even comfort are not enough without fulfillment, and that if her own life is no longer happy, it may still be fulfilling if it helps others' lives.

The following three cases illustrate the difficulty of applying any simple model to understanding traumatic stress phenomena and their treatment. The cases have been previously used to highlight the complexity of stress responses and illnesses (Valent, 1998a). Here the complexity of treatment approaches is added.

CASE 1: A BUSHFIRE

> People responded, as they later said, instinctively. Depending on circumstances they risked themselves to help others, ignored others' needs, and even competed with others such as for the sole exit road or wet towels. States of being stunned fluctuated with superhuman effort. Anger with those who did not help or allow to be helped alternated with guilt for not helping.
>
> An outreach team from a city hospital made contact with known professionals in the area. An advance party assessed local needs. They included the need to be listened to by outsiders who could provide information, empathy, and perspective. Within three days of the fire a community base was established where people could be counseled and from where team members visited all families in the area. Vulnerable people, such as the bereaved, were given priority. Medical examination, information about help, and listening in order to make sense of responses were provided. Physiological and emotional reactions, as well as intense guilts, regrets,

and angers, were put in context of survival needs of self and others. This provided much relief.

Local help groups and networks were facilitated. Local helping personnel were first helped themselves and then briefed on how best to help others. At the same time, information about common responses in adults and children was distributed through pamphlets (Valent, Berah, Jones, Wraith and Hill, 1995—see Appendix 1 for a later version) and the media. Team members were debriefed daily.

It may be seen that intervention was outreach, early, and took into account various social systems (individual, family, etc.) and ages in the community. Interventions were biological, psychological, and social. People were helped to relate their stories and to understand their physical, cognitive, emotional, moral, and meaning responses in context. Team members catered to each other's distress. The team itself was supported by the parent hospital.

People became incensed with bureaucratic insensitivity, though at times the anger was transferred from earlier experiences. Depending on the cause, advocacy, facilitation to be effective, or putting the anger in its earlier context were attempted.

Social, physical, and psychological responses became more wide-ranging and individuals required more tailored treatment. A man who had felt that he had no right to be sad became deeply depressed "for no apparent reason." Giving him permission to cry over his losses allowed him to grieve and his depression lifted. A woman was concerned that she had not noticed her son's squint three years prior. She compounded that experience with not having saved her son from experiencing the fires, and derived the meaning that she was a bad mother. Allowing her to see that she was not responsible for either event relieved her greatly.

A man presented with acute chest pain and fear of a heart attack. Muscle tension due to utter frustration was diagnosed. The man was relieved of his fear and allowed to ventilate his frustration. Later, beside his burnt house he explained how the purpose of his life lay there in ashes. However, he could not grieve his losses without opening up old wounds which had made his house so central to his life. Healing those wounds took months of therapy (Case 13, Chapter 9).

Some pushed their experiences from their minds, but sometimes they intruded against their will. Reconnection with unprocessed painful aspects of their trauma and processing led to relief.

Community meetings were facilitated which dealt with common responses and community problems. The local professionals now informally joined the outreach team.

In this phase, too, interventions were variably biological, psychological, and social and at different social system levels. Treatment of depression and anxiety symptoms, as well as judgments and meanings, needed increased sophistication, because at times conscious connections with the recent trauma were severed or compounded with other traumas. It became more difficult to predict speed of resolution of symptoms. It also required sensitivity to balance attempts to close people's gaps in memory (overcome defenses) at the cost of pain and time out from rebuilding, when not doing so could cost callousness, drinking, physical symptoms, and relationship problems.

> Numerous physical symptoms arose in the following months and local doctor attendances increased. Marital counseling saved some marriages but did not stem the increased divorce rate. A skeleton mental health staff helped numerous victims in various ways over two years.

Symptoms broadened and became entrenched into a variety of biological, psychological, and social dysfunctions requiring a variety of treatments.

CASE 2: ANGINA IN THE EMERGENCY DEPARTMENT

A 48-year-old woman whose chest pain was eventually diagnosed as angina was asked in a routine way, "Of all the things that worry you what worries you the most?" Her husband replied, "Stress" and she added, "It is like rage you cannot express." This was connected with having been dismissed recently after 25 years of loyal service.

However, for eighteen months both she and her husband had attended doctors for many symptoms, both believing they had fatal illnesses. This was connected with the death of their eight-year-old daughter in a vehicle accident seventeen years prior. The substitute daughter was approaching the age of eight. The patient was reliving the rage with her husband she had felt at the time of the first daughter's death.

Pointing out the coincidence of the current daughter now approaching eight, the couple burst into sobs, appreciating the poignancy of that age for the first time. They were able to redirect their attention to their anxiety about the current daughter repeating the old history. The patient also came to understand that with the recent sacking and her daughter's expected death, she came to see her life as having become meaningless. The father saw that his symptoms resembled what he imagined his daughter suffered at the moment of impact just before she died.

Stress levels and the variety of physical symptoms settled in both spouses. The angina was well controlled, and the daughter survived.

This case illustrates that trauma treatment may be beneficial for people who present their traumatic stress with physical symptoms. It also shows how much can be achieved (especially at a time of crisis) with a relatively minor, though well-directed intervention. For further information, see "Spanning Categories of Illnesses," Chapter 10.

CASE 3: A CHILD SURVIVOR OF THE HOLOCAUST

Anne (described in more detail elsewhere (Valent, 1994a and Chapter 10), was a Jewish child orphaned in the Holocaust. She was abused and raped in families which were supposed to hide and protect her. Over many years Anne was treated for depression by antidepressants, for sleeplessness with hypnotics, and for headaches with analgesics.

Forty-five years postwar Anne joined a child survivor group and entered psychotherapy. Through them she gained respect and self-respect for the first time, and a sense that her life was worthwhile. For the first time too, she started to tell her story in therapy. Increased hope allowed her to remember more, in ever greater detail and vividness, piecing together painful meanings. She told her story through a book on child survivors. She hoped her story would help others. She became more involved in the group, more alive, and even happy.

She ceased her medications as her depression ceased with grief for her parents, her headaches ceased when she stopped being angry with them for abandoning her, and she slept somewhat better when she put her night time persecutors back into the past. Her improvement has continued over years.

Anne demonstrates that even after decades of the most horrific events treatment, though complex and prolonged, can be efficacious even if not curative. Peer group and testimony were important adjuncts to treatment (see also Case 38, p. 142).

COMPLEXITIES OF TREATMENT AND THE WHOLIST PERSPECTIVE

The wholist perspective provides a framework for traumatic stress and fulfillment phenomena, and trauma and fulfillment treatment. Its first constituent, the triaxial framework, provides orientation, while survival strategies provide sense and content to both.

The Triaxial Framework

The first or process axis orientates phenomena and treatments at the various points in the process between stressors and illnesses. For instance, biological, psychological, and social responses could be treated by reestablishing memory connections between the fragmented symptoms and their original contexts.

The parameters axis orientates according to the type of traumatic situation, phase of disaster (ranging from preimpact phase to decades later), social system levels (ranging from individuals to communities), and age of victims.

The depth axis locates manifestations and treatment at different levels of human function, ranging from instinctive survival levels through moral judgments including guilt and shame, to refinding meaning, self, spirituality, and life's purpose.

Survival Strategies

Survival strategies such as fight, flight, and goal surrender help to pinpoint and make specific sense of stress and trauma manifestations and their specific fulfillment opposites. They make sense of the great variety of often contradictory stress responses and help their categorizations. Survival strategies thereby facilitate specific counter-trauma and fulfillment therapy (Chapter 7).

In summary, the great variety of clinical manifestations and treatments in traumatic stress were exemplified by three cases. It is suggested that a wholist perspective may provide an organization for such complexity. Before presenting the wholist framework, a historical view of treatments is presented in the next chapter.

Chapter 2

History of Trauma Treatment

In this chapter a brief historical overview will highlight particular treatments found useful in different traumatic situations. This will be followed by a review of commonly used treatments. Finally, some ingredients or principles of treatment common to all situations will be abstracted.

HISTORY TO THE END OF THE 19TH CENTURY

In the Dark Ages catastrophes were blamed on sinners who were tortured and sometimes killed in masses to be rid of the demons inhabiting them (Abse, 1984). Exorcism became a kinder process which drove out inner demons. Exorcists used religious as well as personal charisma, and used altered states of consciousness, ritual, suggestion, and emotional release in their methods.

Two hundred years ago Mesmer and subsequent hypnotists used similar techniques in a secular setting. In the last century Charcot finally wrested mental aberrations from religion and renamed possession as hysteria. He maintained that hysteria developed out of psychic trauma via hypnotic-like "hypnoid" states. Therefore, he maintained, hysteria could be reversed hypnotically (Freud, 1886; Abse, 1984). The bridge was now established from shamanistic to psychotherapeutic techniques of treatment. They were taken up by Charcot's students Janet and Freud.

Janet

Janet believed that hysterias (which actually included a wide psychopathology) were traumatically induced disorders of memory. He believed that retrieval and assimilation of the memories effected cure (van der Hart & Horst, 1989).

The process of memory work, Janet said, required an environment of safety, calm, and a strong trusting relationship, relevant education, physiotherapy, and hydrotherapy, and drugs such as bromides and opium.

Techniques of actual traumatic memory retrieval used hypnosis, imaging techniques, fantasies, and dreams. The relived memories were then "neutralized" or assimilated, through substitution of positive images for the traumatic ones through hypnosis, and reinterpreting traumatic events into less distressing frameworks.

Janet recognized that a fixation on the therapist gave the latter powers of suggestion which could lead to apparent, but only temporary cures. He warned against panaceas, insisted on thorough working through, warned of different layers of traumatic memories, and indicated that therapeutic success may take years and be incomplete, especially in the case of childhood traumas.

Freud

Freud, like Janet, found that hypnosis and suggestion alone were insufficient to cure symptoms. However, unlike Janet, who concentrated on cognitive reinterpretation of traumatic events to complete the process, Breuer and Freud (1893) added emotional abreaction of retrieved memories to neutralize them. They said, "... *each individual hysterical symptom immediately and permanently disappeared when we had succeeded in bringing clearly to light the memory of the event by which it was provoked and in arousing its accompanying affect...*" (p. 6, their italics). The process of emotional abreaction they called catharsis, derived from purging poisons. The poison was forbidden affects.

Breuer and Freud also experienced intense personal patient fixations. It may be because of them that Breuer left psychotherapy and Freud changed his technique from hypnosis to free association (Kleber & Brom, 1992).

However, Freud (1905a) came to see the fixations as an important therapeutic tool. He called it transference, because into the relationship were transferred with ineluctable immediacy earlier traumas. Catharsis then occurred in the poignant transferential situation but, unlike in hypnosis, past and present met in a real piece of life.

Freud warned that transference of authority from earlier parental figures onto the therapist enhanced the latter's power of suggestion, but suggestion-based transference cures faded with loss of positive transference. Like Janet,

Freud became sanguine about the simplicity, immediacy, and permanence of his abreactive treatment (Freud, 1914a). He saw that much time might have to be spent on defenses in order that memories could flow more freely, but noted that it was not wise to push patients to remember. Freud came to give patients more control of their thinking, and conveyed to them that their illnesses were not contemptible, but understandable in terms of the past. He believed that synthesis of the past and new meanings would allow patients to form richer personalities.

In summary, Janet and Freud presaged and often went beyond cyclically rediscovered trauma therapies. While both pioneers overlapped in their conceptualizations and techniques, Janet emphasized a cognitive approach while Freud emphasized emotions. The latter also highlighted the need to overcome defenses and the use of transference. Their theoretical emphases reverberate in cognitive and psychodynamic based therapies to this day.

TREATMENT ACCORDING TO TRAUMATIC SITUATIONS IN THE 20TH CENTURY

Military Psychiatry

Because of the massive numbers of casualties, wars have often led to (re)discoveries of trauma treatment. The last major example was the Vietnam War.

First World War   With the failure of exhortation punishment and electric shocks, recognition of shell shock as a psychological condition led to principles of proximity, immediacy, and expectancy (meaning expectation that the soldier would return to duty) (Salmon, 1919). Kardiner (1941) noted that most acute battle conditions cleared up with rest, sedatives, and hypnosis, if there was a concomitant atmosphere of safety, nurturance, and personal interest in the soldier. Group education about the normality of responses, and tasks and games which returned a sense of control to the soldiers, also helped.

Recovery from amnesia, possibly aided by hypnosis, with subsequent abreaction and catharsis was often used. However, Kardiner noted that recovery of memory was not the prime object of therapy, for it was but a symptom of a crushed ego. Hope and formation of a new ego were needed, into which the trauma was eventually assimilated. Memory was retrieved if the soldier was allowed to tell his story at his own pace. Otherwise, worsening of the condition and even violence could occur. Benefit depended to a large extent on the relationship with the therapist (Abse, 1984; Barker, 1996).

Second World War   Exhortation, shaming, punishment, and forced return to duty again had to give way to proximity immediacy and expectancy, rest, recreation, reassurance, education, and specific trauma treatment. Indeed, Grinker and Spiegel (1944; 1945/1979) and Bartemeier, Kubie, Menninger, Romano, and Whitehorn (1946) warned against return to duty as a measure of outcome, for it could be an artifact measuring psychiatrists' keenness to contribute to the war effort and, by demonstrating their usefulness, to ensure their own safety (Needles, 1946). On the other hand, Grinker and Spiegel (1945/1979) emphasized that psychiatrists within army units with first-hand knowledge of men's experiences and fears could *preempt* morale problems and breakdowns.

Specific treatment for *acute breakdowns* again involved recovery of traumatic experiences (possibly aided by Pentothal injections) and their abreaction. Again, this needed to be done in a nurturing environment and within a protective therapeutic transference in order to avoid aggravation (Lidz, 1946).

Entrenched war neuroses were treated in rear hospitals trying every available drug, but without effect. Two month programs included educative group therapy, destigmatizing, and morale building. Occupational and social therapies aimed to achieve constructive goals and to regain social skills and self-esteem. Focal psychotherapy aimed to desensitize memories through abreactions and educative contrast between past and present.

Grinker and Spiegel (1945/1979, p. 372) quote Kubie regarding what psychotherapy really needed to (and often did not) address. "It is not merely the recovery of an event which releases the patient, nor . . . the recovery of the event plus the feelings and desires which derive from that event. It is the discovery of the totality of the purposes, the hopes, the fears, the loves and the hates which animated the individual at the moment of the event, plus what that event did to those purposes, loves, and fears and hates, and how these were deviated by that event from their initial pathway onto another. This, and not less than this, is the potent discovery."

Military Psychiatry Since the Second World War   The lessons of the world wars were forgotten in Vietnam (Bloch, 1969). For instance, Pettera, Johnson, and Zimmer (1969) reported that their "new therapeutic approach" insisted that soldiers return to duty. Soldiers then came to equate psychiatry with the military machine which forced them to suffer, commit atrocities, and be brutalized (Lifton, 1978). Israeli reports before the Yom Kippur (1973) and Lebanon (1982–85) Wars were also optimistic and judged by return to duty (e.g., Toubiana, Milgram, & Falach, 1986).

Vietnam veterans were slow to receive treatment. At first, only a small number of leading traumatologists ran "rap groups" in "outreach" "street-corner" venues (Lifton, 1978). Then, through unprecedented popular pressure by veterans, PTSD was introduced in the Diagnostic and Statistical Manual of Mental Disorders (DSM) III to validate the veterans as psychiatrically ill, and community-based counseling centers were established. Initially they offered 8–16 session programs using drugs, cognitive behavior therapy, social and other therapies. However, soon treatments were extended to 8–16 months and beyond. As Sipprelle (1992) said, "Chronic, multievent trauma for which treatment was delayed for 10 to 20 years does not respond to a brief course of treatment."

Even intense, months-long residential programs with devoted therapists had only initial positive, but long-term negative, results (Silver & Iacono, 1986; Solomon, Gerritty, & Muff, 1992; Hammarberg & Silver, 1994). This may be because treatments did not address the "totality of purposes" quoted above. This contrasts with an 18-month positive follow-up of 37 veterans whose traumas were dealt with personally and fully, and were made meaningful in new ways (Lindy, 1988).

In summary, the great numbers of war casualties have from time-to-time forced crude simulations of Janet's and Freud's techniques. In favorable circumstances acute breakdowns benefited from them, but entrenched ones needed much more complex trauma and fulfillment therapy than was available.

Holocaust

Treatment of Holocaust survivors highlights countertransference difficulties with severely traumatized people. Yet it also shows that if such difficulties are overcome, hope exists to improve survivors' existential problems.

Countertransference problems manifested as therapeutic nihilism (Tanay, 1968), and fear of unleashing overwhelming feelings and delusional transferences (Klein, 1968; Krystal, 1971). As a result, psychiatry as a whole denied the Holocaust in a "conspiracy of silence" (Krystal, 1971; Danieli, 1985). Hoppe (1968) and Danieli (1980) came to clarify countertransference responses under a number of themes such as guilt, shame, anger, contempt, veneration, over-identification, and defenses such as watering down murder to death, or only intellectual recognition. The overall result was that few survivors had any deep level psychotherapy.

Nevertheless, Holocaust survivors could still be helped if therapists let themselves be involved. Then traumatic meanings such as survivor guilt and sense of abandonment could be mitigated (Krell, 1989). In fact, survivors were less concerned about cures for their symptoms than overcoming traumatic meanings and making their lives somehow purposeful. And this was possible (Frankl, 1967), even to their dying days (Valent, 1994a, p. 141). Recently testimonies have helped to find such purpose (Valent, 1994b). De Wind (1971) concluded that therapy was possible but difficult, and did not aim for a cure.

Survivors are currently reliving their traumas as they face death again in old age. Understanding this can help to provide them with reassurance that illnesses and doctors do not mean extermination, as they did in concentration camps.

Child Survivors of the Holocaust may also be helped by therapy and testimonies, as well as peer groups. They all help validation and integration of childhood memories, and the facing of traumas, issues of identity, meanings, and purpose (Valent, 1994a, 1994b, 1998b; Chapter 10).

Second Generation Holocaust Survivor treatment problems may resemble those of survivors (Bergman, 1982; Steinberg, 1989), but with the added challenge that events are relived for which patients have no memory, and they enact roles of which they have no knowledge (Danieli, 1985; Fogelman, 1989; Albeck, 1994 [Case 43, chapter 11]).

Disasters

Many principles of disaster treatment were transferred from military psychiatry. Thus immediacy, proximity, and expectancy, with early treatment including rest, warm food, and listening to people ventilating their feelings became disaster treatment too (Tyhurst, 1957; Glass, 1959) in outreach programs (Parad, Resnik, & Parad, 1976; Heffron, 1977). Treatment according to phases and social systems (Cohen & Ahearn, 1980; Raphael, 1986) and debriefing (Busuttil & Busuttil, 1997) were also transferred from the army.

Phase-specific interventions usually include preparation, training, and establishment of contacts and services in the *preimpact phase*. In the *impact phase* emphasis is placed on protection, reunion, nurturance, comfort, and reliable information. In the *aftermath and recovery phases* education about normal disaster responses is emphasized. Opportunities may be given for individuals and groups to share and ventilate feelings, conflicts, and put the disaster into understandable contexts and meanings. Victims are given different types of aid, and their own resources for adaptive coping and recovery are encouraged. Children may be given special help to reestablish their routines and to express themselves in painting and play.

Unfortunately, too often services are withdrawn after about a month, a time when people are ready to trust and delve into their problems. Even though helpers and victims may feel good about interventions, as with soldiers, not working through problems may mean that problems persist or return.

Helper debriefs and critical incident management are considered below.

Sexual Assault, Violence and Torture

Treatment issues highlight safety, control, dignity, justice and rights.

Sexual Assault and Violence   The first requirement for treatment is a safe "social envelope" in which victims are validated and protected from "the second wound" of blame and rejection (Salasin & Rich, 1993; Williams, 1995). Social envelopes may be physical refuges and sexual assault clinics, peer groups such as Trauma Survivors Anonymous (Brende, 1993), laws and legal safeguards won by feminist and victims' rights movements. Laws have seen revocation of rape not being able to occur in marriage, establishment of victim impact statements, compensation laws, restitution by offenders, and a victims' bills of rights, which includes counseling (Young, 1988).

Factors which have been found to enhance early psychological treatment for sexual violence are early disclosure to a trusted confidant(e) (Harvey, Orbuch, Chwalisz, & Garwood, 1991), counseling where survival strategies used during the assault are reviewed (Hartman & Burgess, 1988), acceptance of victim identity, and having social networks.

Early intervention is generally considered valuable for violent experiences. For instance, a counseling team may arrive at a bank within an hour of it having been held up (Manton & Talbot, 1990). The team may comfort, hold hands, and listen to what happened. This may be followed up with a more formal debriefing the next day.

Later therapy for sexual assault includes education, increasing coping skills, expression of emotion, retrieval of memories, and integrating the event into new and positive views of self and the world (Dutton, 1992; Resnick & Newton, 1992). The same applies to other victims of violence. All groups benefit from a sense of control and empowerment, and forging new meanings, values, justice, and dignity, all the while progressing from the identity of a victim to that of a survivor (Merwin & Smith-Kurtz, 1988; Ochberg, 1993).

Sexual Abuse of Children: Incest   A "second wound" of disbelief and blame is especially damaging for children. On the contrary, the child has to be reassured that she has done the right thing. Safety from further abuse needs to be ensured, even if it means removal from home (Herman, 1981; 1992). Each family member needs individual and probably peer group help. Mothers may need empowerment to restore their relationships with their children. Perpetrators need to learn the difference between their needs for affection and sexual extortion and the damage caused by the latter. Their treatment may need to be enforced by law.

Therapy of adults who have been abused as children is often complex and long with intense therapist involvement (see below and Chapter 12). Peer group therapy may help overcome feelings of isolation and alienation and help one learn about common abuse responses (Herman & Lawrence, 1995).

Torture   Political torture victims also require safety, recognition, and rights. Counseling may need to be away from state institutions. Patience must be exercised with regard to disclosure and emotions, as both were dangerous and in the past elicited more torture (Simpson, 1993; Cunningham & Silove, 1993). Treatment requires every strategy of humaneness, to counter all the strategies of torture (Chester, 1995). Treatment may also include testimony, bearing political witness, and integrating political, ideological, and universal meanings (Simpson, 1993).

Psychosomatic Medicine

This area highlights the need for a biopsychosocial approach to illnesses (e.g., Engel, 1977). Its advantage is exemplified by the angina patient in Chapter 1 and other patients throughout the book (see also chapters 5 and 6). In addition, many illnesses such as asthma (Groen, 1976), strokes (Goodstein, 1984) and spinal injuries, have their specific psychosomatic treatment literature.

Bereavement and Dying

Death emphasizes the paramount importance of existential meanings (Chapter 1, p. 2).

Bereavement   In some ways bereavement literature preempted current views on trauma interventions. Thus early bereavement counseling (Young & Black, 1997) aimed to facilitate normal grief and mourning. This was done through comforting, acceptance, and explanation of the event and one's responses. Sorrow was given words and a story, helping progression to a new view of self, and a life with a deeper understanding and philosophy. It has been hoped that such early intervention would prevent later pathological grief (Singh & Raphael, 1981; Parkes & Weiss, 1983). Raphael (1986, 1997) speculates that when bereavement is accompanied by other traumas that threaten the bereaved, these traumas need to be addressed first.

Treatment of unresolved or pathological grief (Parkes & Weiss, 1983; Rando, 1993; Young & Black, 1997) may depend on subtypes such as chronic mourning, and inhibited or absent, and conflicted grief. In each type, yearning, sadness, anger and guilt, relationship problems, and other traumas need to be put in perspective.

A more extensive model of grief, depression, and unresolved grief relevant for treatment is presented elsewhere (Valent, 1998a).

Dying   The stresses of the dying are similar to those of the bereaved and other living humans. They include fear of abandonment and loss of control and dignity. Treatment is directed toward mitigating these threats through facilitating contact with relatives, empowerment in treatment decisions, and remembering the dying are still human beings (Valent, 1978; 1979).

As in other traumatic situations therapy may help by facilitating the forging of new integrated meanings of one's life (Kübler-Ross, 1969).

OVERVIEW OF CURRENT TREATMENT METHODS

While each traumatic situation highlights particular aspects of treatment, the following, what will be called "nonspecific," symptomatic, and specific trauma treatments, have been found to be applicable across traumatic situations. Treatments in various social system levels and ages (parameter axis) will be examined at the end of this section.

"Nonspecific" Treatments

All therapies insist on the need for a safe environment. Once established, creature comforts are next in importance. They include warm drinks, food, and rest. Psychosocial comforts include consolation and listening. Together these measures may relieve physical and psychic shock, and provide "counter-trauma" experiences such as trusting relationships. Nonspecific therapy may provide trust and hope for more specific therapy.

Symptomatic Treatments

The goal of these treatments is to alleviate or control specific symptoms.

Pharmacotherapy   Most types of mind-affecting drugs have been advocated for trauma symptoms at some time. The following is a synthesis of some overviews (Silver, Sandburg, & Hales, 1990; Friedman, 1993; Southwick, Bremner, Krystal, & Charney, 1994; Sutherland & Davidson, 1994; Davidson & van der Kolk, 1996).

Antidepressants of both the tricyclic and to a lesser extent monoamine oxidase (MAOI) variety have been claimed to reduce hyperarousal and intrusive symptoms. Recently serotonin reuptake inhibitors (SSRIs) such as fluoxetine have been found to be variably useful in reducing both arousal and numbing effects (van der Kolk, 1994).

Adrenergic activity inhibitors such as clonidine and propranolol were found to possibly replicate and reinforce antidepressant effects. *Carbamazepine and lithium* could be useful in decreasing impulsivity, irritability, violence, and arousal symptoms, while *benzodiazapines* such as diazapam and alprazolam have been used to diminish anxiety and improve sleep. *Antipsychotics* may have a place in paranoid and near-psychotic episodes.

Only five controlled drug trials have been undertaken. They indicated that antidepressants may be useful in PTSD (Sutherland & Davidson, 1994). All reviewers agreed that drug studies were in their infancy, and that the best policy was to use drugs for short-term relief of specific symptoms.

Psychosocial Techniques   Psychosocial techniques vary, but they share a theme of rational education about stress responses and their management.

Debriefing, Critical Incident Stress Management   Debriefing was first used to help emergency service personnel (see also Chapter 11), though now it is applied to victims too. A popular model, which in the 1980s filled a void for helping helpers, is *critical incident stress debriefing* (CISD) (Mitchell & Everly, 1995). Its protocol comprises seven phases. They are introduction, going over the event, description of thoughts, emotions, and signs and symptoms, teaching about them being normal responses, and finally discussion. The main goal is to learn that stress responses are normal survival responses to abnormal situations, and that the situation, not oneself, was crazy. Appreciating this often provides much relief. Other debriefs may add emotional ventilation and integration, and early treatment of conflicts and unacceptable meanings.

Earlier and briefer interventions (Foreman, 1994; Mitchell & Dyregrov, 1993; Raphael, Wilson, Meldrum, & McFarlane, 1996) include *decompression,* brief interventions during rescue breaks, *deescalation and demobilization,* which include food and drink and a short talk on expected responses, and *defusion,* a short group session which reviews the event immediately after it happened. Taken together over time the package is called critical incident stress management (CISM).

Criticisms of CISD and CISM include too much centralized control of organization and packaging, inflexibility mixed with overconfidence in protocols and techniques, and a superficiality in the emphasis only on normal responses. Though both debriefers and the debriefed may feel at first that CISD is helpful (Robinson & Mitchell, 1993), longer term outcomes may indicate otherwise (Hobbs, Mayon, Harrison, & Worlock, 1996; Kenardy et al., 1996). It may be that rational explanations may be insufficient to remove deep reasons for the loss of awareness of the connections between symptoms and their sources (Chapter 3). More research is needed on the potency of particular debriefing ingredients, and the proficiency necessary for their application.

Skills Training Skills training may be seen to be analogous to medical rehabilitation and occupational therapy, where disabled persons (re)learn normal behavior. For instance, Vietnam veterans relearn civilian responses (Siprelle, 1992), and women having escaped abusive marriages may learn how to budget (Dutton, 1992).

Relaxation and Emotion Management *Relaxation and anxiety managements* often use controlled diaphragmatic breathing (Resnick & Newton, 1992) and sequential relaxation of all muscle groups. Structuring rest, exercise, routine, simple pleasures such as walks in nature, accomplishing immediate goals, and learning to obtain social support can also be helpful (Dutton, 1992).

Anger management techniques may use imagined conflict scenarios in which subjects work out alternatives to both aggression and excessive timidity. Learning martial arts may give both confidence and control. *Stress management* programs vary greatly and may include combinations of the above techniques.

Criticisms of the techniques include their superficiality and invalidation of the complexity of people's traumas (Lazarus & Folkman, 1984) through short, trivial, and gimmicky (p. 363) programs in which charismatic people may induce temporary changes. Nevertheless, it may be that all types of symptomatic treatments have a place, in conjunction with nonspecific and specific therapies.

Specific Treatments

Specific therapies focus on the traumas themselves in order to reverse their effects.

Hypnotherapy   Hypnotherapy still resembles the techniques of Janet, in that dissociated fragments of the trauma story are assembled, relived, and restructured through suggestions of new meanings (Kleber & Brom, 1992). The old criticisms of hypnosis are still current—that suggestions may be dangerous, leading only to "transference cures," and that trance states and relivings occur naturally in therapy and are better remembered and integrated, than in hypnosis (Kleber & Brom, 1992).

"Power Therapies"   This is an informal name for therapies which claim to significantly affect the course of PTSD in a small number of sessions. Four such therapies were reported to significantly reduce subjective units of distress for up to six months (Figley & Carbonell, 1994; Carbonell & Figley, 1996; Gallo, 1996).

Traumatic Incident Reduction (TIR)   Here the client is asked to choose an "interesting" traumatic event, to visualize it from just before it happened to the end, and to report on it (Gerbode, 1988; 1995). This is repeated until resolution occurs, through new information and related traumas being viewed spontaneously and assimilated from different perspectives. The process can last several hours.

Visual/Kinesthetic Dissociation (V/KD)   Based on neurolinguistic programming and techniques of Milton Erickson, the subject is asked to hold still (like on a video) an image just prior to the trauma. The image is watched from today (one may even watch oneself watching it today). As the situation is allowed to unfold, commentaries and positive judgments are introduced. The client may relate compassionately to the younger self from the current perspective. Future recall is said to be influenced by these positive reviews, and previously ingrained stimulus-responses are disassociated (Cameron-Bandler, 1978).

Eye Movement Desensitization and Reprocessing (EMDR)   In this technique subjects visualize traumatic events and internally repeat irrational negative self-statements while they track the therapist's finger which moves very rapidly from side to side 10–20 times (Shapiro, 1993; 1995). As distress diminishes, positive self-statements replace the negative ones during eye movements. The process is repeated for other emergent memories. As well as eye movements, tones, light, and physical tapping have been found to be effective. Van der Kolk, McFarlane, and van der Hart (1996) noted that reports of some studies were skeptical, while others were very encouraging of the technique.

Thought Field Therapy   This technique is said to remove traumatic memory perturbations from a thought field by coupling disturbing memories with particular tappings of previously determined acupuncture meridian points (Callahan,

1985; 1993; 1996). This is followed by a "nine gamut treatment"—simultaneous tapping between the little and ring fingers at the back of the hand while doing specific eye exercises, humming, and counting. New emergent memories are treated with the same sequence. Blocks are treated by specific tapping and self-affirmations. This is perhaps the most controversial "power therapy."

Gallo (1996) suggests that the active ingredients common to all these therapies are controlled exposure to the trauma, looking at it from the outside, dual simultaneous attention on the trauma and current stimuli in comfortable environment, paradox where something inconsistent is introduced into the usual view of the trauma, and positive expectation.

Active ingredients may then interrupt and revise prior traumatic stimulus-response bonds. Figley (1996) summarized this in a succinct hypothesis, "Hyperstress is erased by hypostress associated to the same thought." He said that the power of these therapies lay in their extraordinary efficiency in inducing change and hope, shedding as it were, a skin of frozen fear. Later therapy then deals with traumatic changes and losses following this shift (Figley, 1997).

Cognitive Behavior Therapy   Cognitive behavior therapy (CBT) evolved from earlier two-factor and learned helplessness models (Lazarus & Folkman, 1984; Kleber & Brom, 1992).

The Two Factor Model: Exposure and Desensitization   In the two-factor model the first factor is the traumatic experience and fear response (unconditioned stimulus and response). The second factor is avoidant behavior due to generalized secondary conditioned stimuli, which do not actually portend danger.

Treatment is exposure to the latter sources of anxiety and learning that they are in fact not dangerous. Forced exposure to the feared stimuli (flooding) was an early technique, but the intensified traumatic responses could stimulate aversion to treatment. Subsequent techniques combined anxiety management (e.g., controlled breathing and relaxation), gradual imaginal reliving of traumatic memories, and introduction into them of positive incompatible facts, thus changing the quality of the memory (Foa, Steketee, & Rothbaum, 1989).

In *systematic desensitization* based on Wolpe's (1958) reciprocal inhibition, a hierarchy of fear-evoking stimuli are coupled with relaxation and pleasant imaginings. More recently, in so-called *prolonged* (really controlled) *exposure (PE)* (Rothbaum & Foa, 1993) and in *stress inoculation training (SIT)* (Meichenbaum, 1983; Smyth, 1994), the pleasant images may be left out. The safe surroundings, the therapist, and self-control may be substitutes for them.

The Learned Helplessness Model (Cognitive Restructuring or Reframing)
This model draws on Ellis's (Ellis & Grieger, 1976) rational emotive therapy and Beck's (1976) cognitive behavior therapy. Subjects are shown how through selective abstraction and overgeneralization they developed cognitive distor-

tions such as that they are helpless to control their fates or that all is gloomy. These inner premises are cognitively restructured through exposure of the negative self-statements and their illogicalities. Then new self-statements are substituted.

Most therapists use a combination of the exposure and self-talk techniques and include skills and relaxation techniques as well (Foy, 1992). Beneficial results may also be influenced by unstated empathic interactions, trust, faith in rationality and capacity to control one's mind, and expectation of cure in 6–12 sessions (Kleber & Brom, 1992; Smyth, 1994).

Horowitz's Cognitive Focal Psychotherapy   Horowitz (1974; 1976/1992) provides a theoretical bridge between CBT and psychodynamic therapy. He overlapped with CBT in specifying a small number (12) sessions, during which repeated talking about traumas (in the intrusive phase) remolded their significance and meanings. Psychodynamic techniques included interpretation of defenses (in the avoidance phase), use of transference and countertransference, and incorporation of the ending of the therapy into the traumatic experience.

Horowitz (1976/1992) and CBT therapists note that their treatments mostly suit relatively simple anxiety and phobic traumatic responses in adults who remember their traumas.

Psychodynamic Trauma Therapy   Psychodynamic psychotherapy incorporating psychoanalytic techniques is used for complex traumas, especially those which occurred in childhood, have distorted many aspects of personality, and for which memories are variably absent. The therapeutic relationship then may be the crucible in which fragments of the trauma are reenacted (transference) in order that they may be reorganized and understood. Therapists also reverberate with these reenactments (countertransference) and thereby experience the unexpressed soul of their clients' pain and injury (Wilson & Lindy, 1994). The ramifications of these pains may be such as to challenge patients and therapists to be theologians, jurists, and philosophers (Herman, 1992; Pearlman & Saakvitne, 1995). The process can be long and involve an intense existential engagement because it may take a long time to recognize, define name and realign the many fragments of the multiple traumas and their wide-ranging consequences.

The elements of dual attention within a safe relationship are still important. "The therapist must help the patient move . . . from her protected anchorage in the present to immersion in the past, so that she can simultaneously reexperience the feelings in all their intensity while holding on to the sense of safe connection . . ." (Herman, 1992, p. 178).

The crucible of therapy is also the site of conscious exploration of contrasts between present counter-traumatic and past traumatic "nonspecific" experiences. They include safety, boundaries, affect recognition and modulation (Briere, 1992; 1995), client respect, control, autonomy, and rationality.

Eventually the whole trauma story, its aftermaths, and meanings are chronologically owned, integrated, mourned, and replaced by a nontraumatic narrative. Because they often deal with such complex traumas, psychodynamic therapists seldom talk of cures. Perhaps they think in terms of degrees of restoration of humanity.

Psychodynamic trauma therapists recognize countertransference involvements as a secondary hazard to themselves. For instance, overinvolvement or avoidance have been found to lead to "empathic strain" (Wilson, Lindy, & Raphael, 1994). Prolonged empathy is said to inevitably lead to vicarious traumatization, and this includes the range of client symptoms from emotional dysphoria to spiritual despair (Pearlman & Saakvitne, 1995). The specificity of symptoms has been suggested to be due to specific excessive identifications and/or reverberatory responses to victims (Valent, 1995a). To maintain their health and perspective, therapists require supervision and trauma therapy themselves (see also Chapter 8).

The few studies which attempted to compare the efficacies of different specific therapies could only indicate that cognitive behavior, psychodynamic, and hypnotherapies were better than controls (Kleber & Brom, 1992; Sherman, 1998). Obviously much more research is required.

Treatments in Various Social Systems and Ages (Parameter Axis)

Most trauma therapies describe individual adult victims. However, as was already seen in disasters, treatment may include groups, families, and children. Treatment for helpers is considered in Chapter 8.

Peer Groups   Survivors of particular traumatic situations such as the Vietnam War, the Holocaust, and sexual abuse may form peer groups which give their members mutual recognition, identity, siblinghood (Valent, 1994a), shared language and culture, voice, pride, and dignity. They encourage disclosure, testimony, and political action. Group therapy is relatively outreach, egalitarian, and multidimensional, but may be limited in personal depth.

Families   Figley (1988a; 1988b; 1995a; 1995b) noted that family members were also primary or secondary victims. He suggested a five-phase treatment approach.

First, problems are identified and trust established. Then each member discloses the effects of trauma on feelings and meanings. Next, problems such as withdrawal are reframed in terms of trauma symptoms, not lack of affection. The family then develops a healing theory of what happened, why, and how members would react in the future. Finally, accomplishments and lessons learned are reviewed, and therapy is wound up.

This may be the only forum where family members, especially children, express their views and understand each other. Applied even after many years, intergenerational groups may break long-imposed "conspiracies of silence" (Danieli, 1985).

Communities   Communities may be helped in various ways with specific techniques in different phases. For instance, information may be dispersed through pamphlets and the media in the recovery phase. An example of a specifically adapted therapy was the Sweat Lodge purification ritual of Sioux Indian warriors returning from battle, adapted for Vietnam veterans (Wilson, 1989). The ritual encouraged altered states of consciousness, group cohesion, and self-esteem. Community memorials can help grieving and integration, in rebuilding and later phases.

Children   Treatments resemble those for adults, but allowance must be made for children's developmental phases and concentration spans, their expressions of traumatic material in drawings and play, and their reliance on adults (Pynoos & Nader, 1988; 1989; 1991; Terr, 1990). Child counseling may be initiated through parents and schools.

Children from preschool to second grade may need consistent caregiving, repeated concrete clarifications, and help in expressing fears and feelings. Third to fifth grade children may be helped by encouraging expression of secret imaginings and articulation of traumatic anxieties. Older children may, in addition, be educated about expected symptoms and cautioned about impulsive behavior.

COMMON PRINCIPLES IN THE VARIETY OF TREATMENTS

It is suggested that all therapies acknowledge overtly or implicitly the following four ingredients or principles.

1   Recognition   The first step is recognition of trauma, its effects, and their amenability to treatment. Helpers and victims may need education for such recognition to occur.

2   "Counter-trauma" milieu (nonspecific aspects)   Safe and caring environments, and optimistic therapists provide expectancy of improvement, hope, trust, and counter-trauma corrective emotional experiences.

3   Symptomatic treatment   Symptoms such as anxiety, anger, helplessness, shame, and other distressing emotions and behaviors may be specifically targeted by particular drugs, relaxation, assertiveness, anger, and other management strategies.

4   Specific trauma treatment   All specific treatments require remembering the trauma, breaking its falsely learned nexus with present reality by dual attention to both from a new position, and relearning the significance of the trauma story. This may occur in an altered "hypnoid" state of consciousness with close focus on therapists.

In summary, it may be that since Janet and Freud, sensitive therapists have used the basic ingredients of recognition, counter-trauma environment and relationships, symptom relief, and specific trauma treatments. And yet it was seen that aspects of these ingredients were applied very differently in different traumatic situations and in different treatments.

A proper theory or metatheory of trauma and fulfillment treatment requires a model, which provides a framework for the variety of traumatic and fulfillment responses and the variety of treatments and their treatment ingredients. In other words, in order to know when, where, how, and why one may fruitfully intervene with which treatment ingredient modified to what situation, the framework must provide an understanding of biological, psychological, and social trauma and fulfillment responses, and their evolution and ramifications from survival to spiritual levels. It is a further requirement to provide knowledge of when to target which groups (including helpers) with what goals and what means.

Without such a framework treatments may exist in expert, but self-enclosed niches. Or they may overemphasize some treatment ingredients at the expense of others, leading to lopsided results such as temporary transference or partial symptom cures.

The next two chapters elaborate a wholist perspective that provides a meaningful framework for trauma and fulfillment phenomena. Subsequent chapters combine it with treatment principles, providing a heuristic model for treatments. The wholist treatment model is then applied to a range of typical clinical situations.

Part Two

The Wholist Perspective

This section presents the wholist perspective which in turn provides a model for understanding trauma and fulfillment phenomena and treatments applied to them.

The wholist perspective has two main constituents. The first is the triaxial framework, described in Chapter 3. It includes three axes, called the process, parameters and depth axes. They are the skeleton whose concepts provide a framework for the ramifications of the life-trauma dialectic and orientate trauma and fulfillment phenomena. Chapter 4 presents eight survival strategies, which provide the contents or flesh and blood to these concepts. Together they help to explain and categorize the great variety of trauma and fulfillment manifestations which ramify across the triaxial framework.

The term wholist includes whole to indicate a very broad view. It includes holist, which like holistic, indicates an inclusive biological, psychological, and social (biopsychosocial or triadic) perspective. It also includes Koestler's (1983) term holon which includes all steps toward whole (hol), and toward the smallest particle (on) as in an electron, proton, and so on. The perspective, therefore, includes comprehensive and particular views.

The great wealth contained in the triaxial framework and survival strategies is only summarized in this book. They are looked at more fully elsewhere (Valent, 1998a).

Part 3 applies the wholist perspective to explain and categorize the great variety of traumatic stress treatments and applies it to extend practical conceptualization of treatment principles which underlie them all. Part 4 applies the wholist view of therapy to clinical situations ranging from immediate traumatic situations to entrenched symptoms many years later.

Chapter 3

The Triaxial Framework

The triaxial framework (Figure 1) comprises the process, parameter and depth axes. They may be thought of as the coordinates which locate fulfillment and traumatic stress manifestations and treatments.

The *Process Axis* (Axis 1) locates the process from stressors to traumas and illnesses. The *Parameter Axis* (Axis 2) describes what kind of event affects whom or what group, when and at what age. The *Depth Axis* (Axis 3) describes human function levels from survival through morality, meaning, and views of self, to sacredness and purpose.

The major components of the three axes are summarized below in Table 1.

Trauma involves disruptions along all axes, and treatment involves healing along all axes.

AXIS 1: THE PROCESS AXIS

The components and interactions of the process axis are represented in Figure 2.

The figure indicates a process as well as a dynamic system whose components feed into and feed back into each other. However, beyond trauma one may imagine a step in the figure indicating that the prior equilibrium cannot be restored. Indeed, components of trauma and beyond may be stressors in a new

27

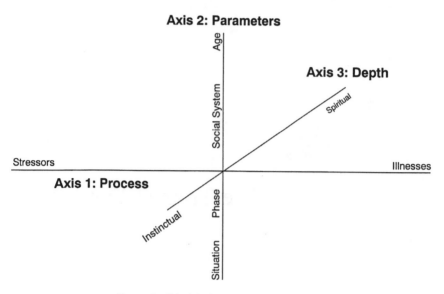

Figure 1   Triaxial view of traumatic stress.

spiral of the figure. All components in Figure 2 have biopsychosocial features, which will be explained later.

Stressors   Stressors have been divided into cataclysmic, "everyday," and "daily hassles" (Eisdorfer, 1985; Davidson, Fleming, & Baum, 1986). *Trau-matic stress* is a common term which is derived from cataclysmic stressors and denotes that they lead to trauma in almost everyone. This is the original mean-ing of the stressor criterion of PTSD in DSM IV (APA, 1994).

Table 1   Components of the Triaxial Framework

Process axis	Parameters axis	Depth axis
1. Stressors	1. Factors in traumatic situations	1. Basic instincts, drives
2. Appraisals		2. Survival strategies
3. Stress responses; stress	2. Phases of traumatic situations	3. Judgments and morality
		4. Basic meanings
4. Strengths & vulnerabilities	3. Social system levels including helpers	5. Ideals, values and principles
		6. Codes, dignity, rights
5. Trauma	4. Developmental phases	7. Spirituality, religion, ideology; beliefs
6. Defenses		
7. Memories		8. Identity
8. Illnesses		9. Symbols
9. Secondary spirals		10. Creativity, esthetics
		11. Sacredness
		12. Wisdom, knowledge, truth

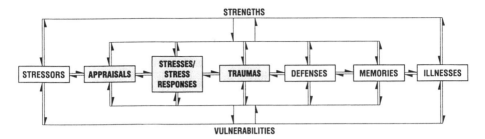

Figure 2 Components of process axis.

Yet "everyday" stressors can also lead to trauma, as was the case in the lady with angina. She also exemplified how stressors may be cumulative (Khan, 1964), or symbolic, such as a child turning eight. As well, stressors may only become significant long after an event when their meaning comes to be understood, as can occur in childhood sexual abuse. Last, stressors may be secondary (Figley, 1995b) or transgenerational (Chapter 2). Hence trauma may develop through a range of stressor dynamics. The following definition captures the different possibilities.

Stressors are actually or potentially noxious events which interfere with the purpose of life; that is, survival and fulfillment of self or others. (See life: trauma dialectic below and Chapter 1.)

Appraisals   Appraisals register and assess the stressor nature of events and initiate stress responses to deal with them. They are influenced by sensory stimuli, past experience, others' interpretations, beliefs (such as that one cannot influence events), and commitments (such as about one's role or ideology).

In traumatic situations perceptions tend to be unambiguous and intense, and appraisals are formed by immediate survival needs. At such times people tend to act "instinctively," often contrary to their past personalities. Furthermore, because situations change quickly appraisals fluctuate, and because events are different from different angles, individuals and others in the same traumatic situation may respond with quite different stress responses at any one time, and over a period of time.

It is suggested that **appraisals register the quantity and quality of stressors in order to elicit appropriate stress responses.**

In the absence of intensely needed information, fantasies may fill gaps. They may lead to rumors, magical thinking, and scapegoating.

Stress Responses: Stress   It is suggested that **stress responses preserve survival and life-enhancing equilibria by countering the noxious potentials of stressors.** They form a buffer state called stress between stressors and trauma.

When stress responses are *adaptive*, previous life-enhancing equilibria are

restored and may even be fortified. In such cases it is said that stress is beneficial (Selye, 1973). However, when they fail, they are *maladaptive*. The situation may be called stress, tension, strain, or distress (Lazarus & Folkman, 1984;
Eisdorfer, 1985; Davidson et al., 1986). It resembles stress in physics, such as
tension which may or may not fracture a bone.

Stress then may be defined as a **state of tension resulting from stressors
challenging life-enhancing equilibria.**

Selye (1973) suggested that the initial stress response may be followed by a
long period of resistance (stress) from which reversal was still possible. After
the third phase, which he called exhaustion and which resembles trauma, reversal was impossible.

Some suggest that the fields of stress and traumatic stress are different
(Shalev, 1996) because in stress, unlike following trauma, many stress equilibria
are still reversible. The position taken here is consistent with physics and medicine. Namely, though a bone or a person may be different when stressed as
against when broken, it is counterproductive to separate fields of study just
before and after the break.

Stress responses are biological, psychological, and social (Figure 3). *Biopsychosocial* indicates their contiguity, but perhaps the word *triadic* should be preferred to indicate their core unity. Stress responses are extremely varied and
they provide the core ingredients for the great variety of manifestations in traumatic stress and fulfillment (Chapter 4).

Biological stress responses are anatomically served by the "old mammalian"
brain including the limbic system and the primitive cortex (MacLean, 1973).

A number of physiological systems and their components respond very
sensitively to a variety of stressors. Examples are the autonomic sympathetic
and parasympathetic nervous systems (Cannon, 1963; Henry, 1986), the endocrine system (Mason, 1968; Panksepp, 1986; Yehuda, Southwick, Mason, &
Giller, 1990; Friedman, 1991; van der Kolk, 1996b), the immune system (Bartrop,
Lazarus, Luckhurst, Kiloh, & Penny, 1977; Calabrese, Kling, & Gold, 1987),
and neurotransmitter and neuroregulator systems (Smith, 1991; Bremner, Krystal,
Southwick, & Charney, 1995).

Faults at individual anatomical sites (such as the hippocampus) or with
particular physiological responses (such as epinephrine and norepinephrine
or cortisol secretion) have been variably marked as "the" stress response or

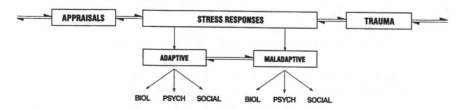

Figure 3 Stress responses.

pathology of PTSD. However, overarching neurophysiological stress response patterns determined by higher psychological goals are likely to be more important (Smith, 1991). Responses are then like muscle contractions whose meanings can only be determined through knowing such goals.

Psychological stress responses include cognitions and emotions influenced by survival needs. For instance, people may be cognitively unconcerned about their pain while rescuing others and feeling the pressure of time. At other times they may see themselves at the epicenter of a disaster, be overconcerned, and time may seem interminable.

Emotions also vary greatly, though fear, anxiety, and depression are most commonly quoted. Cognitions and emotions are interrelated and may vary greatly with circumstances.

Social stress responses are also very variable, spanning engagement and avoidance, altruism and selfishness, cohesion and fragmentation.

Vulnerabilities Vulnerabilities may be defined as **factors which facilitate the noxious effects of stressors.** Though it has been acknowledged that all people have a breaking point (Freud, 1919; Hocking, 1970), vulnerabilities have been used to explain why some react more adversely than others in similar situations.

Background factors such as childhood or old age, being female, low socioeconomic status and education, and previous psychopathology (McFarlane, 1988) may be relevant though they have also been considered to be artifacts. For instance, at times the middle-aged suffer most, and questionnaires tend to obscure typical male pathology. Gibbs (1989) suggested that more pertinent vulnerabilities were what he called underlying structural life theme defects such as unreliability of early environments and growing up with lack of control over affects and behaviors.

Disaster factors predisposing to pathology and PTSD (Shalev, 1996) are suddenness and nearness of stressors, massive destructiveness and mutilation, especially if caused by humans, identification with those killed, and youth of victims. Post-disaster factors include isolation, lack of helping networks, and poor coping styles.

Specific vulnerabilities may arise from previous traumas. In such cases people are vulnerable to cues of the original trauma, even if they are only symbolic of the original situation. Cues of fire, a child turning eight, and cues of abandonment evoked earlier traumatic responses in the three cases in Chapter 1. Vulnerabilities may include threats to defenses which protect against awareness of traumas.

Transgenerational vulnerabilities may be genetic, cultural, and trauma-specific. Examples of the latter include parental-type stress responses in second generation Holocaust victims in response to Holocaust-related cues (Valent, 1998a), and predisposition to vehicle accidents when a relative had died of one (Valent, 1998a).

Strengths   On the other end of the scale **strengths** may be defined as **factors that resist the noxious effects of stressors.** They include stable and happy family backgrounds and capacities to regulate affects and actions. They include training (McFarlane, 1988), learning from past experiences, and accessing of social networks (Shalev, 1996).

Trauma   Trauma is a crucial and germane concept denoting a situation beyond stress, **a state in which a previously life-enhancing equilibrium is irretrievably lost.** It is a central concept in traumatology and is a protagonist in the life-trauma dialectic (Chapter 1).

Trauma is derived from the Greek word denoting wound, or penetration as in stabbing. Its current metaphor incorporated in the logo of the International Society of Traumatic Stress Studies is trauma as a pebble which breaks the stillness of a pond (Figley, 1985a). Freud (1888) described psychological trauma as an event which penetrated the psychic skin (barrier). He went on to say that after penetration, and together with defenses, trauma caused as it were a psychic abscess. The abscess was both a constant reminder and encapsulator (reliving and repression) of the traumatic event (Freud, 1886; 1920). This presaged the reliving and avoidance criteria of PTSD.

Though trauma was so seminal it was often like a black hole which defied description. Horowitz (1976) and van der Kolk, Brown, and van der Hart (1989) suggested that its essential feature was disruption of meaning. Thus unintegrated trauma fragments were relived and avoided until they were integrated in a superordinate meaningful narrative. Benyakar, Kutz, Dasberg, and Stern (1989), on the other hand, saw trauma as a collapse of the self, which explained its wide-ranging unregulated emotions, loss of mastery, shattered assumptions, disruptions of relationships, and loss of identity.

It is suggested that the complexity and energy of trauma stems from its gathering and focusing like a lens previous components of the process axis to then refract them through the filter of defenses into illnesses. The complexity is increased through bidirectional relationships with all components of the triaxial framework at every point. While from a bird's eye view trauma may be seen as a disruption which is relived and avoided, the specifics, dynamics, and ramifications of the relivings and avoidances are indeed very complex. Their understanding and treatment are central to this book.

To clarify some other terms, it is suggested that a *traumatic state* is the state of an organism at the time that trauma is occurring. A *traumatic situation or event* is the external situation in which an organism is traumatized. *Traumatization* is the process of production of trauma.

Defenses   It is suggested that **defenses mitigate the potential and actual effects of trauma and its recurrence.** Traumatology has concentrated on psychological defenses. Their sense is that if traumas cannot be prevented at least they can be made bearable through disconnections between parts of the mind, and thereby mitigate awareness. Breuer and Freud (1893) described the splitting of emotional consciousness where unconscionable emotions were made unconscious (Freud, 1894). Janet used the term dissociation where variable combinations of cognitions, emotions, somatic sensations, and behavior were disconnected from awareness (Braun, 1993; van der Kolk, 1996b). It may be that defenses keep untenable knowledge on hold until the world can provide a realistically purposeful stream of life, at which time reconstituted knowledge can reenter a continuous stream of consciousness.

It is suggested that defenses utilize the triaxial framework and survival strategies and can be categorized by them. A taxonomy of defenses is proposed in Chapter 5.

Memories   Memories are ways of knowing the past. It is suggested that **traumatic memories are reverberations of traumatic events and their defenses.** While nontraumatic (often called narrative or declarative) memories are coherent, can be evoked by will, and can be related verbally and sequentially, traumatic memories resemble right-brain procedural memories, which have no sequence or verbal representation and are evoked in fragments and unconsciously. It is as if nontraumatic memories reside in a web of logical circuitry in the subject's control, while traumatic memories have faulty circuitry and their presence (including intrusive hypermnesias) or absence (variable amnesias) depends on a central switch being thrown which is under tenuous or no subjective control.

Fragmented knowing may be compounded when traumatic events occurred in childhood and before complex adult events could be apprehended. Furthermore, though accurate emotional and somatic encoding and retrieval of events can occur from birth (Tinnin, 1994), early memories are often faulty due to flaws in sequencing, condensation of events, and combination with atavistic images (Pynoos & Eth, 1985; Terr, 1987, 1990; Valent, 1994a; 1995a; Lewis, 1995; Pynoos, Steinberg, & Goenjian, 1996). These features of memory malformation are due to what is called here developmental lags.

In addition, as memories cohere (the circuitry being repaired), original traumatic stress responses, judgments, and meanings threaten awareness. They may be countered by past and current intensified defenses, reliving of outside intimidations to hide events (Case 3, Chapter 1), and current pressures to "conspiracies of silence" (Chapter 2).

Laub and Auerhahn (1993) described different levels of awareness, which increase as memory webs coalesce and defenses are relinquished (and developmental lags are supplemented). Levels of awareness are not knowing at all, reliving in fugues or altered states of consciousness, reliving in fragments, living out in more coherent traits, sense of overpowering narrative, definition in life themes, witnessed narrative, and finally, use of the narrative as metaphor for further development.

While defenses, hypermnesias, amnesias, and their resolutions are everyday clinical fare when dealing with traumatic sequalae (Bremner & Marmar, 1998), the veracity of childhood sexual abuse memories in particular have been repeatedly questioned, with therapists even being blamed for implanting them (The International Society for Traumatic Stress Studies, 1998; Brandon, Boakes, Glaser, & Green, 1998). However, most awareness of sexual abuse is reconstituted outside therapy (Williams, 1995; van der Kolk & Fisler, 1995; van der Kolk, 1996b) and, as in therapy, leads to a sense of deep, even if painful, coherence (Foa, Molnar, & Cashman, 1995). Suggestibility of memory like suggestibility generally can occur for unimportant and peripheral events (Loftus, 1993; Lewis, 1995), but is resistant for traumatic memories (van der Kolk, 1996b; Leavitt, 1997).

Veracity and completeness of memories must take into account the nature of traumatic memory circuitry, developmental lags, defenses, past and present intimidation, and subjective and intersubjective costs and benefits which may influence the presence of different levels of awareness.

Illnesses

Illnesses may be said to be **compromise equilibria established after trauma**. Though what follows concentrates on psychological illnesses, it should be remembered that they are parallel and closely associated with physical and social illnesses.

Psychological trauma illnesses have been conceptualized according to *phenomenological* and *dynamic* approaches. The former classifies illnesses such as acute stress disorder and PTSD (American Psychiatric Association, 1980/1994) according to clusters of symptoms, while the latter sees a great variety of potential pictures resulting from many combinations of traumas and defenses. The two approaches usually overlap clinically.

The Phenomenological Stream

Acute Stress Disorder   Acute stress disorder resembles PTSD in the first post-trauma month; that is, when officially PTSD cannot yet be diagnosed. The disorder also includes at least three dissociative symptoms (Chapter 6). These two features reflect political views of PTSD and dissociative disorder groups (Brett, 1996), and imply that their specific illnesses gel from acute symptom clusters.

However, clinical descriptions of acute stress reactions, such as combat stress reactions (Solomon, 1993; Valent, 1998a), indicate their polymorphous fluctuating unpredictable nature. Furthermore, as so many symptoms and illnesses evolved from acute stress reactions, leading workers concluded that the primary task of traumatology was to understand and specify the uniqueness and variability of acute traumatic responses in a way which made sense of them and their developments (McFarlane & Yehuda, 1995; Solomon, Laor, & McFarlane, 1996; Brett, 1996). In this book survival strategies provide a means to understand the variability of acute stress responses and the triaxial framework provides a framework for their ramifications.

Post-Traumatic Stress Disorder (PTSD)   Post-traumatic stress disorder (APA, 1980; 1994) is the latest version of similar post-traumatic illnesses (Trimble, 1985). It has four criteria. The stressor (see above) criterion involves a threat to life, intense fear, helplessness, and horror. The reliving criterion includes images, thoughts, dreams, actions, flashbacks, illusions, hallucinations, and physiological reactions of the trauma. The avoidance of trauma criterion describes numbing, restriction of interest and interactions, and restricted ability to recall. The last criterion includes arousal symptoms such as sleeplessness, hypervigilance, startle response, and difficulty in concentrating.

Post-traumatic stress disorder gave recognition to the post-traumatic suffering of Vietnam veterans and other victims, and with it rights of treatment and compensation. It is a simple diagnosis able to be operationalized, measured, and understood by lawyers. However, it is suggested that its conceptual abstraction is at too high a level for the clinically important questions of *what* is relived and avoided, *how,* and *why.* It does not list many trauma-related symptoms such as eating disorders and substance abuse (van der Kolk, 1996a), it overshadows other trauma related comorbid diagnoses such as depression, panic, anxiety, and borderline disorders (Herman, 1992; McFarlane & de Girolamo, 1996) and ignores other post-traumatic syndromes, especially those evolving from early and long-term traumatization (Herman, 1992). It ignores physical illnesses, and does not distinguish responses in children or groups.

Last, PTSD does not relate to the rages and guilts, moral conflicts, demoralization, and lost meanings which provided the original thrust to the diagnosis. Trauma, which promised to be the soul of psychiatry (van der Kolk & McFarlane, 1996), in PTSD ". . . does not begin to describe the complexity of how people react to overwhelming experiences" (p. 15).

Dynamic Stream   The dynamic stream with its roots in early psychoanalysis sees the great variety of symptoms and illnesses as stemming from traumas and fashioned by defenses. Treatment includes making historical sense by following the trauma ripples past their defenses to their origins (Figley, 1985; Vaillant, 1992; Herman, 1992; Threlkeld & Thyer, 1992; Braun, 1993; Chapters 2 and 6), establishing ever greater awareness of connections (Laub & Auerhahn, 1993). Memories are then reconciled with current realities, as described in specific trauma therapy in Chapters 2 and 6.

The process of making the unknown known involves a deep immersion in patients' traumas and their existential ramifications. Illness definition becomes less important than issues such as boundary diffusion, transference, and countertransference.

The dynamic stream is concerned with emotions and existential issues. However, the relative lack of classification makes for difficult explanation and communication, and the "soul" is compromised by the many psychodynamic therapists who deny trauma at the center. That is, they deal with the ripples in detail, but ignore the pebble.

In summary, the process axis includes linear concepts, such as progression from psychological traumatic stressors to PTSD, or from physiological responses to physical symptoms and illnesses (see also Chapter 4). It also caters to nonlinear system concepts of multiple components interacting and feeding back to each other with *secondary spirals* potentially occurring within seconds to years. This nonlinearity is further enhanced when the other two axes are added. And yet all traumas have only limited avenues of expression (Weisath & Eitinger, 1993); that is, through limited number of survival strategies and axes.

AXIS 2: THE PARAMETERS AXIS

The parameters axis describes the setting of traumatic situations and of those affected by them.

Type of Traumatic Situation   The cases in the introduction and the various types of traumatic situations in the previous chapter indicated the variable cultures of traumatic responses and emphases in treatment.

Phases of Traumatic Situations   Phases of traumatic situations have different challenges and cultures too. Of paramount importance in the impact phase are saving life and property, in the postimpact phase are ensuring vital resources and preparing for recurrence, later taking stock and rebuilding, and finally healing and building up reserves.

Each disaster phase has its own stresses and traumas. For instance, in the postimpact phase, not being believed or being blamed, callousness and injustices may be experienced as worse than the original traumas. Therefore, in retrospect it is important to reconstruct all phases of the trauma story.

Social System Levels   Aspects of stress and trauma occur at individual, group, family, community, and national levels. At each level they again have different cultures.

Occurrences in larger social units often have correspondingly wider social significance. For instance, ethnic or religious scapegoating may lead to millions of deaths.

Developmental Phases   Stressors have different trauma and fulfillment significance at different parts of the life cycle. For instance, early in life not being gazed and smiled at, not being physiologically attuned to, not having loving impulses returned, and an inability to achieve developmental milestones may be traumatic. Later inabilities to have loving partners or children, and in old age to not make sense of life and move toward a dignified death may be stressful or traumatic. This means that minor hassles at one time of life may be quite stressful at others, and vice versa.

It is important to be aware of normal cognitive (Brainerd, 1978), emotional

(Lane & Schwartz, 1987), and moral (Kohlberg, 1981; 1985) developmental phases, as disruptions at certain developmental phases have characteristic consequences, which later may be traced back to their developmental sources. Characteristics of cognitive, emotional, and moral developmental phases are presented elsewhere (Valent, 1998a).

AXIS 3: THE DEPTH AXIS

From Aristotle (Robinson, 1993) to Maslow (1970) hierarchies of satisfactions, which fulfilled happiness, have been formulated. In what follows, fulfillments and traumas are examined along a hierarchy of human function levels from instincts to spirituality. They reflect evolutionary development of the human brain which is recapitulated in individuals. The levels overlap and they interact bidirectionally. As for the process axis and components of the parameter axis, earlier levels ramify into later ones which in turn subsume earlier levels.

Instincts and Drives   Instincts and drives (which themselves subsume reflexes and automatic physiological responses) are directed to satisfactions of basic needs of security, warmth, shelter, food, and sexuality. Each satisfaction is accompanied by specific biological, psychological, and social pleasures, and lacks with corresponding unpleasures.

Survival Strategies: Acute Stress Responses   Though people may still feel that they reacted instinctively, they have more flexibility of choice with survival strategies (Chapter 4). This is reflected in the polymorphous, often conflicting variety of acute stress responses. Adaptive stress responses are associated with the most intense and sweetest experiences as humans reconnect to what makes life fulfilling. Stress states contain major intense human unpleasures while traumas contain their nightmares (see Chapter 4).

Judgments and Morality   It is suggested that judgments arise when there is potential or actual conflict of survival or fulfillment between self and others. Judgments are external and internal (in which case they are called conscience) feedbacks whose evolutionary function is maximum societal survival. Subjectively, adaptive resolution provides moral gratification while failure leads to moral distress. Compounding philosophical and traumatology literatures, it is suggested that morality consists of three types of judgments, each with specific gratifications and distresses. In trauma the latter are endemic and may be extreme.

1   In **authoritarian** (often called **deontological**) **morality** current or internalized authorities dictate judgments of *good and bad*. Their praise or anger evoke, respectively, a sense of *virtue or guilt*.

2   In **morality of worth** (often called **goods**) judgments are made on the

worthiness of persons and their characters. *Esteem* and admiration or, alternatively, contempt and humiliation evoke alternately high *self-esteem* and *shame*.

3   In the **morality of justice** judgments are made on the fairness or unfairness of events. In this case *rewards* and *punishments* evoke sense of *right* and *wrong*. Because disasters are basically unfair, cries of "Why?!" and "Why me?!" imply wrongs being done to victims.

Basic Meanings   It is suggested that survival strategies and judgmental feedbacks join into basic meanings such as "I am bad if I do not help my neighbor." "I am abandoned because I am unlovable." "I am punished for having done wrong." In trauma unacceptable meanings as well as judgments are endemic. It is suggested that, clinically, the nightmares of traumatic situations (maladaptive and traumatic biopsychosocial aspects of survival strategies), negative judgments, and unacceptable meanings often form basic packages (nodes of information) which are kept out of awareness in later memory.

Ideals, Values, and Principles   It is suggested that ideals, values, and principles are higher-level abstractions of authoritarian, worth, and justice types of morality, respectively.

Ideals contain ultimate virtues such as fighting to the death or turning the other cheek. *Values* (not to be confused with ideals or principles) contain perfections of character such as valor and cunning, honor and humility, ferocity and gentleness, also depending on the situation. *Principles* abstract essentials of justice such as respect for life and property, and equal impartial treatment.

Codes, Dignity, Rights   It is suggested that codes, dignity, and rights are further elaborations of the three streams of morality.

Codes may enshrine authority and ideals. They may be handed down in cultural groups as tradition, or in professions as ethics. (Ethics is sometimes used in the sense morals is used here.) Codes may be laid down in religious or secular laws.

Dignity involves respect of the physical, psychological, and social, value of persons, and their moral meaning.

Rights include universal entitlements that facilitate survival and fulfillment. They include rights to life, security, justice, and freedom to pursue happiness.

Spirituality: Myths, Religion, Ideology   It is suggested that in order to deal with imponderable threats to previous function levels humans evolved a numinous world in which the known was projected to the unknown. Animate qualities were attributed to inanimate matter, human qualities to animals, live qualities to the dead, and inner desires to outer reality. Alongside the objective world ran a cosmology of fulfillment and trauma. The former was governed by spiritual allies resembling parents and leaders who secured eternal satisfaction of all desires. They battled representatives of the latter, represented by monsters resembling earthly predators and enemies. Aided by sorcery, magic, rituals, and human mediums the cosmology gave the impression of knowledge and control over the unknown world.

Modern religions and their secular ideological equivalents evolved from earlier cosmologies. They share with them a simple harmonious theory of causation of problems, social relationships, right and wrong, status and justice, and action for imminent fulfillment (Ingersoll & Matthews, 1986). That is, they subsume solutions to problems at all previous function levels.

Identity, Self Identity is a very complex amalgam of all previous function levels. The amalgam can act with coherence, competence, and self-awareness, and execute roles, in harmony with other identities in various social systems. Trauma can shatter every aspect of the identity amalgam and its components.

Symbols Humans can represent previous function levels symbolically through objects, behavior, or words. Status symbols, medals, territory, flags, rituals, and words can be imbued with the passions of what they represent. Symbols of past traumas can also be treated as the original trauma.

Koestler (1974) noted that symbols can generalize beyond real dangers and enemies to wide populations and have been reasons for the greatest carnages and unhappinesses in history.

Creativity, Esthetics Creativity synthesizes aspects of previous function levels to produce something new. A biological paradigm is procreation. Survival and moral creativity may occur in medicine, science, and jurisprudence. Psychological creativity can occur through dreams, thinking, fantasies, imagination, play, and humor and can be expressed through various art forms.

Esthetics adds delight to creations by connecting them with universal harmony, symmetry proportion, and beauty. In trauma creative synthesis is replaced by disintegration, beauty with ugliness, imagination with past horrors.

Sacredness Sacredness, it is suggested, connects previous function levels to the universe. This is accompanied by a sense of awe, reverence, humbleness, existential joy, cognitive holism, and ethical compulsion (Czikszentmihalyi & Rathunde, 1993). When accompanied by an intense sense of being and significance, this state is called spiritual or mystical consciousness. In traumatic situations sacred connections are disrupted and are replaced by profanities and division. Attempts to abrogate the sacred such as through power over life and death or over others' love and sexuality may reach depths of perversity.

Wisdom, Knowledge, Truth: Existential Meaning Wisdom, knowledge, and truth facilitate pragmatic navigation through the uncertain exigencies of life, and are the highest pinnacles of human endeavor as well (Sternberg, 1990).

They are variably called reason, soul, actualization, existential meaning, and purpose. While providing a glimpse of, or sharing part of the mind of the creator, they also combine awareness of one's limitations and modesty regarding one's significance. It may be said that fulfillment at all function levels provides happiness and meaning, and fulfillment of the human soul, and of life's purpose. Wisdom, knowledge, and truth provide awareness of both life and trauma at all function levels, and give a measure of control over their balance.

In summary, the depth axis provides a means of conceptualizing the "human" fulfillments which trauma shatters. The next chapter explains the great variety of often contradictory human function level contents, such as conflicting morals and values.

A Framework for the Life-Trauma Dialectic

The triaxial framework provides a deeper understanding of the life-trauma dialectic mentioned at the beginning of this book. The purpose of life, it was noted, was to survive and fulfill oneself according to the life cycle and help others to do the same. We can understand now that this takes place in different life situations at various developmental phases, and in different social systems (parameters axis), and at all human function levels (depth axis).

Challenges and threats to life (process axis) may be dealt with successfully by adaptive stress responses whose fulfillments may ramify into the other two axes. The intersection in Figure 1 may then be imagined at the adaptive stress responses point on the process axis (Figure 2). Similar intersecting points may be imagined at different process axis points, such as at maladaptive stress responses or trauma. Contents at such points can also feed (this time their sufferings) into the other axes. Because the three axes are mobile and can intersect each other at any point and because the whole system is bidirectional, each triaxial point can influence any other with its fulfillment and/or trauma ramifications.

The triaxial framework, therefore, theoretically provides an almost infinite number of points on which fulfillments and traumas can play out their dramas, yet it provides exact orientation for the points as on a three-dimensional map. The specific patterns, contents, and reasons for the dramas are described in the next chapter.

Chapter 4

Survival Strategies

While the triaxial framework provides a framework for orienting fulfillment and trauma responses, survival strategies help to categorize their great variety and to make sense of them. To use a musical analogy, the triaxial framework provides the musical instruments, orchestra, audience, concert hall, time, composer, and creativity. The eight survival strategies are the octave whose notes, overtones, and harmonics make a complex symphony. The notes themselves are well-known survival biobehaviors, but they could only be assembled following the untying of an evolutionary theory conundrum.

Evolutionary Background of Survival Strategies   Fight and flight have long been recognized as survival strategies and they are implicit in many trauma formulations. For instance, soldiers' use of these strategies underpins concepts of what is relived and avoided in PTSD, and the arousal criterion includes their physiological aspects. However, it is unlikely that only two survival strategies are the repertoire of the means to respond to traumatic situations.

Inclusion of other means of survival was hampered by evolutionary theory, which assumed that the fittest individuals (e.g., with superior fight and flight capacities) survived and reproduced selectively. The theory was stalemated by

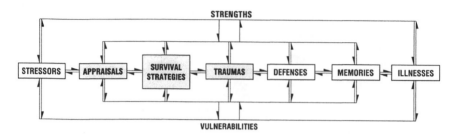

Figure 4   The place of survival strategies on the process axis.

noting that these fittest individuals often sacrificed themselves for their inferior brethren. The stalemate was broken with the realization that units of evolution were not superior individuals, but naturally occurring, interbreeding populations of some hundreds. Not only could positive mutations spread rapidly in such small populations, but it made sense that at times the evolutionary calculus was better served by sacrifice of a few superior individuals if the community was preserved, than the reverse (Scott, 1989). This opened possibilities to include survival strategies which involved altruism, mutuality, and help.

Definition and Characteristics of Survival Strategies   It is postulated that **survival strategies are biopsychosocial templates which have evolved to enhance maximum survival within social units.** Their level of operation is in the "old mammalian" brain (MacLean, 1973), between instincts on the one hand, and abstract functioning on the other. That is, they coincide with acute stress responses. Thus, in Figures 4 and 5 survival strategies replace the stress responses in Figures 2 and 3 (Chapter 3). Specific adaptive and maladaptive biological, psychological, and social responses of the eight survival strategies are categorized in this chapter (see summary in Table 2). The contributions of adaptive and maladaptive survival strategies to the life-trauma dialectic is depicted in Figure 6. Survival strategy ramification across the triaxial framework (the wholist view) is depicted in Figure 7. Heavy stippling in that figure denotes unambiguous survival strategy responses, while lighter stippling denotes derived nuances.

It can be seen that survival strategies are crucial elements which help to

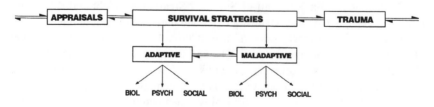

Figure 5   Survival strategies.

Figure 6   Survival strategies in fulfillment and trauma.

accomplish the "primary task of traumatology," that is, to understand, specify, and make sense of acute traumatic stress responses and their developments (Chapter 3).

Sense and Categorization of Survival Strategy Manifestations   Table 1 (Chapter 3) and Table 2 should be referred to while reading the rest of this chapter.

Table 2 lists specific appraisals which evoke one or another of the eight survival strategies. The latter are, respectively, rescuing, attaching, asserting, adapting, fighting, fleeing, competing, and cooperating. Survival strategies are arranged in pairs such as fight and flight, separated by double lines. This denotes their reciprocity, social complementariness (e.g., one rescues, the other attaches), and frequent fluctuation as alternative strategies.

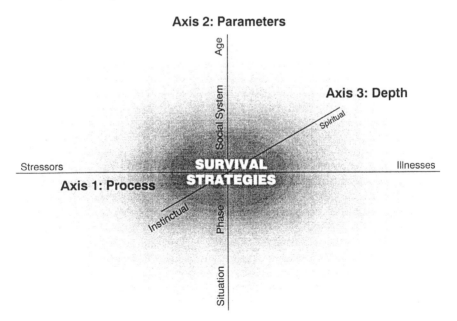

Figure 7   Wholist (triaxial and survival strategies) view of traumatic stress.

Table 2 Survival Strategy Components

APPRAISAL OF MEANS OF SURVIVAL	SURVIVAL STRATEGIES	SUCCESSFUL/ADAPTIVE RESPONSES				UNSUCCESSFUL/MALADAPTIVE RESPONSES				TRAUMA RESPONSES
		BIOLOGICAL	PSYCHOLOGICAL	SOCIAL	JUDGMENTS	BIOLOGICAL	PSYCHOLOGICAL	SOCIAL	JUDGMENTS	
MUST SAVE OTHERS	RESCUING PROTECT PROVIDE	↑ESTROGEN ↑OXYTOCIN ↑OPIOIDS	CARE EMPATHY DEVOTION	RESPONSIBILITY NURTURE PRESERVATION	RESPONSIBLE GIVING ALTRUISTIC	SYMPATHETIC & PARASYMP AROUSAL	BURDEN DEPLETION SELF-CONCERN	RESENTMENT NEGLECT REJECTION	IRRESPONSIBLE NEGLECTFUL EGOTISTIC	ANGUISH COMPASS FATIGUE CAUSED DEATH
MUST BE SAVED BY OTHERS	ATTACHING PROTECTED PROVIDED	↑OPIOIDS	HELD, CARED FOR NURTURED LOOKED AFTER	CLOSE SECURE CONTENT UNION	WORTHY DESERVING LOVABLE	↓OPIOIDS	YEARNING NEED CRAVE ABANDONMENT	CRY INSECURE DEPRIVED SEPARATION	UNWORTHY ENCUMBRANCE REJECTABLE	HELPLESSNESS CAST OUT LEFT TO DIE
MUST ACHIEVE GOAL	ASSERTING COMBAT WORK	↑E, NE ↓CORTISOL ↑IMMUNOCOMP	STRENGTH CONTROL POTENCY	WILL HIGH MORALE SUCCESS	STRONG CAPABLE SUCCESSFUL	↑E, NE DEPLETION E, NE ↑BP, ?CHD	FRUSTRATION LOSS OF CONTROL IMPOTENCE	WILLFULNESS LOW MORALE FAILURE	INADEQUATE INCOMPETENT FAILURE	EXHAUSTION "BURN-OUT" POWERLESSNESS
MUST SURRENDER GOAL	ADAPTING ACCEPT GRIEVE	PARASYMP AROUSAL ↑CORTISOL	ACCEPTANCE SADNESS GRIEF HOPE	YIELDING MOURNING TURN TO NEW	PITIFUL SYMPATHY TRIBUTE	↑CORTISOL ↓IMMUNOCOMP ↑INFECTION, ?↑CA	OVERWHELMED DEPRESSION DESPAIR	COLLAPSED WITHDRAWAL GIVING UP	WEAK PATHETIC DESPICABLE	DAMAGED GIVEN IN SUCCUMBING
MUST REMOVE DANGER	FIGHTING DEFEND RID	SYMP AROUSAL ↑N, NE ↑BP	THREAT REVENGE FRIGHTEN	DETERRENCE WOUNDING RIDDANCE	BRAVE NOBLE HEROIC	↑↑SYMP AROUSAL ↓CORTISOL	HATRED PERSECUTION KILLING	ATTACK ERADICATION DESTRUCTION	VIOLENT WICKED MURDERER	HORROR EVIL "MURDER"
MUST REMOVE ONESELF FROM DANGER	FLEEING RUN, HIDE SAVE ONESELF	SYMPATHETIC & PARASYMP AROUSAL	FEAR TERROR DELIVERANCE	RETREAT FLIGHT ESCAPE	PITIABLE VULNERABLE REFUGEE	NE DEPLETION ↑E & CORTISOL	PHOBIA PARANOIA ENGULFMENT	AVOIDANCE PANIC ANNIHILATION	TIMID PANICKY COWARD	"INESCAPABLE SHOCK," BEING HUNTED, KILLED
MUST OBTAIN SCARCE ESSENTIALS	COMPETING POWER ACQUISITION	↑↑TESTOSTERONE SYMP AROUSAL	WINNING STATUS DOMINANCE	CONTEST HIERARCHY POSSESSION	SUPERIOR RESPECTED HONORED	↓TESTOSTERONE ↓FEMALE HORMS ↑CORTISOL	DEFEAT GREED, ENVY EXPLOITATION	OPPRESSION STRUGGLE PLUNDER	INFERIOR CONTEMPTIBLE HUMILIATED	TERRORIZATION MARGINALIZATION ELIMINATION
MUST CREATE MORE ESSENTIALS	COOPERATING TRUST MUTUAL GAIN	↑OPIATES ↓BP, E, NE	MUTUALITY GENEROSITY LOVE	INTEGRATION RECIPROCITY CREATIVITY	TENDER POIGNANT BEAUTIFUL	↓OPIATES ↑↑PARASYMP AROUSAL	BETRAYAL SELFISHNESS ABUSE	DISCONNECTION CHEATING DISINTEGRATION	DECEIVER ROBBER PERVERSE, UGLY	FRAGMENTATION ALIENATION DECAY

E, epinephrine; NE, norepinephrine; Immunocomp, immunocompetence; Parasymp, parasympathetic; Symp, sympathetic; BP, blood pressure; CHD, coronary heart disease; CA, cancer.

Survival strategies are listed according to their adaptive and maladaptive, biological, psychological, and social characteristics. The lines between them are for the sake of clarity, rather than depiction of facts. Adaptive and maladaptive survival strategies oscillate, and biological, psychological, and social responses act as functional biopsychosocial units. Similarly, the apparently static divisions in the table belie the dynamism within it and its triaxial connections.

The first line for each psychological and social description of survival strategy responses (and the first line under the survival strategy name in column 2) refers to physical survival, while the second to provision of resources. The third lines (bold and underlined) are combinations of both. Words may appear to be ambiguous or relevant across survival strategies. This may reflect some characteristics which survival strategies share, or insufficient honing of language. On the other hand, the wealth of available words compelled me at times to pick what I considered the most apt of a range of words. The reader may choose other valid words.

The table also lists traumas which may arise from each unsuccessful survival strategy. In addition, adaptive and maladaptive judgments of worth are included to give a sense of survival strategy ramifications along the depth axis.

Brief descriptions of survival strategies and their manifestations on the three axes follow. Broader descriptions including their theoretical underpinnings are described in another book (Valent, 1998a).

RESCUING: CARETAKING

In this Survival Strategy one person saves the life of another. The paradigmatic picture is a man carrying another person to safety or a mother breastfeeding a baby.

In the pressure cooker of disasters the cues of the helpless may become imperative motivators to instant bonding and helping (MacLean, 1985; Zahn-Waxler, Cummings, & Ianotti, 1986). In later disaster phases, and in caretaking, the bonding may take longer to develop.

Process Axis

Appraisals that one must save another evoke stress responses which lead to protection and provision of essentials.

Adaptive Stress Responses
Biological The thalamocingulate division of the limbic system, female sex hormones (Rosenblatt, 1989), opioids (Panksepp, Siviy, & Normansell, 1985), and cortisol may be involved.

Psychological The feeling of *care* (Table 2), it is suggested, originates in the chest as an outgoing protective feeling. One is propelled with extended arms which crave to hold the other to the chest. Provision is associated with a sense of convex fullness in the chest desiring to fill the other's emptiness. In that sense it resembles breastfeeding. In tandem, *empathy* is the cognitive and emotional giving, and through preoccupation and attunement (Batson, 1978) helpers understand the "soul" of the pain and injury of others (Wilson & Lindy, 1994). *Devotion* combines care and empathic giving to the point of self-sacrifice.

Social   Responsibility for the other is associated with a sense of a special role and self-image. *Nurture* includes provision as well as tending, making the other prosper and help toward self-care. *Preservation* of the whole other person is the final success.

Maladaptive Stress Responses
Biological aspects of maladaptive rescue-caretaking have not been sufficiently studied, though the intense distress must be reflected physiologically.

Psychological   Aspects reflect a swing from self-sacrifice to *self-concern,* as a result of the other feeling to be a *burden,* a literal weight, to the extent of a sense of collapsing under it, or being dragged down to one's doom by it. Helpers may feel "milked," used up, drained, and *depleted.*

Social   Resentment takes over from responsibility. It may be manifested by irritable words, gestures pushing away, or by passive withdrawal. Empathy and care are withdrawn, resulting in *neglect* of the other. *Rejection* may manifest in stiff body and straight arms in a gesture of rebuffal or actual aggression.

Trauma   Failure to rescue and care arouses *anguish,* an agonizing worry that one may (have) *cause(d) the death* of another. It is associated with intense survivor guilt. The fullness of adaptive giving in the chest feels wrung and distorted, and this is reflected in the wringing of hands which cannot care. *Compassion fatigue* (Figley, 1995a; 1995b) is the cost of ineffective empathy and caring (Chapter 11).

Illnesses   Figley (1995a; 1995b) formulated compassion fatigue and secondary traumatic stress disorder (STSD) as helper illnesses. The latter was the equivalent of PTSD in victims, with the difference that the stressor criterion was derived secondarily from traumatized victims. Helper illnesses are considered in more detail in Chapter 11.

Parameters Axis

Rescue/caretaking varies according to *type of disaster* and *disaster phases.* In the impact phase it is often directed to preservation of life, postimpact to provision of resources and later to reconstruction of prior reserves and buffer states.

Rescuing also varies according to target *social system levels* such as individuals, families, or communities.

Developmental Phases   Children help each other and attempt to help helpless parents from a very early age. Their failure may lead to inappropriate guilt. Children develop sufficient empathy by six to nine years to respond appropriately to others' plight (Batson, 1978). Later devotion may have features of idealism in adolescents, giving way to pragmatism as they become parents.

Depth Axis

Fulfillment   To save or be the source of another's life is one of the most meaningful and purposeful of human satisfactions. It satisfies moral feelings of goodness, worthiness, and doing the right thing, fulfills ideals of altruism, maintains values and principles, and provides dignity and an identity which is part of the sacred stream of creating life. This may be symbolized by Jesus on the cross saving humanity, and Mary feeding Jesus. Wisdom understands the balance between vulnerability and giving life, and propagates knowledge which enhances the saving and fulfilling of even more lives.

Trauma   It includes the anguish, agony, guilt, and shame for causing suffering and death to others. One feels one has abrogated basic ideals, principles, and values. Having interrupted the universal law of giving life, one's purpose in life loses meaning.

In summary, preserving life gives life meaning and purpose. Failure removes them.

ATTACHMENT

In attachment one's life is saved by another. The paradigmatic picture is being carried to safety, and a breastfed infant being held securely. Attachment reciprocates rescue-caretaking bonding, and like it, can form quickly in traumatic situations. Attachment and caretaking are present in all animals beyond reptiles (MacLean, 1985). As a survival biobehavior, attachment was first described by Bowlby (1971).

Process Axis

Appraisals that others are needed to protect and provide evoke attachment.

Adaptive Stress Responses
Biological   More research is needed in this area, but probably the thalamocingulate division of the limbic system and similar hormones and opioids to the ones described for bonding (see above) are involved.

Psychological The person feels *held and cared for* by a special other. This includes being seen, recognized, held by gaze and mind, and being empathically responded to in a constant and reliable manner (Winnicott, 1960b). Feeling *nurtured* includes physical and emotional satisfaction of needs, while the sense of being well *looked after* provides a combination of physical security and emotional satiety.

Social One may see a *closely* held (in the narrow or wide sense of the word), *secure,* and *content* person in a life-giving *union.*

Maladaptive Stress Responses
Biological Separation anxiety seems to be associated with sympathetic activity, while yearning with parasympathetic. Separation calls, and a sense of separation and isolation are associated anatomically with the cingulate gyrus, and physiologically with opioid withdrawal (MacLean, 1985; Panksepp, 1989b), elevations in ACTH and adrenal cortical secretions, and depression of the immune system (Field & Reite, 1985). Separations may lead to irregularities and vulnerabilities in short- and long-term attunements for many physiological functions. For instance, they may compromise immune function and lead to vulnerability to cancer (Coe, Wiener, Rosenberg, & Levine, 1985; Panksepp et al., 1985).

Psychological *Yearning* has been called a separation pain (Raphael, 1984), one which rivals most intense physical pains. It is felt as an intense longing in the chest directed towards the absent person. Lack of nurturing leads to specific physiological *needs* and *cravings,* perhaps the most intense being the one to be held, rating above hunger. Continued separation leads to a sense of *abandonment* and aloneness in the world.

Social Intense *insecurity* is accompanied by separation calls (distress vocalizations), which may be heart rending to those who hear them. Arms reach out to be picked up and to belong. The body may follow in search. *Deprivations* lead to various biological and psychological deficiency states. *Separation* is the final state of not being attached.

Trauma Attachment trauma has been characterized by *helplessness* (Freud, 1926; van der Kolk, 1987; Allen, 1995), which in addition to maladaptive attachment features has a sense of being *cast out* into a bondless, unconnected universe dominated by threat (Lifton, 1980). Psychological casting out is into a mental vacuum, unrelatedness, and nonentity (Guntrip, 1973). The person feels that he or she is *left to die.*

Illnesses
Biological Autonomic nervous system manifestations can present as various breathing, stomach, and bowel symptoms. The latter may range from "three

month colic" themselves to peptic ulcers (Dunn, 1942; Folks & Kinney, 1995). Skin conditions such as neurodermatitis and eczema have been suggested to be preceded by separation traumas (Alexander, 1950; Taylor, 1987), as has asthma (Weiner, 1977; Moran, 1995). Severe early emotional deprivation can lead to a wide variety of illnesses and even death (Spitz, 1965; Kraemer, 1985), and predisposition to later illnesses, such as cancer (Chapter 3).

Psychological Freud (1926) postulated that depending on defenses used, separation trauma could lead to separation anxiety, phobias, and obsessional neuroses. Later, workers noted attachment failures to lead to psychological deadness, false self, anorexia nervosa, and borderline disorders (Winnicott, 1960a; Kohut, 1971; Kernberg, 1975).

Social Attachment failures can lead to dependence, school refusals, symbolic comforting through food (leading to obesity), drugs, and a variety of actings out of internal tensions.

In addition, the great variety of potential attunement failures may contribute to vulnerabilities to a further great variety of symptoms and illnesses.

Parameters Axis

Developmental Phases Discriminate biological bias towards an individual caretaker at birth (Stern, 1984), and the attachment bond is clear by two months. It is most intense between three and 12 months and remains intense until three years. It diminishes thereafter, but in humans never extinguishes.

Phases of childhood separation studied include first early clinging and searching, followed by "despair" for some days, followed by "detachment" (Robertson & Robertson, 1967–1973; Bowlby, 1975). However, it may be that grief and the defenses against it add to the appearance of despair and detachment. Reunion after prolonged separation may lead to hostility and "anxious attachment." On the other hand, adaptive attachment bonds may serve as lifesaving mental anchors through lonesome travails (e.g., Dimsdale, 1974).

Social units may attach to ever bigger ones, such as families to government services, nations to powerful allies.

Depth Axis

Fulfillment To the pleasures of being cared for and nurtured are added self-esteem judgments of being good, lovable, and deserving, and meanings that the world is abundant and benevolent. Carers are seen as ideal, and their care for oneself is seen as a core value, principle, and right. When such earthly carers are absent, they may be substituted by magical and divine carers, and indeed heaven is often pictured in terms of adaptive attachment. Ideologies may promise heaven on earth. Real security and nurturing lay foundations for a mature, satisfied and creative identity, with a sense of belonging in a sympathetic universe. Wisdom acknowledges one's need of other people. It accepts with appreciation, knowing that gifts of life may not continue forever.

Trauma Added to the torments of abandonment and helplessness one experiences guilt and shame for deserving such punishment. One feels unlovable and unworthy, basically not worth caring for. Alternately, when the good, vulnerable, and innocent are made to suffer, this leads to collapse of the sense of benevolence and justice of the universe—its values for life. One feels abandoned by God and ideology. There is no meaningful nurturing, no love shining down on one to live for.

In summary, fulfilled attachment is the vision of paradise. Attachment trauma is like being cast out from it.

ASSERTIVENESS: GOAL ACHIEVEMENT

In assertiveness life is preserved by achieving essential goals. The paradigmatic picture is of competent individuals hunting, working, or soldiering. Hunting is the evolutionary precedent (Laughlin, 1977; Isaac, 1977; Lee, 1977), which underpinned the recent spurt of brain evolution and has also resulted in increased competence in combat. Work derived from hunting, often still maintaining biases toward territoriality and small male groups.

Process Axis

Appraisals register that one must achieve essential goals in order to survive.

Adaptive Stress Responses
Biological The lateral perifornical hypothalamus, and ventral and lateral tegmental areas of the brain (Shaikh, Brutus, Siegel, H. E., & Siegel, A., 1987) are involved in association with sympathetic nervous system activation. The latter leads to elevations in blood pressure, serum epinephrine (E), norepinephrine (NE), cholesterol, and fatty acids, and decreased coagulation time (Smith, 1991; Panksepp, 1993). At the same time the cortisol-producing axis HPA (hypothalamic pituitary adrenal cortex) is suppressed (Ursin, Baade, & Levine, 1978; Hoch, Werle, & Weicker, 1988).

Psychological Goal-directed activity rallies mental and physical *strength,* whose energy radiates into concentrated effort. *Control* over mind, body, and environment gives a sense of *potency,* mastery, and capacity (McClelland, 1975).

Social Control is reflected in *will,* authority, leadership, and forcefulness. Group will is reflected in *high morale.* Ultimately, these features lead to the goal being *successfully* achieved.

Maladaptive Stress Responses

Biological Responses are intensified, but exhaustion of components such as opioids (Friedman, 1991) and NE (van der Kolk & Greenberg, 1987) may occur.

Psychological Thwarted efforts lead to *frustration*. *Loss of control* at times experienced as "going over the top" or "nervous breakdown," may progress to a sense of *impotence*.

Social Manifestations may include *willfulness*, often resulting in folly (Tuchman, 1983; Lifton, 1973). *Demoralization* manifests in loss of confidence and dedication to the task. These features lead to *failure* to achieve goals.

Trauma *"Burn-out"* involves attrition of energies and capacities, as if one's flame of energy was going out (see also Chapter 11). *Exhaustion* denotes extreme fatigue which is, however, not amenable to resolution through rest and sleep. In combat exhaustion (Bartemeier et al., 1946) soldiers looking older than their years were bent with tiredness, but were also smoldering with resentment and frustration. *Powerlessness* underlies total impotence to achieve essential goals. It is sometimes confused with helplessness, as in the concept learned helplessness.

Illnesses

Biological Sympathetic nervous system manifestations include the arousal symptoms of PTSD, as well as of every body system. For instance, muscular tension can manifest as head, back, and chest pains. Palpitations, blurred vision, breathlessness, restlessness, arrhythmias, and even sudden death (Niaura & Goldstein, 1992) are manifestations in other systems.

Long-term physiological responses to sustained hostility have been implicated in hypertension (e.g., Niaura & Goldstein, 1992/1995), and coronary artery disease (e.g., Boman, 1982a; Appels & Mulder, 1989; Goldstein & Niaura, 1992/1995). The same factors may also be relevant in strokes.

Psychological Burn-out is becoming recognized as an illness (Figley, 1995b). Its social manifestations may include aggression and substance abuse to release tension (see also Chapter 11).

Parameters Axis

Different work and combat groups have different cultures. Many share training in the preimpact phase, peak effort in the impact phase, and unwinding and enjoyment of the results in later phases. Goals may express themselves differently in different social system levels such as groups, families, and nations. Last, developmental goals change over the life cycle. Efficient control of the breast may develop into mastery of complex skills. The last goal may be a good death.

Depth Axis

Fulfillment   Contrasting with attachment, assertiveness pleasures and judgments favor autonomy and achievements by oneself. These are esteemed, admired, and rewarded. Independence and self-sufficiency are values and ideals for which one strives, while achievements provide dignity and identity. Actualization of one's full potential is an accepted principle, and may be enshrined in ideology. When success is uncertain and hazardous as in hunting and wars, magic and religion may fortify the sense of control. Such activities and rites of passage are associated with sacredness, stemming from being part of a chain of life, sometimes killing to acquire life. Wisdom appreciates the satisfaction of one's achievements, while acknowledging that one day one will be reaped oneself.

Trauma   It is characterized by powerlessness, impotence, and failure. This is made worse by judgments of inadequacy, loss of esteem, worth, and dignity. Ideals of achievement and making a mark in the universe collapse. One becomes a failed human being without purpose.
In summary, achieving life's goals gives a sense of pride in one's being, while failure leads to ignominy.

ADAPTATION: GOAL SURRENDER

In adaptation, life is preserved by relinquishing unachievable goals in order to turn to new ones. The paradigmatic pictures are soldiers who retreat to regroup, and the bereaved, who grieve and refind love. Grief seems to be a recent evolutionary phenomenon though mourning rituals occur in all cultures (Stearns, 1993). Tolerance and understanding of grief and depression varies. Anglo-Saxon cultures developed a disdain for open crying.

Process Axis

Appraisal includes the need to surrender a life goal for the sake of a higher priority one. Unambiguity of losses, such as viewing a dead body, makes such appraisals easier.

Adaptive Stress Responses
Biological   Responses involve the hippocampus and septum (Panksepp, 1986a), parasympathetic nervous system, and the HPA axis. The latter results in increased cortisol secretion and suppression of the immune system. Selye (1936, 1973) called this a universal "general adaptation syndrome," but it is only one specific stress pattern (Henry, 1986).

Psychological   There is *acceptance* that something terrible and irretrievable has happened. Initial shock and outcry give way to *sadness* and *grief*. The pangs of grief are among the greatest pains humans have to endure (Bowlby,

1981). The heart feels wrenched, torn, and wounded. Tears of sobbing are a salve for the wounds. After a sometimes long process loss is accommodated, *hope* returns, and love turns to the new.

Social *Yielding* to superior forces allows adaptation to them. *Mourning* what has been yielded may be seen as the social equivalent of grief, and the healing of physical wounds (Engel, 1961; Parkes & Weiss, 1983). Funerals and other ceremonies formalize a social structure for comforting and healing, provision of hope, and moving on after a time.

Maladaptive Stress Responses

Biological Adaptive stress responses are accentuated. For instance, depression is associated with increased levels of corticotrophin releasing factor, ACTH, and cortisol (Panksepp, 1993), and diminished immunocompetence in both cellular and humoral parts of the immune system (Bartrop et al., 1977; Irwin, Daniels, & Wiener, 1987; Calabrese et al., 1987).

Psychological Being *overwhelmed* has been thought to be the hallmark of the trauma response (Freud, 1920; Figley, 1985a). However, like shock, it can be reversed. Without adaptive grieving and mourning, unresolved grief and *depression* may result. Unlike the pain of an open wound, depression feels like a heaviness in the chest with compressed hurt and tears, whose connection with loss is often lost. When connection and grief are refound, depression often disappears (Chapter 1). Even hopelessness and *despair,* which may feel like depression encased in immovable concrete are reversible.

Social Subjective shock from outside appears as *collapse,* sometimes called being stunned, the disaster syndrome (Wallace, 1957), or conservation-withdrawal (Engel & Schmale, 1972). People feel extreme weakness, though, if asked, they can move. Lack of will makes them suggestible and docile, enabling groups to be herded to safety. Otherwise, people may *withdraw* and curl up in bed, *giving up* hope (Schmale, 1972).

Trauma When loss wounds are too great, *damage* to the torn heart leaves at the least some later scars. In unremitting situations, as in concentration camps, people may *give in* and *succumb* through a loss of desire to live (Bettelheim, 1943; 1960) ". . . the sudden loss of hope and courage can have a deadly effect" (Frankl, 1959, p. 75).

Illnesses

Biological Physiological manifestations of shock and conservation-withdrawal are dizziness, tiredness and fatigue, cold and nausea, and arrhythmias even leading to death (Steptoe, 1981). Suppressed sobs may feel like a lump in the throat.

Mortality rates (Rees & Lutkins, 1967; Levenson & Bemis, 1995) and incidence of a variety of severe illnesses (Parkes & Weiss, 1983; Levenson & Bemis, 1995) increase markedly over controls in bereaved spouses. It may be that immune system dysfunctions contribute to infections, cancer, and autoimmune diseases.

Psychological   *Unresolved griefs* result from fixations within the grieving process (Chapter 2; Rando, 1993). It is suggested that inhibited or absent grief may be due to fear of adaptation trauma (including despair and succumbing) and other survival strategy traumas, such as flight in cases of horrible multiple deaths. Chronic mourning and conflicted griefs typically include unresolved attachment and rescue-caretaking traumas, sometimes in ambivalent relationships with unacknowledged angers and guilts. Types of unresolved griefs often overlap. In each case the various survival strategy traumas need to be dealt with before grief can proceed.

Depression as an illness is the most common post-traumatic diagnosis (Yehuda & McFarlane, 1995), and comorbid illness with PTSD (Sutker, Uddo, Brailey, Allain, & Errera, 1994). It is suggested that depression includes the mood depression (see above), and dissociated elements of unresolved grief. As noted, the latter may contain symptoms from other survival strategies. For instance, attachment symptoms may include agitation associated with impulse to search, and suicidal ideas or assumption of the symptoms of the dead in a bid for union with them.

Social symptoms include drug-taking and other dependencies to ease psychic pain, promiscuity, pregnancies, and premature marriages to substitute lost objects, delinquency in children, and shoplifting in adult women, as well as accidents and suicidal attempts to draw attention to one's distress.

Parameters Axis

Phases of grief have been described as shock and denial, anger, bargaining, sadness and depression, acceptance and hope (Kübler-Ross, 1969). In fact, clinically such progression is rare (Vargas, Loya, & Hodde-Vargas, 1989). In order to avoid above confusion of emotions, defenses, judgments, and survival strategies, it may be more useful to apply usual disaster phases with shock and other adaptation stress responses in the impact phase, needing to go over every detail of the loss and ventilating sadness and other emotions in the postimpact phase, and finding new meaning in reconstruction and recovery phases. Bittersweet nostalgia and full acceptance of new goals may take years (Kleiner, 1970; Parkes, 1972).

Social systems of grief and depression may be individual, family, communal, national, or even international. Secondary and transgenerational symptoms are common.

Developmentally, grief and weeping appear first around six months and take on, if allowed ever more adult forms by 16 months (Bowlby, 1981). Grief may be obscured by adults, children's shorter attention spans, and their concerns for their current survival. The meaning of death develops over the life cycle. Children under five see it as living in a different place, later death is personified, while after nine it can be seen as final. Adults may hark back to earlier developmental interpretations of death.

Depth Axis

Fulfillment in loss may seem to be a paradox. However, sobbing and grief provide relief, and tears salve wounds of the heart. Grief is also a gift of love, a virtuous tribute to the departed, which is esteemed by others. At the same time ideals of stoicism and dignity are valued, too. The justice of death is explained in terms of the principle that life is borrowed and the lender takes back his goods. Magic, myths, and religion mitigate and deny loss. Indeed, heaven is a place of eternal reunion with no losses. However, with acceptance of earthly reality existential meanings became redefined. One is then part of the sacred rhythm of life, death, and regeneration, the latter leading to new hopes and loves. Wisdom accepts grief and tears as crossing a river from the dead to new life. It accepts the vicissitudes of loves and losses and one's own ultimate death, hopefully in its own good time.

Trauma   There is an absence of satisfying grief, morality, or justice. Traumatic loss offers no solace; perhaps it even earns stigma and blame. Death has no value, follows no principle, is undignified, bizarre, profane, and meaningless. The rhythm of life is permanently disrupted for no purpose. The only wisdom is to not love in order to not lose.

In summary, grief is like a weeping but healing wound. Without weeping life stays ripped apart.

FIGHT: DEFENSE

In fight life is preserved by removal of danger. The paradigmatic picture is driving out enemies, or killing in order to not be killed.

Cells already kill foreign cells which intrude into their territories, and the xenophobic (Wilson, 1975) and territorial (Ardrey, 1967) principles have persisted throughout evolution. In early societies defense was very important with death from wild animals contributing to a life expectancy of only 25 (Laughlin, 1977). Riddance of internal enemies such as parasites and poisons was through body wastes. Disgust of enemies signifying such poisons and body wastes, and fighting them in sorcery through such wastes, is a human phenomenon (Rozin, Haidt, & McCauley, 1993).

Process Axis

Appraisals of others' postures, vocalizations, and intrusions evoke responses whose goal is to tilt the fear—aggression balance (Shalit, 1994) toward enemy fear and withdrawal. Killing indicates failure of adaptive defense.

Adaptive Stress Responses

Biological The hippocampus, medial amygdala, medial tegmentum, and hypothalamus are involved in fight (Shaikh et al., 1985; Heath, 1992). The sympathetic nervous system is intensely aroused (Cannon, 1939; Panksepp, 1986), while the HPA and cortisol secretion remain level or are even inhibited (Henry, 1986). Androgens may increase aggression and territoriality (Yahr, 1983; Olweus, Mattsson, Schalling, & Low, 1988).

Psychological *Threatening* words and actions convey the rage felt, which is akin to a furnace in the chest radiating energy to muscles which are ready to attack. Once blood is drawn or a wound (including psychological such as to honor) has been inflicted on onself, *revenge* is highly desired. Successful defense *frightens* off potential attackers.

Social Here threats accomplish *deterrence*. In retaliatory revenge this may incur *wounding* in kind. If successful, threats and retaliation achieve *riddance* of the enemy. Release of body fluids may be a way of fighting disgust with disgust, forcing withdrawal of even powerful attackers.

Maladaptive Stress Responses

Biological arousal, especially of the sympathetic nervous system, is intensified.

Psychological Rage may intensify to fury and *hatred*. They may feel like turmoil in the chest and twisting of the gut which demand elimination, and evoke *persecutory* desires to *kill* the enemy.

Social This results in *attack*. Killing may still be averted if a thrashed enemy is seen to have "learned his lesson" and ceases to be a threat. Otherwise *eradication* may seem to be the only solution, leading to *destruction* of life, potential avengers, and even of a whole people and culture.

Trauma Any doubt about whether killing was necessary to not be killed leads to *horror* and traumatic responses such as numbness, unreality, nausea, and severe headaches (Lifton, 1973; Browning, 1992). The horror is associated with the sense of having become *evil* through trespassing the taboo of *murder*.

Illnesses

Biological Sympathetic nervous system symptoms and illnesses resemble those responses in assertiveness, and may be even more intense and long term.

For instance, suppressed arousal may contribute significantly to hypertension and coronary artery disease (CAD) (Barefoot, Dodge, Peterson, Dahlstrom, & Williams, 1989; Kubanyi, Gino, Denny, & Torigoe, 1994). Disgust-related symptoms include nausea and vomiting, and possibly defecation.

Psychological Aggression and violence are common constituents of antisocial personality disorders. Aggression has been central in psychoanalytic formulations (e.g., Freud, 1917; 1920). Its combination with projection leads to paranoia, turned inward towards self-destruction; fused with sexuality, it leads to sadism and masochism.

Social Misplaced violence has been a pervasive tragedy of humankind (see below).

Parameters Axis

Phases In the preimpact phase definitions of enemies and friends, territories and "lines in the sand" take place. Fantasies supplement ambiguities of such definitions. Aggression and its discharge in the impact phase may be abetted by prior oratory or watching violence. After the fight, the cost is counted and the future assessed.

Fight occurs at all *social system levels,* ranging from individuals to groups, communities and nations. The same can be said for enemies and scapegoats.

Developmental Phases Infants already split, good and bad, project their own aggression onto others, and displace it onto scapegoats. By four to seven months, parental parts and parents as whole are attacked physically, with body fluids and fantasies. Targets for attack may be dehumanized into objects or demonized into predators. Hatred evoked by childhood abuse and traumas can smolder, and be expressed and displaced even after many years (Athens, 1989; Collins & Bailey, 1990; Walsh, 1991; Zaidi & Foy, 1994). Adults also split, project and displace, dehumanize and demonize. When consequent killings do not accord with real dangers, they are murders and atrocities (Lifton, 1973; Browning, 1992).

Depth Axis

Fulfillment Defense of life and its ramifications such as justice, ideals, values, principles, honor, and dignity, even if it means killing or being killed, are sensed as fulfilling and purposeful. Their defense takes on the characteristics, such as honor and principles, of what is defended. Killing and self-sacrifice are also seen as virtuous, justified, brave, and heroic, and may occur according to warrior codes. Comrade bonds are forged through blood into intense love, with special love and obedience for the leader. In just wars God is on one's side, and in religious wars he provides wonderful rewards in the next life. Cult figures and ideologies may be substituted for religion. People may fight for symbols of all of the above, such as flags and crosses. The warrior feels whole in his identity and proud of his creative tactics, and weaponry. Killing may assume sacred qualities by risking and inflicting death in order to achieve eternal life. Knowledge is that of taking human life. Yet wisdom sees the truth that killing may have predator fear at its core, and these days such fear can be resolved differently.

Trauma   Killing is not self-defense, but murder and atrocity. It is immoral and wicked, violating basic human ideals, values, principles, rights, and dignity. It violates law and divine commandments, and disrupts the sacredness of life. A minority of perpetrators counter traumatic horror with what is called virulent violence (Athens, 1989). They come to enjoy the power rush, thrill, even ecstasy of killing. By breaking the ultimate taboo, they may see themselves as gods who decide who shall live and die. But they require ever greater heaps of dead (Canetti, 1973), and killing becomes profane, banal, as it did in Auschwitz (Lifton, 1986). That is even more horrifying.

In summary, fighting in self-defense was an essential survival strategy against predators. It may be misapplied and perverted through extant primitive fears.

FLIGHT: ESCAPE

In flight, life is preserved by removing oneself from danger. It is the reciprocal survival strategy to fight. Escape may involve running, hiding, freezing, camouflaging. Similar avoidances may occur psychologically.

Process Axis

Appraisals register that one must escape danger.

Adaptive Stress Responses
Biological   Flight is associated with the anterior hypothalamic, medial preoptic regions, and dorsomedial hypothalamus (Panksepp, 1989b; Henry, 1986a). The sympathetic nervous system is activated, though it may be admixed with parasympathetic activity and mild elevation of cortisol (Henry, 1986a).

Psychological   *Fear* is a cold constriction clutching at the heart. Its sympathetic nervous system accompaniments include shivering and trembling, palpitations, hard breathing, butterflies in the stomach, weakness in the knees, and the need to defecate and void. Fear may lead to *terror* and an imperative need to escape, hide, or freeze. Startle may be sudden terror motivating movement, while fright a surge of frozen terror. Successful flight leads to a sense of *deliverance.*

Social   Posture indicates a lack of threat in smallness, the voice squealing, the eyes downcast. *Retreat* may follow, though this may be intensified to *flight* itself when terror seizes. Successful flight effects *escape.*

Maladaptive Stress Responses

Biological   Adaptive physiological responses are accentuated (Friedman, 1991). In inescapable shock NE depletion and subsequent NE sensitivity may occur. Associated opioid mediated analgesia (van der Kolk & Greenberg, 1987), increased cortisol secretion, and diminished immunocompetence (Knapp et al., 1992) may occur.

Psychological   Unsuccessful escapes may turn into *phobias* of the original situations and cues reminiscent of them (Öhman, 1993). Evolutionary fear, relevant stimuli such as darkness, aloneness, and fear of predators have natural biases to become phobias. On the other hand, derived fears of people, often displaced from earlier times, may lead to *paranoias*. *Engulfment* is the sense of being caught and about to be destroyed.

Social   Retreat from dangerous situations manifests as *avoidance.* Intense avoidance associated with terror may lead to *panic,* an impulse to flee without curbs (Quarantelli, 1954). *Annihilation* is the final dreaded outcome, often conceptualized in primitive predator or poison terms.

Trauma   *Inescapable shock* (Maier & Seligman, 1976; van der Kolk, Boyd, Krystal, & Greenberg, 1984) is the sense of being caught "This is it!". Those who escaped such moments describe them in terms of frozen terror, dissociation, numbness, resignation, and bewilderment. There is a sense that one has been *hunted down* and is about to be *killed.*

Illnesses

Biological   Sympathetic nervous system arousal can produce widespread symptoms (see above) similar to those described in assertiveness. Furthermore, anxiety may accentuate symptoms of all illnesses, and hyperventilation can mimic any psychophysiological symptom (Lum, 1975). Prolonged sympathetic arousal may also contribute to hypertension and CAD.

Psychological   Fear, terror, panic, and associated arousal are central features of PTSD and the anxiety disorders of DSM IV—panic, phobia, and generalized anxiety disorders. Separation of these disorders may be somewhat artificial, as on close examination they have similar precedents (Öhman, 1993), and differences between them may only reflect different traumatic situations and defenses. For instance, claustrophobia may be related to fears of engulfment, drowning and choking, while agoraphobia, school phobia, and phobia of darkness may avoid predator-like vulnerability. Displacement of fear on to people may lead to paranoia, and on to the body to hysteria (Breuer & Freud, 1893; Freud, 1921). Both Freud and PTSD theorists have sometimes seen fear and flight-type anxiety as central to all trauma illnesses. However, in this book I maintain that all survival strategies have their specific trauma anxieties (Chapter 6).

Social illnesses involve fearful and avoidant behavior which may come to be entrenched in timid, paranoid, or schizoid traits.

Parameters Axis

Each *phase* has a characteristic means of escape. Preimpact may involve evacuation, impact phase running and hiding, while avoidances characterize later phases. Flight may occur at individual, family, and community *system levels.*

Developmental Phases Infants already withdraw their gazes, heads, and limbs from fearful situations. Atavistic fears in children's tales may reflect realities of high infant mortality till recently. Sources of danger vary through the life cycle, but some remain constant. Adult fears often include earlier atavistic ones.

Depth Axis

Fulfillment Ingenious escapes alternate with heroic fights as sources of admiration. Escape and refuge provide great relief and hope of resuming a fulfilling life. The promised shores of a sanctuary country such as the U.S. or Israel are imbued with high values and idealism. Codes and obligations of giving refuge provide for dignity, rights, and entitlements for refugees. Religion may provide spiritual refuge, heaven being an eternal sanctuary. Ideologies provide security on earth. Wisdom is an awareness of human vulnerability and of eventually being reaped, but in the meantime, appreciation of safety and vigilance to ensure it.

Trauma In it one may be trapped physically, or morally when escape is deemed as cowardice. Refuges and sanctuaries may be shot or violated. The world is seen as unsafe, callous, insensitive to one's human value, and dignity, and the right to safety. No magic, religion, or ideological sanctuary works. One is senselessly hunted down for no good purpose.

In summary, while escape results in continued life, being trapped has qualities of paranoid nightmares.

COMPETITION: STRUGGLE

In competition, life is preserved by obtaining scarce essentials. The paradigmatic picture is of two individuals contesting a prize. In adaptive competition the prize is dominance in a pecking order, which in nature provides first access to food, females, attention, and comforts (Tiger & Fox, 1971; Laughlin, 1977). Hierarchies regulate competition and maintain peace. When hierarchies break down, all struggle against all. The paradigmatic picture is then a scramble for food.

Process Axis

Appraisals assess hierarchical status and access to scarce resources.

Adaptive Stress Responses

Biological   The medial preoptic and anterior hypothalamic sites, which also selectively take up testosterone, are involved in intermale competition, which has been studied the most. Increased testosterone levels are closely associated with high status and winning across species including humans (Knol & Egberink-Alink, 1989; Booth, Shelley & Mazur, 1990). Interfemale dominance may be facilitated by female sex hormones as well as adrenal testosterone (Henry, 1986a).

Psychological   The ambition to *win* is accompanied by ambition, enterprise, and striving. Triumph brings exhilaration and a feeling of bigness, as well as *status* and *dominance*. They in turn provide a sense of superiority, power, and privilege. However, this is associated with noblesse oblige which requires making sure that all in the pecking order have enough to survive.

Social   In *contests* similar postures and actions to those in fight may be used establish superiority. However, here the intention is not to be rid of the opponent, only to show "who is who." *Hierarchy* ensures lack of internal struggle and smooth distribution down the line, but more *possession,* and ahead of others, is the ultimate prize.

Maladaptive Stress Responses

Biological   Defeat may be associated with the hippocampus and septum (Henry, 1986a) and is sensitively reflected in low testosterone and high corticosterone and ACTH levels (Henry, 1986a; Blanchard & Blanchard, 1988). Defeat may also compromise immunocompetence (Fleshner, Laudenslager, Simons, & Maier, 1989).

Psychological   *Defeat* may lead to feeling small, inferior, and in extreme cases crushed. Strains in possession exhibit *greed*, felt as an insatiable craving, *and envy,* felt as a torment of spite and acid vindictiveness in the chest or gut. Greed and envy take others' status and resources and *exploit* them.

Social   Power used to *oppress* and exploit may lead to hierarchical *struggles.* Social disorganization may lead to "each man for himself," "dog eat dog." Losers get nothing, and their remaining resources may be *plundered.*

Trauma   Forceful dominance is accompanied by *terrorization* (Bauer, Priebe, Häring, & Adamczak, 1993). The oppressed are stripped of possessions and privileges, and may themselves become exploitable commodities. Those on the lowest hierarchical rungs are *marginalized*, meaning that nothing is owed them, not even their lives. They slip into oblivion or are *eliminated*.

Illnesses

Biological   Low socioeconomic status is associated with increased rates of morbidity and mortality for a wide range of illnesses. Unwinnable conflicts may contribute to hypertension and CAD (Niaura & Goldstein, 1992) and a sense of defeat may precede coronary heart disease (Appels & Mulder, 1989).

Psychological   No specific competition illnesses are mentioned. However, psychoanalysis recognizes greed and envy and intrafamilial rivalry as important ingredients in neuroses and psychoses.

Social   Illnesses include corruption, tyranny, class struggles, and wars.

Parameters Axis

Phases of contests and struggles include preparation, execution, and subsequent hierarchical readjustments.

All *social systems* can have hierarchies and struggles. Oppressions and struggles have made up much of human history.

Developmental Phases   Envy and greed may already occur at the breast (Segal, 1975). Competition between siblings and peers is well established by the age of two (Cummings, Hollenbeck, & Ianotti, 1986). Oedipal and Electra struggles involve rivalries with the same-sex parent for the other parent. Castration anxiety may then be seen as paternal terrorization of the son. School and work rivalries follow in later life.

Depth Axis

Fulfillment   The joy of winning is augmented by the virtue of one's superiority, others' esteem and respect, and just and deserved preferential rewards. Yet, the principles and ideals of free competition allow all to achieve status and wealth according to their abilities and effort. Once achieved, status defines an important part of identity, and status symbols may be secondary sources of contest. The comforts of possession may provide resources for creative excellence and the esthetics of good taste, elegance, etiquette, and wit, all of which may become status symbols. Hierarchies may be reinforced by myths of divine lineage. Heaven itself is hierarchically arranged. Thus knowing one's place may seem to be part of a sacred, universal hierarchical order. Wisdom sees the good fortune of privilege and maintains enjoyment of it by sharing it with others.

Trauma   Defeat leading to oppression and exploitation is coupled with injustice and humiliation. A derived basic meaning may be that one is inferior, and defeat breeds defeat. Power becomes the ideal value; envy and greed manifested in gluttony, avarice, rapaciousness, and lust are ruling principles. Laws and dignity are for the dominant. Religion and ideologies use their earthly powers for extortion and depravity. Creativity and esthetics become self-indulgences. Sacredness of universal order is profaned with self-glorification and humans pretending to be gods. Wisdom to see that this is the seed to self-destruction is lost.

In summary, hierarchical order favors survival of the superior yet maintains order and preservation of those lower in the pecking order. Its breakdown leads to "jungle mentality," exploitation, and struggle.

COOPERATION: LOVE

In cooperation, life is preserved by pooling resources to create more essentials for mutual gain. The paradigmatic picture is procreation, and reciprocal giving and sharing.

Reciprocal giving is present from insects on and favors mutual survival (Trivers, 1971). Giving and taking (Youniss, 1986), exchanges and making deals (Tiger & Fox, 1971), are essential human activities which form the glue or social bonds.

Love, like grief, may be a recent evolutionary development in which special exchanges and affectionate bonds are the vehicle for procreation and mutual growth.

Process Axis

It is *appraised* that one needs another to gain essentials.

Adaptive Stress Responses
Biological   Sexuality and affiliation are associated with the amygdala, temporal pole, and orbital frontal cortex (Steklis & Kling, 1985). They have highest concentrations of opioids which enhance social comfort. Sex hormones promote sexual desire and bonding in both sexes (Panksepp, 1993). Serotogenic and cholinergic systems lower blood pressure as well as E and NE secretions (Henry, 1986a).

Psychological   Giving and taking build *mutuality* and trust. Giving occurs with a *generosity* which does not deplete, because the other is as precious as oneself. In *love,* too, one feels an overflowing heart wanting to give to the other. Reciprocated love is exciting, happy with a sense of unbounded future, and is characterized by a glow of health (Liebowitz, 1983; Hatfield & Rapson, 1993).

Social Love bonds *integrate* on the same social level. That is, *reciprocity* is nonhierarchical, giving being sensed as necessary as taking. Out of such sharing something new is *created* for both.

Maladaptive Stress Responses
Biological Sense of isolation may be associated with the cingulate gyrus and decreased opiate levels (Panksepp et al., 1985). Little is known about the physiology of sexual aberrations though suppression of male sexual hormones may diminish sexual desire and crime.

Psychological Lack of reciprocity and especially cheating are felt as *betrayal*, a stab in the back or the heart. *Selfishness* has replaced, generosity and the victim feels taken advantage of and *abused*. Abuse includes that of one's trust, love, and one's generous gifts. Physical and sexual abuse, especially of children, is an extreme extension of this.

Social *Disconnection* replaces integration. Love is replaced by lies, deceit, *cheating,* seduction, thieving, and robbery. *Disintegration* of bonds results.

Trauma Disintegration of relationships can lead to loss of psychosocial coherence and *fragmentation.* A world without significant relationships feels barren, *alien,* stagnant, and *decaying* (Lifton, 1967; 1980).

Illnesses
Biological Loving relationships may protect through soothing and increased immunocompetence (Jemmott, 1987). In contrast, relationship difficulties and breakdowns underlie a wide variety of psychophysiological symptoms, sexual disorders, and other illnesses.

Psychological Relationship problems lead to much human unhappiness, to the extent of underlying much clinical suicide behavior. Childhood love deprivation, and especially sexual abuse, predispose one to a wide variety of later psychiatric disorders (Chapter 3).

Social Attempts to substitute for love, alleviate alienation, and to feel alive include use of drugs, sex, violence, and self-mutilation.

Parameters Axis

Phases Altruistic giving may be most intense in the impact "post-disaster utopia" phases of disasters (Siporin, 1976). Love bonds are similarly most passionate during falling in love, requiring much work before settling to companionate love with its long-term loyalty, intimacy, and give and take (Lilar, 1965; Hatfield & Rapson, 1993).

Different *social system levels* have different mutual gains and loves. Male-female bonds lead to progeny, parent-child ones promote growth of progeny and parental fulfillments. Families, friends, and communities all provide a matrix for reciprocal giving and gain.

Developmental Phases Already in early infancy mothers and babies exchange looks, smiles, and body products, and babies develop gratitude and generosity (Klein, 1957/1975). By the second year, exchanges with peers and friendships begin. By nine, selected friendships develop which demand fair and equal treatment (Youniss, 1986). Sexual, adult, and parental bonds develop throughout the life cycle.

Depth Axis

Fulfillments Loving, sexual and other affectionate relationships provide much human happiness. In such relationships generosity is accompanied by a sense of goodness and self-worth, while the recipient feels reciprocally beautiful, worthwhile, and lovable. Relationships thus provide much meaning and sense of identity, even if at times they are over-valued and idealized. Yet, cooperative relationships are based on equal partnership, trust and honesty, principles of fair give and take, which may be codified in laws of trade and marriage vows. Even with gods fair exchanges involve trading sacrifices and prayers for generous returns. Both earthly and spiritual love are imbued with a mystical and sacred dimension of a creative stream of life inherent in the universe. Wisdom ensures that all love is enjoyed in its place and season.

Trauma Breaking, distortion, and betrayal of love bonds are among the worst human pains. They are aggravated by the immorality of unfair one-way betrayal, cheating, and exploitation. The world may come to be seen as untrustworthy, unloving, and oneself as worthless and unlovable. Ideals and principles of love are devalued, dignity and identity degraded. One feels alienated from oneself and the world. Sex and love may be seen as dirty and wrong. The magic of love, one's creative force, and spiritual connections with the universe are desecrated. Even procreation may be spiritually barren, and the world is esthetically ugly and vulgar. The truth seems to be that love turns in on itself and destroys life.

In summary, love and its creativity are among the most beautiful and purposeful of life's fulfillments. Their damage makes life seem empty and purposeless.

THE WHOLIST PERSPECTIVE AND MAKING SENSE OF STRESS RESPONSES

The wholist perspective can help orientate and categorize the huge diversity of survival strategy responses over the triaxial framework and explain their sense.

For instance, orienting the initial description of responses in Case 1 (Chapter 1) as survival strategies in adults in the impact phase of a bushfire allows making sense of people hosing down fires, risking themselves for others, competing for wet towels, and feeling stunned, as respectively assertiveness, rescue, competition, and adaptation survival strategies are used in changing circumstances. Later chest pain associated with frustration, and depression associated with blocked grief could be orientated in the postimpact phase, with assertiveness and adaptation survival strategies, respectively, which were moderately disconnected from awareness.

Seeing assertiveness and rescue angers in connection with being sacked and losing a daughter, ramifying to angina could help make sense in Case 2. Similarly, in Case 3, Anne's late recovery phase phobias and paranoid psychosis were traced back to flight responses to threats from fire, water, and people threatening to kill her if she disclosed. Muscle pains, headaches, and nausea emanated from suppressed fight. Tiredness, despair, and depressive disorder emanated from her ungrieved losses (adaptation).

Second, the wholist perspective can help to categorize fulfillment and trauma phenomena and their ramifications. Thus Table 2's columns categorize physiological, emotional, and social acute stress responses, traumas, and judgments of worth. The same can be done for other depth-axis components, such as virtues and guilt, justice and injustice, generalized meanings, ideologies, and the sacred and sacreligious (Valent 1998a); and trauma anxieties, angers, guilts, basic meanings, values, and religion (see Chapter 5).

In summary, the wholist perspective can help to understand the great variability of fulfillment and trauma manifestations by pinpointing their triaxial positions and tracing them back to acute stress responses evoked for survival in particular contexts. It can also help categorize phenomena by collecting various survival strategy manifestations at particular triaxial points (Chapter 5). Application of the wholist perspective to treatment ingredients is explored in the next section.

Part Three

The Wholist Perspective
Applied to Common
Treatment Principles

This section applies the wholist perspective to the four treatment principles which have been distilled in Chapter 2 and have been seen to apply to trauma therapies generally.

The four treatment principles or ingredients are recognition, and nonspecific, symptomatic, and specific treatments.

Chapter 5 is devoted to recognition. The relatively large space devoted to this ingredient acknowledges its prime importance, being a foundation for the other ingredients. The wholist perspective is applied to different tools of recognition. They include gathering information, reading and categorizing it, and sorting it into diagnoses. The wholist perspective will also provide a framework for understanding the variable treatments found in traumatology (Chapters 1 and 2).

Chapter 6 applies the wholist perspective to nonspecific, symptomatic, and specific treatment principles and their components. Nonspecific aspects of treatment such as therapeutic relationship, maintenance of boundaries, and support become more understandable and specific through the wholist perspective. So do symptomatic treatments, such as drugs and anxiety management. Application of the perspective to components of specific therapy such as recovery of memories and breaking the nexus between past and present also enriches their conceptualization and enhances control over them by increasing specificity. Finally, the perspective is applied to tailoring of treatment and research. Applications to treatment through clinical demonstrations are the subject of the following section.

Chapter 5

The Wholist View and Language
Applied to Recognition

In this chapter the wholist perspective or view is applied to recognition, the first treatment ingredient of trauma therapy. The first stage of recognition is acknowledgment that a trauma had indeed occurred. This chapter concentrates on subsequent recognition of trauma and fulfillment sequelae.

The first part of the chapter examines how a wholist attitude facilitates the modes and means of gathering information. The next part examines ways of reading the wholist language in order to make sense of it and categorize the information gathered on traumatic stress and fulfillment manifestations (including defenses). Last, the wholist perspective is applied to understanding and categorizing the wide variety of diagnoses and treatments in traumatology. Introducing both linear and nonlinear paradigms, a wholist conceptualization explains the range of such diagnoses and treatments.

WHOLIST RECEPTIVITY APPLIED TO MODES
AND MEANS OF COMMUNICATION

The wholist perspective seeks to understand how and why the lives of victims have been disrupted, in order to help remove the effects of the disruptions, and to reconstitute for people their paths of life and fulfillment.

Wholist Receptivity and Wholist Language   Wholist receptivity recognizes that disruptions are expressed through fragmented biological, psychological, and social ramifications of survival strategies along the triaxial framework (the wholist language), and that availability of one's own wholist self (willingness to read the wholist language) facilitates victims' expressions, and making connections between what happened and wherever they are "at." Translation of the wholist language to ordinary language allows symbolic coherence of the trauma story within one's life narrative (see also pp. 75–76).

Modes and Means of Communication

Wholist receptivity will now be applied to different, usually clinically overlapping modes and means of client communication. They are telling the trauma story, professional history and examination, transference, and countertransference. Verbal and nonverbal means of communication, used in all these modes, will be examined.

Facilitating Telling the Trauma Story   From the very first meeting wholist receptivity may clear a royal road to description of central traumatic events and their sequelae. As part of the receptivity, the opening question must be broad and nondirective. In intense situations a "So?" or "Well?" may unleash a gush of communication. At other times, a well-tried opening question, used in Case 2 (Chapter 1), is "Of all the things that worry you, what worries you the most?" This may be accompanied by looking in the person's eyes and a gesture indicating breadth when saying "Of all the things . . ." and the hands coming together to focus on the trauma when saying ". . . what worries you most."

On the other hand, "Tell me about your pain/depression." may establish an environment whose language is restricted to "passport symptoms" leading to particular helper biased biological or psychiatric diagnoses (see below).

The following case indicates how a lack of wholist receptivity may limit treatment, and how its presence can enhance it.

CASE 4: SUPPRESSED GRIEF AS SHORTNESS OF BREATH

An elderly woman kept returning to the emergency department with shortness of breath, to the point of being given oxygen. This time she was asked what worried her most. She paused and surprisingly said, "My son died six months ago." She had left her mentally retarded son in respite care for a weekend for the first time. He set the house alight, and died of smoke inhalation. The mother had not cried nor told this story to any doctor; she just suffered extreme guilt and shortness of breath. The latter may have been due to suppressed sobs and identification with her son choking (Chapter 9). As she talked she cried for the first time. Her shortness of breath gave way to deep sobs, and her breathing normalized. This process was repeated two more times. After discussion she accepted grief therapy with gratitude. She left without shortness of breath and did not need to return again.

The following two cases are further typical examples of how the wholist approach opens the path to central traumatic issues which are otherwise undiscovered. In the process, the presenting "passport" symptoms often dissolve.

CASE 5: ALONENESS AND ASTHMA

A man thus far simply treated with drugs for his asthma said that his greatest worry was that he anticipated being jailed in court that day. He was terrified of being confined alone, and aloneness was the usual trigger for his asthma. Through contacting the court he was able to be reassured that in case of imprisonment he would not be in solitary confinement. He was accompanied to court by a friend, free of asthma and confident that it would not recur.

CASE 6: SEPARATION AND CAR CRASH

The greatest worry of a taxi driver treated symptomatically for car crash injuries was that his wife had left him three days prior. He had driven continuously since then till he crashed. He rested, and was given help to deal with the separation.

The initial interview may resemble initial potential disclosures of traumatic events to family members. Nonacceptance may lead to compromise acceptable symptoms, or "second wound" intensification of symptoms with deterioration in clinical relationships.

CASE 7: SUPPRESSED DISCLOSURE OF ABUSE

A young woman was admitted to a psychiatric ward for supposed depression, but she quickly disclosed that a friend of the family had seduced and abused her sexually for a long time. Now that he married she was distressed more than ever, realizing how she was betrayed and exploited. Her parents were embarrassed, blamed the patient, and imposed a conspiracy of silence. The treating psychiatrist reinforced this and concentrated on treating the depression. However, the patient's "depression" worsened, she became uncooperative, and slashed herself. She was then diagnosed with a borderline personality disorder and received high doses of drugs and electroconvulsive therapy. Much later in psychotherapy the original depression was treated in terms of her deep realization of abuse and betrayal, and grief for the loss of her hope for love.

It should be emphasized that the wholist approach does not "open a can of worms," but rather leads to what is central, concentrates multiple symptoms, and saves time. It is both a human approach dealing with what is most important and meaningful to patients' lives, and is clinically efficient and comprehensive.

Frequently, the trauma story may not be unveiled through receptivity alone. Yet in retrospect such receptivity discloses a more transparent, and symbolically closer story than would be otherwise obtained. The first session, and especially the first things said, often have condensed in them matters of special significance.

In practice, a dynamic interplay exists between coherent narrative of life and its disruptions, and partial communication of disconnected narratives (see also Defenses below).

Professional Histories   Professional histories follow up developments of presenting symptoms and a wider perspective of the sufferers.

Histories and observations can provide connections in trauma stories, even if outside patients' awareness, through contiguity of events and onset of symptoms, evocation of symptoms as the person is talking about such events, and similar gestures and expressions associated with talking about symptoms and the original events. Families and agencies are another source of information. It is important to not press for trauma histories which the examiner may suspect, but which the patient is not ready to face (Pearlman & McCann, 1994). Wholist histories include the following.

Following Up the Nature, History and Development of Symptoms   The exact nature of the symptoms is determined, including their qualitative and quantitative characteristics, location, onset, offset, duration, radiation, and associated features.

Specific Question About Traumas and Disruptions   Taken as part of a routine history, significant traumatic events may be discovered for the first time. One may ask, "Has anything major disrupted your life, or someone very close to you, in the last two years/ever?" "Were you at any time scared for your life or for the life of someone close to you?" "Have you ever suffered major disillusionments in your life?" One may specify major traumatic situations, such as bereavement, serious illnesses, accidents, physical abuse, or sexual abuse.   The events can then be explored in detail, such as what survival strategies were used, and how responses and other matters developed over time.

Family History   As disruptions are transmitted psychosocially as well as genetically, it is important to ask about both in the previous two generations, and in other significant figures. Has anyone in the family, especially the same gender parent/grandparent, older sibling but also spouses and close friends, suffered similar symptoms, stresses, and traumas as the patient? What was going on in the lives of those relatives and friends when they were the patient's current age, the age when the patient's symptoms started, and when the patient's traumas occurred?

Personal History; Culture: Strengths, Defenses and Fulfillments; Vulnerabilities, Personality Traits   This part of the history scans the three axes for so far unasked information. What prior biological, psychological, and social fulfillments and disruptions left what strengths and vulnerabilities, defenses, personality traits, using which preferred survival strategies at which triaxial points (see also defenses below)?

Specifically, what is the person's sense of morality, self-esteem, identity, and meaning? What provides pleasure, creativeness, and purpose? What are family, group, and community relationships like? How congruent are fulfillments with the person's point in the life cycle?

Wholist Examination This involves physical, mental, and social examinations.

Transference Freud (1895) described transference as the transferring of early childhood affects and relationships into the therapeutic relationship. However, both adult and recent events can similarly be transferred, such as when anger is transferred from the impact phase of disasters on to helpers in later phases. Transference and countertransference may be the only way infants or severely traumatized persons can communicate their stories of distress, and are therefore central tools for discerning unprocessed or defended events.

It is suggested that transference may be thought of as a creative dramatization of something inexplicable or overwhelming which cannot be described in words. The client enacts a script which the therapist is asked to decipher. For instance, terrified, aggressive, and clinging behaviors may reflect past threats and abandonments.

Transference awareness may be facilitated by asking oneself, "What is the person doing, enacting, why, and what may it mean?"

Countertransference When transference dramas cannot be interpreted externally by the therapist, then akin to stage dramas they must be allowed to resonate within oneself, and then oneself be deciphered. In such cases helpers use their own selves to empathically reverberate with victims in a wholist dyad. The wholist perspective is then used on one's wholist self as CAT scan and magnetic resonance imaging instruments, to pinpoint the orientation and nature of client responses.

While the question "What is the client doing, enacting?" gives clues to transference dramatizations, questions "What is the client doing to me?" "Is what I am feeling a reverberation with the client?" give clues to countertransference. Different aspects of a scene may be dramatized in sequence, with client and therapist cast in different roles. For instance, at one moment the therapist may be cast to empathically identify with a victim, at another time he or she may be cast as their rescuer. Thus countertransference responses may identify with, or be complementary (Valent, 1995a), to a client dramatizations.

Helpers must have the capacity to immerse themselves in their clients' experiences, and to emerge from them to take stock. They link their body sensations, feelings, thoughts, fantasies, and impulses to client transferences. The following case illustrates the subtle personal nature of countertransference.

CASE 8: COUNTERTRANSFERENCE
(see also Case 38, Chapter 10)

An adult incest survivor was reminiscing how in her family all conversation was sexually tainted, so different from the "nice" talk in therapy. Then she momentarily retreated into herself and reemerged with a sexual leer. She said that she just remembered how she had sexually craved the therapist over the weekend. The therapist felt rebuffed and tainted. Recognizing this as a countertransference response, he asked after a while what had happened to the "nice" talk. The patient looked terrified. With great apprehension she remembered how nice talk was denigrated in her family and accompanied by threats of being thrown out. She had enacted in the transference her intimidation and compliance to "rectify" nice talk to eroticized talk. The therapist used his feelings of rebuff and taint as a means of the patient discovering similar feelings in herself when leered at and forced into eroticism. This led to exploration of how terror of being cast out (attachment trauma) had kept her thinking in an eroticized mold.

It requires openness and self-knowledge to be able to pinpoint clients' effects on oneself, ranging from physical sensations to spiritual doubts (Pearlman & Saakvitne, 1995). Such maturity and self-knowledge are never complete, so helpers are left with internal undigested material. That is why they are prone to become secondary victims (Chapter 11), and need supervision and help to resolve their own traumas.

It may be seen that wholist receptivity, history-taking, transference, and countertransference are powerful modes of communicating trauma and fulfillment.

Means of Communication   Each mode of communication utilizes a variety of verbal and nonverbal communication means, which subtly communicate what is inside and outside awareness. Each means of communication has an intuitive component, whose translation to conscious understanding may require special training.

Speech: Verbal Communication   While verbal communication may relate whole narratives through words, metaphors, analogies, descriptions of emotions, and of complex pictures, words may also be used to convey only fragments of stories, and even to obfuscate.

Speech can overlap with nonverbal communication in its use of intensity, rhythm, and tone of voice. Furthermore, words may be put together in special ways such as in free associations, and slips of the tongue, indicating connections between apparently disparate factors. Interruptions of speech and diversions may indicate defenses (see below).

Nonverbal Communication   Nonverbal communication includes physiological reactions, affects, gestures, mien, postures, behaviors, clothes, and the person's environment.

Especially after early life traumas and where dissociation and other defenses are prominent, enactings and body language may be a prevalent means of communication. In the following case a physiological response is communicated in countertransference.

CASE 9: PHYSIOLOGICAL
COUNTERTRANSFERENCE RESPONSE

Described more fully elsewhere (Valent, 1994b), while interviewing a child survivor of the Holocaust the interviewer had an uncontrollable need to empty her bowels. This physiological response came to be seen to represent the survivor's childhood response to unclear but pervasive terrors of annihilation.

Altered States of Consciousness and Art Symbolizations Altered states of conscious-ness and use of artistic expression add to verbal and nonverbal means of partly telling traumatic stories. Altered states of consciousness (see also Chapter 6) include hypnosis, fugues, flashbacks, nightmares, and dreams. Art symbolizations include drawing, painting, playing, and dramatizations.

It may be seen that the wholist perspective enhances information-gathering of trauma stories and their disconnected fragments. It will now be applied to understanding traumatic stress and fulfillment manifestations.

WHOLIST READING AND MAKING SENSE OF TRAUMATIC
STRESS AND FULFILLMENT MANIFESTATIONS

It is suggested that information gleaned by all the modes and means of communication can be interpreted by the wholist perspective. The latter acts as a dictionary, which translates from trauma, or wholist, language into common language. Thus it makes sense of traumatic stress and fulfillment manifestations.

The structure of the wholist language may be pictured as points on ripples in a pond (pp. 32, 35) located in particular length, breadth, and depth (triaxial) situations with specific turbulences (survival strategies) in the waves (relivings) and troughs (avoidances, defenses). An alternative metaphor is a three-dimensional (triaxial) web of bulbs whose positions are defined by the triaxial framework. Each light emits different survival strategy colors, informing what is happening at the triaxial point. Switched-off bulbs represent defenses. Colors and darknesses are most intense near the center (as in Figure 7).

Each combination of point and color is a word in the wholist language, which can be translated into common language and becomes available in the trauma narrative. For instance, most words in Table 2 are translations into common language of survival strategy bulbs at acute stress response triaxial points.

It may be possible to trace prospectively developments of ripples or lighting up of the triaxial web. On the other hand, one may be presented with a wide variety of contradictory manifestations, or an apparently random mix of flashing

76 TREATMENT PRINCIPLES

bulbs whose original currents are obscured. Yet understanding the circuitry of the wholist perspective and significance of the location and color of bulbs (places in the dictionary) facilitates making sense of them. For instance, if modes and means of communication light up the feeling color and triaxial point which translates into yearning (Table 2), the circuitry may suggest an attachment distress due to unwelcome separation in the past. Similarly, lighting up the bulb signifying the word inadequate, indicates a negative assertiveness judgment, which may relate to past failure and impotence.

In other words, *by recognizing, translating, and tracing survival strategy manifestations at particular triaxial points along the triaxial framework back through acute stress responses to their origins, sense can be made of the great variety of fulfillment and trauma manifestations* (see also p. 81). The near infinite potential combinations and permutations of triaxial components and survival strategies is mitigated by the limited number of axes and survival strategies, and their typical arrangements in patterns such as biopsychosocial. Furthermore, because the wholist language is in some ways richer, and organizes human nature more logically than the common language, its translation can help to hone and categorize human phenomena.

Honing of Symptoms

The wealth of the wholist language may enable clearer definition of symptoms often covered by an umbrella word in the common language. For instance, the clinical word depression stands for a variety of manifestations such as sadness, despair, being overwhelmed, feeling defeated, oppressed, unloved, cast out, and alienated. Similarly, chest pain is too often restrictively associated with coronary occlusion, when it may also represent muscle tension, yearning, craving, oppression, envy, and betrayal. The wholist perspective can hone and help make sense of such symptoms.

CASE 10: HONING OF CHEST PAIN SYMPTOM

The recently widowed wife of a famous man complained of chest pain. Encouraging an intimate description of the pain, she came to describe it as an oppressive constriction in the heart. Asked what could produce such a feeling, she said, "As if someone was standing on your chest, not allowing you to sob." Tracing what might disallow her sobbing, it was the insistence on a public funeral, where she would have to maintain her composure. During discussion she realized that she had the right to insist on a private funeral, and allow a public memorial. The constriction lifted and she sobbed.

Modes and means indicated here a psychophysiological symptom of unexpressed grief (adaptation psychophysiological illness), which could be quickly traced to the recent loss. Confirmation of the correctness of wholist language translations may be gained by cognitive and emotional relief leading from its translation, and presence of other manifestations at the same or adjoining triaxial points. For instance, the above patient had associated weakness and despair, which also lifted with the sobbing. (For further examples see Chapters 9–11.)

To repeat, the huge variety of traumatic stress and fulfillment manifestations can be honed and made sense of through the wholist perspective.

Categorizations of Traumatic Stress and Fulfillment Phenomena

It is suggested that many words used in traumatic stress and fulfillment such as stress, stress responses, trauma, anxiety, anger, guilt, justice, and values are generic terms at particular triaxial points, and that specific categorizations of their contents can be obtained by collating ramified survival strategy manifestations at such points. The vertical columns in Table 2 for appraisals, adaptive and maladaptive biological, psychological and social stress responses, traumas, and judgments of worth are such categorizations.

Clinically, it is useful to recognize generic terms such as anxiety and values, and to then hone their specific survival strategy types. Each category type is a triaxial bulb shining with a specific color and can be traced back to its origins. However, much wider philosophical applications arise from heuristic categorizations, perhaps for the first time of very important human issues.

Theoretically, contents of every triaxial point can be categorized by collating survival strategy manifestations at that point. Categorizations of virtues and guilts, justice and injustice, generalized meanings, ideologies, and the sacred have already been presented elsewhere (Valent, 1998a). Categorizations of trauma anxieties, guilts and angers, basic meanings, values, and religion are considered below.

Categorizations of Trauma Anxieties   Categorization of traumas in Table 2 indicates that traumas are not undifferentiated inchoate states but specific survival strategy failures. Each traumatic state has been denoted as *the* essence of trauma at some time, and similarly, each related anxiety has been seen at some time as *the* hallmark anxiety of trauma.

It is suggested that categorization of types of anxieties in order of the survival strategies in Table 2 is, respectively, anguish, separation anxiety, anxiety of powerlessness and failure, of being overwhelmed and giving in, of one's murderousness, annihilation, defeat, and disintegration. It is suggested that each anxiety has a somewhat different feel and probably physiological variation. While some anxieties have specific designations, others need to be described longhand, because of lags in common language. The same is true for other categorizations.

Categorizations of Angers and Guilts   In order of listed survival strategies, angers include, respectively, blame (for irresponsibility and self-concern), protest (for lack of presence and care), frustration and exhortation (to perform better), admonishment (to not break down and give in), rage and fury (at enemies), condemnation (of cowardice and lack of moral fiber), outrage (at greed and lust), and anger at disloyalty and abuse of trust.

Corresponding guilts are survivor guilt, guilt of disobedience and being "bad," guilt of failure, guilt for "breaking down" and giving in, for wickedness, cowardice, and fear, for greed, envy, and priority guilt, and guilt for having cheated, lied, betrayed, and abused.

Categorization of Meanings   The following basic (as against existential) meanings develop out of adaptive/maladaptive survival strategies. It will be remembered that meanings include survival strategies and their judgments. Contradictory adaptive and maladaptive meanings are presented side by side.

I preserve and nurture, I do the right thing when called on to do so / My selfishness causes others to suffer and die. I am precious and my needs are always met somehow / I am unworthy and cast outside others' help. I succeed when I put my mind to it, I control my destiny / I am inadequate. Others control my destiny, I can take what life doles out, I can roll with the punches / I am weak and hopeless, I give in because the world is overwhelming. I can defend against danger / I am a dangerous killer. I am fleet-footed and cunning, and can escape danger / Danger is always ready to engulf me. I am superior and deserve more, though I give of my largesse to the less fortunate / I am a loser, and must rely on the benevolence of the powerful. When I give, others reciprocate, My love begets love / My trust and love get exploited and abused.

Categorization of Values   Positive and negative values arising from adaptive and maladaptive survival strategies are, respectively, the following: pity, charity, patience, selflessness, and martyrdom / unconcern, meanness, selfishness, and callousness. Amenability, obedience, cleanliness, orderliness / demandingness, overdependence, disobedience, disorderliness. Prowess, intelligence, industry, perseverance, effectiveness / laziness, unreliability, immaturity, slovenliness, ineffectiveness. Acceptance, humility, fortitude, faith, stoicism, stiff upper lip, as well as heartfelt grief / "breaking down" (crying), giving in, as well as riling against and ignoring loss and the inevitable. Formidableness, reputation, courageousness, deadliness / aggressiveness, violence, murderousness, heinousness. Cunning, adroitness, deftness / timorousness, faint-heartedness, cowardice. Ambition, excellence, superiority, honor, prestige, knowing one's place / venality, corruption, lust, exploitativeness. Trustworthiness, fidelity, honesty, generosity / dishonesty, betrayal, abusiveness, and lecherousness.

Religion   The following survival strategy ramifications present hopes of certainty in an uncertain universe. Cross-cultural similarities of myths and religions reflect cross-cultural similarities of survival strategies. In traumatic situations the hopes may be dashed. The following manifest adaptive survival strategies.

Gods and priests are parental figures who protect, provide, and direct the world. Apparent failures are made up for in the afterlife (*rescue*). According to *attachment* mythology, divine parents reward being good and obedient. Misfortune indicates disobedience or disrespect, such as slovenliness with prayers and rituals. Penance and sacrifice may bring forgiveness.

Hunting and combat (*assertiveness*) may be seen as divine struggles abetted by ancestors and gods. Work may also be sacred, especially when building churches. Religion counters death and loss *(adaptation)* in terms of eternal life and union. In *fight* the enemy is dehumanized and despiritualized, or demonized as the devil. One's own fight for life is sanctioned by God. *Flight* including hiding may be aided by magical potions, amulets, rituals, and prayers. Heaven is the ultimate sanctuary. Religion affirms *competition* through a strict hierarchy spanning heaven and earth. Knowing one's place ensures that benefits are passed down the line. Finally, religion can fulfill a sense of ephemeral mutuality *(cooperation)* and spiritual love, whose fertility may be manifested in religious creativity.

Categorizations of moral components manifest both their naturalness and contradictions (puzzles for philosophers). Both are explained by different underlying survival strategies serving survival in different circumstances. Assumption of unwarranted guilts, shames, and injustices can also be explained, as ways of avoiding traumas of knowing about an apparently immoral, unprincipled universe.

Reading the Absence of Traumatic Stress Phenomena; A Taxonomy of Defenses

Like troughs beside ripples, or darkness where light should be, absence of expected phenomena can be as important as their salient counterparts. Such absences may also be traced to their origins.

CASE 11: DEFENSE AGAINST UNACCEPTABLE FEELINGS

A 33-year-old woman with depressive moods and hypochondriacal fears of death, had been prevented at the age of 9 from attending her father's funeral, and her mother forbade any expression of grief thereafter. The patient was adamant that she held no anger against her mother. However, in sessions she could not speak, because as it became clear, a volcano of fury might erupt against her mother. She might also collapse into eternal grief for her father. For the first time she became aware of an internal wall which had caused her to lead a double life over many years. Behind the wall she was aggrieved, furious, and panicked that mother would reject her should her feelings be known. She maintained the wall through work addiction to distract herself, and kept contact with her father through having symptoms like he had before he died.

Stories such as these indicate human capacities to arrange degrees of awareness (see also "Memories," Chapter 3) and symbols as compromises to inner and outer survival pressures. Suppression of impulses to express survival strategies may ramify triaxially and leave their traces. In this case lack of natural anger and grief were traced to their original contexts. Defenses are often not experienced as such subjectively, though people may experience themselves as walled off or shut down. To the observer, defenses may appear as silences, interruptions to lines of thinking, compulsiveness, give-away slips of the tongue, or gestures unaccompanied by congruent feelings.

Defenses mitigate awareness of past traumas, and the sense of the potential for their ever-present recurrence (see also Chapter 3). The wholist perspective may help to classify defenses.

A Taxonomy of Defenses   It may be that primary psychological defenses are concerned with elemental disconnections and not knowing on the process axis, and secondary ones with distorting knowledge using the other two axes.

Primary Defenses   Primary defenses of *dissociation* and *fragmentation* disconnect and scatter elemental (nodal) functions of cognition, emotion, body sensation, self, and other. It is suggested that different combinations of dissociation are called by different names. Dissociation of feeling has been called *psychic numbing.* Together with cognitive awareness it has been called *detachment* or *isolation of affect.* Lack of cognitive representation may be called *disavowal.* Disavowal of one's person while acknowledging external reality is *depersonalization* while acknowledgment of self, but not of external reality, is *derealization.* Dissociation of all but somatic representations is *somatization*, while actions being sole remnants in awareness are *acting out*. The various disconnections lead to fragmentation or disintegration of function. Dissociation at the time of trauma has been found to be an important precursor and predictor of PTSD (Shalev, Orr, & Pitman, 1993; Marmar et al., 1994; van der Kolk, 1996a).

Splitting may be seen as polarization of maladaptive and traumatic survival strategy realities and fantasies of corresponding adaptive fulfillments. Thus an abused child may fantasize a contemporaneous good parent. *Repression* on the other hand, may exclude a whole traumatic survival strategy with all its components, appraisals, and contexts.

Secondary Defenses   Secondary defenses may be conceptualized as additions to primary defenses across the triaxial framework. *Projection, introjection,* and *displacement* do not fragment core mental functions but may transfer them, and more complex information, across the parameter axis. For instance, anger may be projected and displaced on individuals, families, groups, nationalities, as well as across time and place. Replacement of a split off or repressed maladaptive survival strategy by another in another time or place is *undoing.* For instance, compulsive helping may attempt to undo prior guilt of having caused death. *Precociousness* and *regression* may be ways of dealing with stresses by sliding up and down developmental phases. Changing survival strategies at higher function levels may see *substitution* of values, ideologies, religions, or nationalities. *Sublimation* may be seen as a defensive shift up the depth axis. For instance, alienation may be obfuscated by political allegiances or quasi-religious and sacred groups.

Although primary and secondary defenses often interact, predominance of primary defenses may contribute to relatively severe psychotic-like phenomena or psychoses, while secondary defenses to more benign conditions (Vaillant, 1992; 1993). However, this cannot be said for some projections and displacements (see "Fight," Chapter 4).

Having applied the wholist perspective to client communications, it may be opportune to look at the reading of communications in the other part of the wholist dyad.

THE WHOLIST PERSPECTIVE APPLIED TO CONCEPTUALIZING DIAGNOSES AND TREATMENTS

While for patients it is important to find words for their trauma narrative, for clinicians it is important to find words for ailments so that matching treatments can be instituted. It is suggested that the wholist perspective can contribute to the understanding of the language of diagnoses and treatments. In order to help do this, the concept of point, line, and volume diagnoses derived from the triaxial framework is introduced. It should be noted that in practice the three overlap.

Point (Phenomenological) Diagnoses and Treatments

Diagnoses   Point diagnoses are common language names or words which denote the characteristics of symptoms and illnesses. They are listed in textbooks such as DSM, under names such as angina, depression, or conduct disorder. In the wholist perspective such diagnoses apply to survival strategy manifestations at particular triaxial points, like points on ripples, bulbs or stars in the triaxial web (p. 75). Constellations of such points may be described as illness syndromes, often named after the brightest star, such as anxiety in anxiety disorder and dissociation in dissociative disorder. It may be that the tension of PTSD in DSM stems from it being a philosophical threat to point diagnoses, being a generic, uncertain star or ripple with reliving and avoidance potentially covering a great variety of symptoms and illnesses. It also introduces dynamic line diagnoses (see below) by insisting that the illness develops from prior events.

The wholist perspective naturally traces connections between points in its web to their origins. By tracing survival strategy ramifications at particular triaxial points along the triaxial framework back to their acute stress response survival strategy origins, definitive sense can be added to the point diagnoses of the wide range of traumatic stress and fulfillment phenomena (see also p. 76).

Treatments   Point treatments may be said to be applied to salient biological, psychological, or social survival strategy fragments at particular triaxial points. Point treatments overlap with symptomatic treatments (Chapter 6). Examples of point treatments in Cases 2 and 3 have been anginine for angina, analgesics for headaches, and antidepressants for depression. Point treatment for phobias may be desensitization; for PTSD it has included fluoxetine and thought-field therapy.

It is suggested that specialist treatments may be applied at particular triaxial points. On the *process axis* in order of components in Figure 2, rescue and emergency work address traumatic stressors, debriefing treats acute stress responses, stress management treats maladaptive stress responses, psychodynamic therapy treats defenses and retrieving memories, and a variety of biological, psychological, and social treatments target specific symptom and illness fragments.

On the *parameter axis* different specialist treatments cater to different phases. Different therapies cater to individuals, families, groups, and different ages such as adults and children. On the *depth axis* justice, compensation, advocacy, empowerment, testimonies, and homecoming ceremonies for soldiers are examples of particular point treatments.

Line Diagnoses and Treatments

Line Diagnoses   Line diagnoses trace survival strategy ramifications between two triaxial points prospectively or retrospectively. Points may be close such as suppressed rage and high blood pressure, or more distant, such as suppressed rage at a child's death and angina (Case 2, Chapter 1). Post-Traumatic Stress Disorder can also be seen as a line(ar) diagnosis, reliving and avoidance being linked to earlier traumatic events. Lines may have connecting points. In PTSD they have been variably suggested to be dissociation, aloneness, helplessness, being overwhelmed, and so on. Sometimes such connecting points have different diagnostic labels like hypertension and angina, which may be waystations between suppressed rage and coronary artery disease. Similarly, between stressors and illnesses, stress responses can be called acute stress disorder; maladaptive stress responses may be called by a variety of adjustment disorders (see also Chapter 9). Clinically, linear diagnoses are not simple causes and effects, though simple links are often sought. It may be acknowledged that lines are part of a system of inputs and feedbacks as is suggested in Figure 2.

Line Treatments   Line treatments may be applied at the recognized points of symptom and illness developments. For instance, in Case 2 treatment could have been applied at the initial time of rage at the husband for the death of their daughter, during the long period of suppressed anger when high blood pressure possibly developed, when rage returned with anticipation of another death, and, ultimately, when angina supervened. Similarly, PTSD may be amenable to treatment by removal of stressors, treating maladaptive stress responses, defenses, memories, and finally PTSD itself.

Volume Diagnoses and Treatments;
Nonlinear Wholist View

Biopsychosocial, holistic, and complex dynamic diagnoses have taken into account complex interlinking factors in symptoms and illnesses. It is suggested that the wholist or "volume" approach contains and extends them, as well as point and line diagnoses.

Triaxial (Volume) Enrichment of Point and Line Diagnoses   It is suggested that clinically, point and line diagnoses can be enriched by taking note of their triaxial extensions. For instance, the point diagnosis of yearning has different nuances depending on parameter axis disaster phases, ages and social groups, and depth axis levels. For instance, yearnings for rescuers, approval, and spiritual yearnings have different connotations. Similarly, triaxial expansion of angina in Case 2 (Chapter 1) brought out the whole contextual story.

Taking PTSD as a line diagnosis on the process axis, it may be seen to contain a rich dynamic amalgam of biopsychosocial stressors, stress responses, strengths and vulnerabilities, traumatic states, and memories (each with their own triaxial contributions). In addition, the parameter axis influences PTSD qualities by different disaster phases, ages and social system levels, and the depth axis by judgments, principles, spirituality, and existential meanings. Further, PTSD has bidirectional interactions with all these components.

As for PTSD, it may be seen that the wholist perspective subsumes and enriches phenomenological (point) and dynamic (line) diagnoses by extending them across the triaxial framework. At the same time it increases their specification and sense through defining their triaxial positions, survival strategy contents, and original contexts.

Wholist Notation of Diagnoses   It is suggested that the wholist perspective helps to assume control over the tension between a desire to control with one or two words and the need to almost relate the trauma narrative to obtain a full picture. According to circumstances, it is possible to choose sectors of the wholist picture to describe point, line, and volume diagnoses.

For instance, point diagnoses in Case 11 above may be depressive and somatoform disorders. Line diagnoses may connect them with suppression of grief at her father's death, and terror of the illness which caused it. In PTSD terms this was what was repeated and avoided. A thumbnail volume diagnosis is the description given above, which includes point and line diagnoses and adds their dynamics, defenses, and some triaxial interactions.

The wholist perspective also conceptualizes what has not been diagnosed by doing a check of the triaxial framework and survival strategies. On the process axis, for instance, it has not been said what symptoms the father had and which she reproduced, nor details of rescue, attachment, adaptation, fight, and cooperation biopsychosocial symptoms over time. On the parameter axis it has not been mentioned how her symptoms affected her family, and on the depth axis how her life was distorted by guilt for hating her mother, leading a double identity, and the uncertain purpose of life when death and hate reign.

Volume Treatments   Volume treatments extend point and line treatments into the other axes. For instance, Horowitz (1976/1992) extended line treatment of PTSD to include judgments and meanings on the depth axis. Figley (1988a; 1988b) added to this treatment of families (parameter axis) as well. Most types of treatment, in fact, embrace various degrees of triaxial volume. Wholist treatments, examined in detail in Section 3, favor selections of volume treatments.

A NONLINEAR PARADIGM

It is suggested that point and line diagnoses and treatments rely on linear paradigms while more complex systems and volume concepts on nonlinear ones.

In the nonlinear paradigm, the pebble hitting the pond (trauma) may be visualized as akin to big bang or a quantum mechanics event of great energy. Akin to time, matter, and space "freezing" out of this quantum energy, so the triaxial framework "freezes" out high energy polymorphous stress responses across the length, breadth, and depth of the pond.

Like the laws which limit the near infinite potential combinations and permutations of quantum and chaos events, so the apparently unlimited effects of trauma are mitigated by the limited number of traumatic situations, axes, survival strategies, and codes (such as biopsychosocial). Thus the ripples freeze out into a wide variety but nevertheless limited, relatively stable manifestations.

This paradigm explains the uncertainty (inherent in quantum events) in predicting which of a wide variety of biological, psychological, and social symptoms, illnesses and fulfillments will occur, and yet being able, retrospectively, to trace a wide variety of manifestations to the different aspects of the pebble hitting the pond. For instance, as has been shown for Anne (Case 3, Chapter 1, end of Chapter 4), her many symptoms and illnesses could be traced to different details of her childhood abuse.

Thus, whether followed prospectively or retrospectively, a wholist perspective enables a variety of symptoms and diagnoses to be connected to various facets of single or related traumatic events, and to see them as part of a bigger, more meaningful whole.

In summary, the wholist perspective enhances recognition by increasing the capacity to receive complex information and sort it. In combination with wholist receptivity through all modes and means of communication, the wholist perspective allows helpers to make diagnoses of manifestations from their origins to their end points, through their emergence, and in their triaxial contexts and meanings.

In other words, the wholist perspective and its language deepen and extend the definitions, source, and sense of point diagnoses, their linear development from traumatic events, and their nonlinear connections and meanings over the triaxial framework.

Recognition is the first treatment ingredient, and of itself can provide major relief. Further, the wholist perspective provides a range of recognition tools and diagnostic options. The latter span single-word diagnoses to relatively complex descriptions. The capacity for a range of types of diagnostic sorting of information is further important because each type has a language which reflects a scientific philosophy and consequent choice and lack of choice of treatments. Because the wholist perspective subsumes and can make choices between point, line, and volume diagnoses and treatments, it overcomes philosophical dichotomies which have bedevilled diagnosis and treatment. The dichotomies are reductionist/whole, mind/body, scientific/humanist, and linear/nonlinear. (For a fuller discussion see Valent, 1998a.)

The next chapter shows application of the wholist perspective to the other treatment principles.

Chapter 6

Wholist View of Nonspecific, Symptomatic, and Specific Treatments

In the last chapter the first treatment principle, recognition, was seen to be a complex process of information-gathering and sorting, helped by the wholist perspective. In this chapter the wholist perspective will be applied to the other treatment principles. Nonspecific treatments will be seen to utilize specific survival strategies at particular triaxial points. Symptomatic treatments are more specific still dealing with biological, psychological or social symptoms at such points. Nonspecific and symptomatic treatments correspond to point and line treatments. Specific trauma and fulfillment therapy adds nonlinear volume approaches. Its task is to break the conjunction between past trauma and present at all triaxial points and within all survival strategies, and to help establish a new meaningful narrative. It is important to note that, in practice, all four principles are used in various combinations. For instance, all types of therapies utilize recognition, and in practice specific therapy uses all treatment principles.

Applied treatment principles, the wholist perspective can add a further dimension to point, line, and volume treatments. It can do for clinicians with treatments what it does for patients with traumatic stress and fulfillment manifestations—recognize, hone, categorize, enrich awareness and sense of treatments, and thus enhance control over them. Unlike in Chapter 2, in this chapter particular treatments are not addressed. The wholist perspective is applied to their distilled commonalities.

All four treatment principles are presented in Table 3. Helper aspects will be considered further in Chapter 11.

"NONSPECIFIC" (COUNTER-TRAUMA) TREATMENT

It is suggested that many apparently nonspecific aspects of treatments such as safe environment, therapeutic relationship, boundaries, and trust may be understood in terms of specific replacements and, hopefully, neutralization of maladaptive and traumatic appraisals and survival strategies, with their adaptive counterparts. In this sense this is counter-trauma therapy. It overlaps with what is generally called corrective emotional experience. However, applying the wholist perspective, counter-trauma experiences also include cognitive, biological, and social, as well as intersecting axial aspects. For instance, fight and flight

Table 3 Principles of Trauma and Fulfillment Therapy in Victims and Helpers

Victims	Helpers
1. **Recognition**–Need for symptoms and their origins to be seen and understood. Opposed by lags and defenses.	1. **Recognition**–Wholist receptivity to survival strategies at triaxial points. Recognize client and own lags and defenses.
Communication *Modes*–Story, fragments, enactments, projective identification.	*Reading of communications* *Modes*–Wholist language, history, transference, counter-transference.
Means–Verbal, dreams, flashbacks, body language, dramatization, symbols, art. *Ramifications of survival strategies across the triaxial framework*	*Means*–Reading verbal, free association, dreams, body language, actions, symbols. *Wholist diagnosis including point, line, and volume diagnoses*
2. **Nonspecific**–Need security, hope, trust, boundaries, relationship.	2. **Nonspecific**–Outreach, empathy, counter-trauma environment for all Survival Strategies.
3. **Symptomatic**–Need relief from suffering.	3. **Symptomatic**–Counters to symptoms at particular triaxial points.
4. **Specific**–Remember, understand, separate past trauma and present, narrative with new meanings.	4. **Specific**–Balance hope and retrieval of memories, dual focus, hold, break nexus, help new narrative meaning.

boundary issues may involve personal, group, or national intrusions, and involve security, justice, law, identity, and spiritual aspects. Nonspecific therapy thus involves particular survival strategies at certain triaxial points. Indeed, the more "nonspecific" therapy is defined, the more specific it becomes.

Safe Environment   A safe therapeutic environment counters past traumatic intrusion trapped and engulfment experiences of flight, by providing sanctuary and escape from danger. For instance, women's refuges offer safety from violent men. Safe environments usually also include the following.

Space and Boundaries   Respect for physical and mental territory coupled with constancy and reliability counter perceptions of threat and need for flight. At the same time they allow definition of threats, enemies and allies, and possibilities of fight and other survival strategies. For instance, friendly, effective helpers, constancy, routine, and kept promises encourage seeking help, and counter mistrust; that is, they encourage adaptive attachment and cooperation.

Space to Think and Communicate   Suppressed survival strategy responses such as hopelessness, murderousness, guilts, and shames may enhance thinking and processing them.

Therapeutic Relationship   The therapeutic relationship is often called the cornerstone in trauma therapy. The wholist language may help translate its often nebulous terms.

"Being Human," "Being There"   This may be interpreted as therapists being receptive with their own wholist selves to wholist language communications, through whatever modes and means clients may use.

Empathy, Caring, Holding, Nurturing   These adaptive attachment features counteract the frequent attachment traumas of clients. Because they often occurred in early life, trauma and fulfillment therapy is particularly prone to transferences from childhood, and may attract descriptions in terms of parent-child interactions.
    The responsive attunement of therapists to client emotions can relieve and modulate physiological, emotional, and behavioral arousals. In this sense helpers are variably called good mothers, environmental buffers, safety membranes, or alter egos.

Kindness, Comforting, Support   These are therapeutic gifts providing and promoting different adaptive survival strategy experiences. Kindness and comforting may be part of attachment care or grief support. Encouraging achievements promotes assertiveness, uplifting the defeated aids competition, while generosity promotes cooperation.

Nonjudgmental attitudes and respect counter specific negative survivor self-judgments.

Hope in the generic sense involves replacement by adaptive survival strategy appraisals of their traumatic equivalents. Good cheer, confidence, and positive expectations counter adaptation giving in, and hopelessness. Promoting achievement counters sense of failure, winning the hopelessness of defeat.

Helpers may act as hopeful role models, especially if they were past victims themselves. However, it is important that hope finally be focused within the subject. If centered on helpers, charismatic leaders, or cult figures, tenuous "transference cures" based on attachment dependence may collapse when hopes in therapists are not fulfilled.

Respectful Collaboration   In trauma and fulfillment therapy it is acknowledged that victims and helpers have specific roles in their work towards a common goal. Role distribution between equally vulnerable humans depends on luck at the time, therapists happening to have their wholist selves relatively more intact and available for help at this time. In the therapeutic process the relative differential decreases, and both partners emerge wiser.

Professional remuneration also maintains boundaries. It enhances mutual dignity, lack of client debt and obligation, and enables dissolution of bonds when goals of therapy are achieved.

SYMPTOMATIC TREATMENTS

Symptomatic treatments are frequently "point" treatments (Chapter 5) of symptoms and illnesses, directed towards removal of particular biological, psychological, or social survival strategy ramifications at specific triaxial points. The following is a more detailed examination of some common symptomatic treatments.

Education, Clarification, Advice   Preimpact training, briefing, and preparations help to deal intelligently with later stressors. Clarification, explanation, and advice on particular events can be helpful in all phases. Postimpact education and debriefing (Chapter 10) that explain the nature of certain acute stress responses and their source in survival strategies, can ameliorate fears of physical illness and irrationality. The same may apply to specific symptoms in later phases. Explanation of particular guilts, shames, and maladaptive meanings as based on survival of past trauma can also be helpful. However, without the whole "package of information" (p. 38), including emotional understanding, explanations and reassurances may be too narrow and unconvincing over time.

Drugs   Drugs may alleviate particular survival strategy symptoms at certain triaxial points. Just as analgesics relieve pain and anginine angina pain, antidepressants treat depression, anxiolytics anxiety, major tranquilizers psychotic symptoms, and carbamazepine aggressiveness. Specific drugs for PTSD are still being sought.

Relaxation, Stress, Anxiety and Anger Management: Skills Training   Perhaps the psychosocial equivalents of drugs, and often part of cognitive therapies, specific techniques can counter specific symptoms at various triaxial points. For instance, relaxation techniques may counter fight and flight tensions. Anxiety and anger can be further managed by awareness and avoidance of situations which evoke them. Thought blocking by screaming "No!" when unwelcome thoughts surface is another technique used, as are various other devices and games. For instance, falling backward into another's arms may counter paranoid fight or flight wariness, and encourage adaptive cooperation.

Skills training may enhance specific adaptive survival strategies. For instance, assertiveness may be enhanced by job training, learning to handle money, talking in public, acquiring social skills. Self-talk may help in specific situations, such as "I can do things. I am not inadequate." Ticking off lists of achievements may enhance a sense of success and adequacy.

"Treatment packages" often use different combinations of nonspecific and symptomatic treatments. The apparent disparateness of all these treatments makes sense if they are seen to address dispersed symptoms on dispersed triaxial points.

It may be said that while the above treatments overlap with what is generally called supportive therapy, specific trauma and fulfillment therapy overlaps with insight psychotherapy. The implication is that insight is gained into something previously hidden, which may be the crucial aspect of traumatic events and their links with current symptoms.

SPECIFIC TRAUMA TREATMENT

It is suggested that specific trauma therapy is directed at the basic irrationality, the "appendix in traumatology," that is, (re)living inappropriately what were normal responses in times of trauma in current normal conditions. The apparent irrationality is increased with disconnections of memory for the original events (see Defenses and Memories, Chapters 3 and 5).

It is suggested that the requirements to remedy this central ailment are to recognize and name the traumas and their initial contexts, define them and their sequelae in words, break the nexus between their past context and current reality (by intense dual focus of attention), and relearn the significance of the traumas as part of one's narrative story rather than it still being lived. Life's purpose can then turn from concerns for survival, which is assured, to fulfillment. In clinical practice these steps overlap.

"Remembering"–Recognizing and Naming
the Trauma: Making Sense of Its Fragments

Recognition and naming of trauma and its sequelae has been examined in the previous chapter. Its subjective equivalent is often called "remembering" the trauma, with the implication that it had been forgotten. However, as was seen earlier (Chapter 3, see also Chapter 10), it is more correct to say that ever greater awareness is achieved, whether through relaxation of defenses or making up for developmental lags when traumas happened in young children. However, even in adults who seem to remember their traumas vividly (even too vividly), integration of the event may be prevented by some hidden core vulnerability, judgment, or meaning being defended from awareness. Generally, the more and more severe the traumas that occurred, the more intense the defenses, and the greater the original developmental lags, the more arduous is the task of achieving a logical, fully aware memory sequence.

Retrieval of awareness and fleshing out of memories may be gradual, with events sensed as ever more "revealed." It is as if they had always been there, but now they move as it were from an "imprinted" nonverbal to a more discernible, verbal memory. This results in a sense of control and, even if painful, memories or awareness form part of a joyous retrieval of self. Alternately, developmental lags are made up and gaps in knowledge are filled with a deep and logical coherence.

Achievement of memory is helped greatly by the synergistic use of previous therapy ingredients. It may be held back by their absence, as well as past and present intimidations, and fears of being plunged back into the traumas.

The Power of Words   It is suggested that words both dissect out and put together what trauma shatters. They are both scalpels and building blocks of the soul.

One patient said, "Words have taken it out of my body. It is out there now (indicating her hand where her fingers as it were manipulated the words)." For another patient the word imprint (relating to traumatic memories) provided spontaneous relief. "Yes, it is as if my father's wart has been imprinted in my vagina. He stamped his finger in me. It has always been there, but now I know it." (see also Case 38b, Chapter 10). Correct translations of experience can provide immense relief and control. A therapist's words which dissect and interpret experience are indeed like the surgeon's scalpel which can reach the bottom of psychological distress, expose it, and in this case cut out the distress of ignorance.

The more exactly words signify human experience the more powerful they are, because they act as symbols which lift awareness from animal-like feeling and acting to human experiences of making meaning, self-awareness, and a quest for coherence. Like mathematical symbols depict physical nature, words depict human nature. It is in this sense that words are the building blocks of the soul.

Furthermore, it is a soul owned by the person. Another patient said, "When I lived my unhappy life I did not know about it. Therapy was like writing it in a book. When I read the book it caused me much grief. Now I own the book in my library."

It has been said that words alienate from the essential human by providing an observer rather than an experiential perspective. However, words used correctly do not detract from experience but supply it with another dimension.

Words such as those above, direct attention to human essence, and are felt as poignant, specifically human and spiritual. Such can be the effect of a correct translation from the wholist language.

True, like scalpels, words also have the potential to injure and infect. Words that take away dignity and that humiliate may be even more wounding than the shedding of blood. Much training is necessary for the correct use of words.

For helpers who struggle with their work, words such as those involved in diagnoses can also provide control, power, and spiritual beauty. Or they may hide truth and injure patients (Case 7, Chapter 5; Chapter 10).

Breaking the Nexus Between Past and Present

In order to be aware of painful traumas, and to relinquish learned survival modes including arrangements of the mind, people need to have hope that doing so is safe and will enhance their happiness. In order to check on the hope, relaxation and reversal of defenses occur, enabling increased awareness of both past trauma and current adaptive possibilities.

Hope and Fulfillment Therapy: Relaxation and Reversal of Defenses   The background for new hope may already have been established through previous treatment ingredients. In this case specific traumatic fears are identified and countered by hopeful survival strategy alternatives at different triaxial points. For instance, the fear of eternal crying and despair with awareness of loss is countered by explaining the physiology of limited pangs of sadness and weeping, giving words to the relief the client actually craves, but above all exploring hopeful opportunities beyond ungrieved losses. Putting fears and hopes into words often helps clients to see that they can control the risk to hope. Hypothetical scenarios and their risks may be played out in fantasy, and practical small steps may be devised to test hope in reality. The therapeutic relationship is often the first place for testing new ways.

At times defenses such as withdrawal and substance abuse may need to be treated ahead of establishment of hope in order for just engagement to occur. Yet hope cannot linger far behind, because without it more primitive defenses may intensify, or patients may decompensate or cease therapy. Therefore, it requires skill and tact to know how much to facilitate dismantling defenses without prior establishment of hope.

It may be that in therapy specific defenses are reversed in specific ways. For instance, *splitting* and *repression* are reversed when good and bad (trauma and hope) combine in the effort to assess both, and *fragmentation* is reversed when a number of such assessments on the triaxial framework cohere. *Projection* and *projective identification* are reversed when therapists feed back transference and countertransference information. Even *dissociation* may be reversed, often aided by certain techniques. For instance, clients may be encouraged to view their traumatic experiences from outside like a film, or as a train passing through a landscape. Or they may be asked, "What would you think if you observed another person say exactly what you just said?" "What would you say to the desperate child?" or "Let us now see what we have gone through." In each case *depersonalized* or *derealized* fragments are integrated as belonging to oneself.

The wholist perspective helps to put into words specific traumas, their hopeful adaptive survival strategy alternatives, and defenses. By simultaneous attention to both sides of the equation and the central defensive buffer, trauma therapy is also hope and fulfillment therapy.

Controlled Exposure to the Trauma   With increased memory and awareness of trauma, controlled exposure to ever more evocative cues, responses, and aspects of trauma are contrasted with current realities or possibilities. Exposure must be controlled, because it may become a stressor which results in retraumatization. Because of this danger patients may be afraid of their thoughts and of therapists who may expose them. Control is achieved differently by different techniques (see Chapter 2), though they overlap. Cognitive therapies emphasize rational explanations, strategic goals, and controlled guided imagery with anxiety management (see above), while psychodynamic therapies emphasize secure therapeutic relationships, empathic attunements, and verbal interpretations.

Altered State of Consciousness   Exposure to trauma tends to reevoke the intense energy and focus of the original situation in which traumatic imprints were established. The energy and focus when traumas are relived may appear as an altered state of consciousness. Based on the hypothesis that such states are necessary to alter traumatic engravings, hypnosis, abreactions (aided by drugs such as Amytal) and flooding have been used to encourage such states. Risks include retraumatization, intense flashbacks, fugues, nightmares (Chapter 5), and decompensation. It is more usual to try to control altered states of consciousness with controlled exposure (see above). In such cases traumatic emotions of the past still arise and can be learned about but are tempered sufficiently to be able to be processed.

Nevertheless, it may be that, with earlier traumas especially, relatively more vivid relivings are necessary in order to understand the traumas. Much skill is necessary to obtain the necessary information without regression, retraumatization, and decompensation.

Dual Focus of Attention   Past traumatic imprints and new opposite realities are now jointly focused on in the homogenizing therapeutic prism. The dual focus of attention involving simultaneous reliving and observing one's trauma from a perspective of safety creates a high-energy paradox, which helps to break the nexus between past trauma and current reality.

It is suggested that various techniques enhance dual focus of attention.

Thus, while reliving traumatic events, simultaneous eye movements, tappings, therapist presence, and interpretations emphasize contrast between them and the present. It is suggested that irrespective of technique, treatment is more powerful the more exactly particular triaxial point survival strategy opposites are experienced simultaneously, and validated in mutual awareness. It is this which finally challenges the nexus of established stimulus-response patterns.

It is also suggested that dual focus of attention must address all components of nodal information (Chapter 3)—that is, perceptions, cognitions, sensations, emotions, relationships, judgments, and basic meanings. Partial "repackaging" of one or another aspect such as rational explanation, cognitive restructuring, appeasing sensations, emotional catharsis, or conflict resolution, are insufficient on their own.

Relearning the Significance of the Trauma and of Current Reality

Achieving dual focus of attention in the high-energy therapeutic prism means that past and present are refracted from it separately, and realigned in new patterns of experience. All nodal components such as biological, psychological, and social stress responses, unconscionable judgments, and unacceptable meanings are reassessed according to past traumatic situations and survival needs, and reshaped according to objective history to the current day. All triaxial ramifications are reassessed similarly, forming a new network of deeper meanings.

With full awareness of what happened and what is, previous traumatic fragments become poignant stations of coherent narrative memories. The significance of the trauma is placed in context to the whole life story. The previously trauma-disrupted life resumes its existentially meaningful purpose.

A paradigmatic example may illustrate briefly the treatment principles described.

A PARADIGMATIC CASE ILLUSTRATING TRAUMA THERAPY

In this highly simplified case only one survival strategy, assertiveness, is considered.

CASE 12

Suppose a small child falls down the stairs and screams its sense of powerlessness. Intuitively, the mother *recognizes* the situation, picks up the child, and provides a counter-trauma environment. This is equivalent to *nonspecific* therapy. She provides *symptomatic* relief through rubbing, bandaging, giving aspirin. In *specific therapy* she names and connects the child's feelings with the event. She brings the child to the stairs and shows that they are safe. She contrasts feelings of inadequacy by her confident judgments of the child. She teaches better stair climbing skills, and conveys the significance of the event as a minor necessary step in the child's growing competence. The child feels hopeful, does become more competent, and remembers the event with overall pleasure. It is part of a model for interpreting setbacks as challenges in the context of ever greater achievement.

In contrast, suppose that as one of many such experiences, the mother reviles the child as clumsy and inadequate. The later adult presents with phobia of heights, recurrent limb pains, and a deep sense of inadequacy, all of unknown origin.

First, the person's problems need to be *recognized* as serious. The therapist listens with all modes and means of communication, and together with the client the symptom fragments are traced along assertiveness circuitry to their origins, and are verbalized. *Nonspecific* treatment includes empathy, kindness, respect, and expectation of success. *Symptomatic* treatment may include pain killers, relaxation exercises, anxiety management, deconditioning for fear of heights, and tasks which improve a sense of adequacy.

Specific therapy extends recognition and provides words for increasing awareness of fears, powerlessness, humiliation, unfair judgments. Coupled with hope that knowing the truth will help, events such as the one falling down the stairs are remembered. Further fleshing out of memories leads to deep understanding that as a child the client was denigrated and reviled by mother. The symptoms of inadequacy and failure now make 'nodal' sense. New judgments and meanings are experimented with. Trauma and counter-trauma experiences are intensely joined. For instance, the person may feel simultaneously reviled in memory and respected by the therapist. The person sees the paradox and may separate past and present and their different realities. The client may test out new self-views, and with success symptoms recede. The process may be repeated at different triaxial points, until a coherent story evolves in which past traumas are but memories in an otherwise successful life.

It may be seen that trauma treatment cannot be captured in cookbook recipes or protocols (Turner et al., 1996). However, the wholist perspective can extend understanding and hone application of treatment ingredients. It can also help to indicate which specific treatment techniques use which aspects of the wholist perspective and which treatment ingredients. This can help in planning and tailoring treatment, and in refining and extending research questions.

Planning of Treatment

A wholist approach makes sure that all triaxial points are covered for potential intervention. On the process axis biological, psychological, and social arenas of stress and illness with variable subjective awareness of their sources are prepared for. On the parameter axis preparations are made for each disaster phase, social system, and age group, and individual and community strengths are harnessed. Depth axis preparation includes readiness to respond to angers and guilts with understanding, and making sure that justice, dignity, and people's roles and identities, values, and spiritual structures are maintained or restored.

Planning involving application of available resources, including the human and conceptual armamentarium for wholist treatment needs. Lack of a wholist perspective may lead to important omissions in treatment. For instance, biological, psychological, or social distress, different disaster phases, particular victims groups, and the spiritual needs of the helped may be ignored.

TAILORING OF TREATMENT: WHOLIST TREATMENT

Although most clinicians may agree that debriefing can be useful in early disaster phases for adults, and more complex insight therapies may be necessary for adult survivors of severe and chronic early traumas, few guidelines exist for choice of treatments for particular situations, symptoms, and illnesses.

In current circumstances where actual treatments vary greatly, it may be asked what determines what treatments are used, and how can the wholist approach help in choice of treatment?

Choosing Treatment Ingredients for Point, Line, and Volume Treatments

It may be that points of intervention and choice of treatment ingredients have been influenced by a complex cultural interaction of client and helper recognition and desires (see Table 3, p. 88).

An example of a combination of helper recognition and desire may be the anticipation that akin to first aid splinting a fracture or disinfecting a wound, early intervention may prevent later traumatic ramifications and complications. While this may well be valid, it is also possible that too much desire may deny the wholist complexity of trauma and lead to deleterious or insufficient treatment through application of wrong or too few treatment ingredients at too few triaxial points.

In practice, various combinations of point, line, and volume treatments (pp. 81–84) may follow complex interplays of mutual need, desire, capacity, taste, and negotiation. Thus, some treatments may stop short with strengthened defenses which cause tension but less direct trauma threat, others with the resolution of a major symptom, and others still explore client's whole wholist selves.

At times the most efficacious triaxial (such as political) points of intervention may be least exploited because of lack of a treatment ingredient such as recognition or hope. A contrary example was the worldwide publicity of the likely effects of nuclear war on health by an international society of physicians, which contributed to nuclear weapon deescalation agreements.

Ideally, all treatment ingredients are applied across the whole triaxial framework as necessary. It is suggested that a wholist overview can help to tailor the best point, line, and volume possibilities of intervention under the circumstances. In other words, the wholist approach with its honed yet extended diagnostic range of both traumatic stress manifestations and treatments, may help to apply trauma therapy ingredients at the right triaxial points at the right times.

Application of a pragmatic abridged wholist treatment checklist, based on Tables 1 to 3, may read something like this. Have all symptoms (biological, psychological, and social) been made sense of and treated and all survival strategies been considered? Have all victim and disaster parameters been accounted for (such as children, families, communities in different phases)? Have "human" issues such as guilt, shame, fairness, and justice, meanings and purpose, been addressed?

Is recognition of all symptoms and their sense complete? Have all modes and means of information gathering and diagnosis been utilized? For instance, have helper-victim dynamics (transference, countertransference) been assessed? Have all helper parameters, capacities, lags and blind spots been taken into account? Have all possible treatment ingredients been applied? Have past and present been delineated, understood, worked through? Have treatment ingredients been applied throughout the triaxial framework? Are new paths of fulfillment established? Have secondary helper effects been recognized and dealth with?

The checklist provides a speedy means of ensuring, applying, and tailoring treatment to maximum advantage in the circumstances, as well as of knowing which treatments are wanting.

RESEARCH

The wholist perspective can provide some understanding of current research dilemmas. For instance, the usual linear measurements of treatment outcomes have limits because of the unmeasurable nature of inputs such as empathy and hope, outcomes such as aliveness, and the nonlinear nature and combinations of treatment ingredients in the wholist framework. Linear research must specify or keep constant such triaxial points, survival strategies, and influences from each axis.

Because of unpredictable linkages in the triaxial web, the usual outcome measure of symptom disappearance may not be quite suitable, because it may be associated with new symptoms in other parts of the web. If such symptoms are merely substitutes for the original one, claims of cure are unfounded. On the other hand, even increased symptoms may indicate progress, as they may represent a therapeutically useful relaxation of defenses. It should be noted that symptoms may not be a valid outcome measure in any case. For instance, a person may have more symptoms as a result of therapy, but feel more existentially alive.

Last, because it is difficult to predict what mix of ingredients at which point may have what strategic effect in the web, single interventions with one treatment may have marked benefits, while at other times the most astute mix of treatment ingredients needs to be applied for a long time for any benefit. Yet this may not reflect the efficacy of treatments; as in other circumstances their efficacies may be reversed, or some treatments in some circumstances of necessity take time.

Research is indeed in its infancy, with little known about relative power of specific interventions. One may speculate that perhaps there is a need for non-linear research methods analogous to those in quantum mechanics and chaos theory.

For the moment it is as well to maintain a measure of humbleness, open-mindedness, but also skepticism. For instance, claims for fast cures should not be written off as nonspecific "placebo," "bedside manner," and "transference" cures, but rather should be critically examined for therapeutic value. On the other hand, care must be taken to not accept apparent cures which result from enthusiasm and charisma, but which may only channel symptoms away from therapists' views.

In summary, akin to aiding recognition and making sense of the wealth of traumatic stress manifestations, diagnoses and treatments, the wholist perspective aids honing and making sense of each treatment principle. More precise definitions of "nonspecific," symptomatic and specific treatments opened up opportunities to better plan and tailor treatments, making sure that all possible aspects were considered. The wholist perspective also extended research questions regarding efficacies of treatments.

In conclusion, simultaneous awareness of the pebble and ripples in the whole pond and awareness of the various means of intervention, brings one a step closer to conceptualizing the mix of experiential wholist resonance and scientific understanding which contribute to trauma and fulfillment therapy. The following section hopes to demonstrate this in greater detail, both for victims and helpers.

Part Four

Clinical Applications: Wholist Treatment

Previous sections dealt with descriptions of the wholist perspective and its application to treatment principles. In this section it is shown how the wholist view is applied clinically.

Chapter 7 serves as an introduction to the section and highlights general questions such as length and prognosis of therapies, and specific applications of the triaxial framework and survival strategies. Subsequent chapters describe typical clinical situations ranging in time from the occurrence of traumas. Chapter 8 describes trauma alleviation almost in the happening, Chapter 9 of sequelae at stages of setting or recently having set, and Chapter 10 examines long-term ramifications of early severe trauma. Finally, Chapter 11 examines stresses and traumas in helpers.

Chapter 7

Introduction to Clinical Application
of the Wholist Perspective

This chapter attempts to give a feel of applying the wholist perspective to common clinical experiences and issues. Issues addressed are predictions of length of therapies, possibility of cures for long-term problems, and hazards of therapy. Clinical examples then highlight applications of survival strategies, the triaxial framework, and fulfillment aspects of therapies. In this chapter all trauma therapy ingredients are implied as present. Subsequent chapters highlight the treatment ingredients.

GENERAL ISSUES

In this section of the chapter the uncertainties of trauma and fulfillment therapy are addressed.

Length of Therapies: Can one Predict?

It is suggested that because victims and helpers represent two nonlinear systems, it is difficult to predict the therapeutic fit and extent of benefit of particular types of interventions. On the one hand, interventions in the triaxial web may occasionally be so strategic as to reverberate beneficially throughout the whole structure. On the other hand, apparently strategic and early interventions may not prevent serious sequelae. The following two cases exemplify this.

CASE 13: WELL-TARGETED STRATEGIC INTERVENTION

A 59-year-old widowed saleswoman presented with intrusive post-traumatic anxiety and phobic symptoms related to a burglary four months previously. She had been awakened from her sleep by noises of broken glass. Then she heard footsteps and rummaging noises, which eventually reached the hall next to her bedroom. She had called the police immediately after awakening and they arrested the intruder in her house at gunpoint.

The woman wanted crime compensation in order to be able to build a high wall around her house. However, reviewing her life, she noted that she had always had a psychosocial wall around her so she could not be hurt. I commented that the essence of her symptoms was fear resulting from having had the walls of both her physical and psychological fortress broken through (maladaptive flight).

At the next session the lady seemed much relieved. She smiled, "I know when I first put up my fortress." She related her first memory, seeing her (depressed) mother having hung herself after attempting to kill her. "I know that is when I closed off from the world on a deep level." The lady noted that when the intruder entered, she froze (flight) as the young three-year-old had done She associated this with survival, "That way snakes don't bite you."

However, this time she had called the police, and the predator was captured. In this sense she became the hunter (adaptive assertiveness). Further, having called the police (adaptive attachment) brought them to the rescue! And having opened herself to me in the previous session reinforced the image of helpful parent figures. Contrasting this with her mother led to great turmoil. She then reassessed her mother as ultimately well meaning to her, wanting to relieve her of the miseries of the world as she saw them, but then rescuing her from herself instead.

We validated new rescue, attachment, and cooperation cognitions and feelings, which had welled up in her. With surprising speed the patient realigned in the same session meanings and values of excessive self-reliance and avoidances in relationships. She felt mellow for the first time in her life and she determined that she would henceforth avail herself of opportunities of friendship and affection. In the next session she was symptom-free. Four years later she was still well, and markedly more open and affectionate.

CASE 14: EXPANDING LEVELS OF TREATMENT

Four days after a bushfire a man (see also Case 1, Chapter 1) was terrified that his chest pain signified a heart attack. Medical examination established only muscle tension. The symptom was exacerbated as the man described how he had worked hard to build his house and then all his efforts were frustrated to save it (maladaptive assertiveness). The symptom was meaningfully and emotionally put in context with relief. Other maladaptive assertiveness symptoms were explored—loss of control, impotence, willfulness, sense of failure, powerlessness. He was much relieved at the end of the interview. In the following weeks various other responses to his bushfire experience were placed in context, but he could not grieve.

At the site of his house he desultorily poked a shovel into the charred rubble. "This is my burnt-out life." he said. To grieve his losses (adaptation) he had to remember previous traumas which had made his house represent the purpose of his life. This involved therapy over almost two years, following which he was able to resume the threads of his life in a fulfilling way.

Comment   These two cases indicate the necessary uncertainty under which one operates and makes comments which may have different unbeknown point, line, and volume reverberations. It may be that in the first case a comment targeted at engulfment panic at the identity triaxial point, together with her counter-trauma experiences, fortuitously touched a point in her triaxial web which led to widespread reverberations and reworkings.

On the other hand, in the next case a number of triaxial points were sufficiently resolved for symptom reduction. Such success could have been considered as successful debriefing. However, this would have ignored the parameters of the man's social isolation, and on the depth axis the collapse of his identity, meanings, and life's purpose. It required longer time and therapy for the man to become aware and grieve (adaptation) these losses and to develop hope for new alternatives.

Long-Term Multiple Problems: How Much Can One Hope?

While interventions in acute traumas may at times be overoptimistic, lack of them in long-term chronic trauma sequelae may be based on excess pessimism. This may be rationalized as "They are too old." "It is too entrenched." "There is too much pain and despair to experience." or "It is better to maintain defenses." Holocaust survivors were often placed in such a category. Yet it will be shown (Chapter 9) that even survivors of most extreme traumas such as Anne (Chapter 1) can benefit greatly from trauma therapy. The following is another case in point.

CASE 15: RESOLUTION AFTER 70 YEARS

A 74-year-old man had been investigated for a variety of chronic pains over many years. During his last hospitalization he asked to see a psychiatrist who "understood trauma."

The man related his experiences in an orphanage between the ages of 3 and 13. They included severe physical and sexual abuse, violent deaths of friends, hunger, and other forms of cruelty.

Over the years the man married, had children and grandchildren. He formed and became a *de facto* father figure to a national network of orphanage survivors which still meets annually.

For the last 20 years and especially after retirement as a bus driver, the man started to have both flashbacks and a variety of physical pains. Some were related to spinal injuries and arthritis, but others to what eventuated to be relived traumatic experiences (see also Chapter 9). The patient sensed the connection, but was distressed that his doctors did not and were not interested in his experiences. They diagnosed the symptoms as "in the head," and further, discounted the organically based symptoms. A variety of psychiatric diagnoses added to the distress of nonrecognition.

At last the man was able to both reexperience his symptoms and relate connected stories in an atmosphere of belief and sympathy. In the process his symptoms, flashbacks, and apparently bizarre actions cohered for the first time in his understanding. He came to clearly distinguish memory pains and current physical pains. Processing each memory relieved him of symptoms he had carried for years. The last symptom to disappear was a pain from the front of his chest in a direct line to his back. During an accentuation of it at a survivors' meeting he believed that a movement on his part would kill him. In the session he reexperienced this as being stabbed with a hat pin by a nun in the orphanage. After 20 sessions the patient felt better than ever in his life. This has continued so far for 15 months.

Comment   This remarkable man demonstrates that even after 70 years multiple and severe childhood traumas could be successfully treated in trauma therapy (see also "Anne," Chapter 9).

HAZARDS OF TRAUMA THERAPY

It should be remembered that trauma treatment, like any other can have side effects and may even be hazardous. Just as one may hit a lucky spot which has a beneficial domino effect, one can also hit an unlucky spot.

CASE 16: STROKE WHILE IN THERAPY

A 36-year-old middle-executive woman presented some months after the death of her mother in a car crash, thought to be caused by a sudden stroke.

The patient could not grieve properly because of the hurried nature of the funeral, not having seen the body, but also because of prior childlike dependence on the mother. The result was chronic mourning, characterized by constant bewailing of mother, and inability to function in life.

At a special session on the anniversary of the mother's death, the client imagined washing, dressing, talking to, and laying her mother to rest—that is, all the things she had been prevented from doing. She started to grieve for the first time and was very grateful for the opportunity to do so.

At the next session, on the anniversary of the mother's funeral, she complained of a headache and nausea, which she remembered were exactly what she had felt at the time of the actual funeral. She thought that perhaps her mother had suffered such pain and nausea before she died. That evening the patient had a stroke. Heroic surgery saved her life. Luckily, she was able to recover physically to near her previous function and, amazingly, she completed her grieving process.

Comment   This case illustrates inadvertent hazards of trauma therapy, in this case in association with the apparently uncanny biopsychosocial unity of transgenerational symptoms. It was not expected that adaptive grief in a young woman would be almost fatal, but, in retrospect, perhaps she had stopped grief at the funeral because of a sense that it was physically dangerous. It is also incidentally ironic that the hemorrhage served her desires of being united with her mother, but it also facilitated eventually surrendering her.

In summary, the last three cases illustrate the need for humbleness in predictions of cure and incurability.

Applications of the triaxial framework and survival strategies are highlighted in following cases.

HIGHLIGHTING TREATMENTS ALONG THE AXES OF THE TRIAXIAL FRAMEWORK

Examples highlighting each of the three axes in turn follow.

Treatment Along the Process Axis

The following case indicates how dismantling defenses allowed connection to be established between symptoms and illnesses, and preceding traumas, stress responses, and their contexts.

Much therapy preceded and followed this session. A subsequent session with this patient is presented in detail (Case 17/38, Chapter 10).

CASE 17: THAWING DEFENSES ENABLING FREE FLOW

A 40-year-old woman previously treated for major depressions expressed in previous sessions that now that things were better, she needed to see more clearly the impact of her father's sexual abuse on her, as it interfered with her current relationship.

In the first part of the session the woman demonstrated a gamut of her usual defenses. She first explained in obsessive detail how busy she had been at work (obsessive-compulsive distraction). She then described how a sleazy man offered her a partnership but the terms were exploitative (displacement). After a blank silence she turned on herself, saying how useless and pathetic she was, how she could not remember anything, was confused and exhausted (dissociation, displacement on self); she just wanted to sleep and never wake up (flight); she felt she was bad and evil (turning judgment on self). She complained of severe back pain (displaced somatization) which was clarified to be pelvic pain (fragment of her trauma). She burst into tears saying she was going crazy with the different feelings (fragmentation) which she could not understand. She mentioned that she had watched the last episode of Dracula the night before, but went to sleep in terror, so she did not know the end (dissociation).

The therapist summarized the described defenses and their context to previous sessions. He asked if she wanted to know their significance. She nodded fearfully and hopefully. The defenses were given (lay) words. It was suggested that perhaps they defended against Dracula-type fears for herself. The patient wanted to go on.

She was encouraged to look at herself as the woman who wanted to understand herself for the sake of her relationship with her partner.

With intense pain she described a small child whose heart was broken, because she realized that her father was not going to make her his princess, but crumpled and tore her apart physically and emotionally instead. As bad, her mother hated her, and blamed her for being bad. Nothing could be done to make them love her. These were the feelings present since childhood, the depressions treated over the years, the different symptoms in the session. Words were found for them all. The adult woman felt pity for the poor child, betrayed and unloved by her parents. She said, "I would have died as a child had I had words then." She digested the session before she left. In the next session she looked bright and lucid.

Comments   Business, displacement, self-blame, dissociation, fragmentation, confusion, going crazy, even despair, and depression were all used as shields against knowing about abuse, betrayal, and lack of love. Reminder of the well woman who needed to know, facilitated understanding her defenses and giving them up in order to know her past. This was necessary in order to contrast it with current realities and achieve future fulfillments.

Treatment Along the Parameters Axis

Treatments in different phases at different social system levels have been highlighted for the bushfires in Case 1, Chapter 1, and will be taken up in cases in Chapters 8–11. Below, the importance of parameters is highlighted in the power of group treatment. This is exemplified in the exclamation of a child survivor of the Holocaust when first coming to a group, and a type of survivor hymn shared in groups (Ochberg, 1988, p. 17).

My liberation is beginning today–6th March 1995! For the first time in my life I am in a room with Jewish people. I am able to admit that I am Jewish and you seem to accept me. Even though I don't know who, or what I am, I have hope, and I am glad I came to this meeting, though I nearly chickened out.

I have been victimized.
I was in a fight that was not a fair fight.
I did not ask for the fight. I lost.
There is no shame in losing such fights, only in winning.
I have reached the stage of survivor and am no longer a slave of victim status.
I look back with sadness rather than hate.
I look forward with hope rather than despair.
I may never forget, but I need not constantly remember.
I *was* a victim.
I *am* a survivor.

Ramifications Along the Depth Axis

It is suggested that spontaneous progression of presenting problems (see below) can occur from one survival strategy to another and occur along components of an axis of the triaxial framework. The following case indicates developments along the depth and parameter axes. This time the progression was over some months.

CASE 18: TREATMENT ALONG THE DEPTH AXES

A 35-year-old survivor of domestic violence was initially consumed with memories, flashbacks, and nightmares of her abuse, and fears of her husband claiming her back (maladaptive flight) (survival level).

As she gained confidence in her security and capacities to manage her and her two children's affairs on her own, she reexamined her assumptions of guilt, shame, and beliefs that she was deserving of her abuse (judgment level/personal, family, social system). She became incensed at the injustice of her victimization, and took legal compensation action. She came to understand that she had been an innocent victim of her husband's violence (basic meaning of victimhood). She recognized and grieved her lost ideals of marriage, her dignity, values, principles, and rights, and abrogation of her identity and symbols of her hopes, such as her husband having squandered the house she had worked for. In a peer group she came to understand the sociopolitical phenomena of wife abuse. During this process her fears diminished, and she gained increasing peace, stature, dignity, and recovery of values and liking of herself.

At this stage her younger sister sought refuge from her violent partner. The now ex-victim gave her sanctuary and tried to convey the lessons she had learned to her sister. Her hope was that her mother, sister, and herself would form a bastion against the wrongs of female abuse (political identity, ideology). Instead the mother took her sister back to her partner, and the patient realized that her mother had similarly encouraged her to return to her husband in the past. She now also remembered mother having been directly cruel to her.

This realization hurt "more than the abuse," because the patient had to revise all her meanings in terms of her mother being a perpetrator and covert ally of her daughters' perpetrators. Confronting mother revealed that she had been perpetuating experiences of her own abuse and cruelties. And then the patient realized that she herself had out of fear turned a blind eye to ill treatment of her children by their father. To complete the transgenerational nemesis, her son was suspended from school for bullying behavior, and her own neglect of him was blamed for this. She commented bitterly, "I had spent nights at the police station with my children, so yes, they may have been late, and unsupervised. But the school refused to give him extra attention, saying they would then have to do the same for all their conduct-disturbed kids" (family, social nelgect). But she also improved communication and discipline with her child. He grieved the loss of his father with whom he tried to maintain contact through his behavior. His behavior improved.

The patient changed her own attachment hopes and dependency on her mother. She saw that in the past she had transferred them to her husband, and this, together with his violence, had held her hostage to him.

These hard lessons added to the patient's deep knowledge of violence, its transmission and perverse effects on well-meaning people like herself. She contrasted this with the sacred transmission of protection, nurture, love, and growth. She saw how she had spanned both sides and why. She put her wisdom to good purpose. She broke the generational cycle with her own children, helped mother and sister patiently with their own traps, and became imbued with the sacred principle that people not be oppressed. She changed her government department's work habits which exploited power over people it was meant to serve.

Comments   It may be seen that for effective treatment depth and parameter axis ramifications of especially traumatic flight and attachment had to be negotiated. Extensive, especially depth axis processing of the trauma, allowed the patient to replace maladaptive depth axis components with adaptive ones, inlcuding a deep sense of herself and her purpose.

A CASE HIGHLIGHTING SURVIVAL STRATEGIES

The following case demonstrates how in traumatic situations all survival strategies may be attempted. In turn recognizing each may provide a grip on them which may mitigate their maladaptive ramifications. Here raw, intense survival strategies are presented.

CASE 19: VALIDATING ACUTE SURVIVAL STRATEGIES

A 78-year-old woman was brought to the emergency department after she collapsed while identifying her daughter's body. The daughter had been killed hours earlier by a drunken driver after visiting her mother. The patient's physical condition was currently stable.

As soon as she realized that there was an interested person beside her, the mother spontaneously expressed the first cycle of unsuccessful survival strategies. First she expressed intense anguish and guilt for having caused her daughter's death by her having visited her (rescue). Then she felt intense naked pangs of yearning for her daughter (attachment). Next she ground her teeth loudly (they could be heard in the corridor) in rage at drunken drivers, saying they should be killed (fight). Then she rued the fact that it was her daughter, rather than so many others who were more expendable to society (such as the drunken driver), who should have been killed (competition). Then she cried in frustration, "What can I do? There is nothing I can do!" (assertiveness). She despaired of living further (adaptation). She wished the whole thing was a dream and had not happened (flight). Last, she was distraught that she had been cheated of the rewards of all the love she had poured into her daughter (cooperation).

Over an hour and a half the therapist said very little but responded softly to each survival strategy. "You feel you should have somehow prevented her from visiting you. Then she would be still alive." "You miss her with all your heart." "There is nothing that can be done." "Drunken drivers who kill innocent people should be killed."

The mother returned to each survival strategy in subsequent cycles, and eventually, even at this early phase, adaptive aspects made their appearance. For instance, she sobbed in unabashed grief (adaptation). She wondered whether mothers could prevent drunken drivers from killing (rescue) in the future. Then she made provisional plans for the daughter's body (assertiveness). She was very grateful to the therapist (cooperation). She decided to see her daughter's body again (attachment) and go on to a friend who had herself lost a child and who would understand her current state (cooperation).

Comments   It may be that in traumatic situations one scans and evokes each survival strategy to see if it may be applied. Therefore, trauma sequelae manifest different adaptive and maladaptive proportions of all survival strategies. Perhaps the intervention facilitated the appearance of adaptive aspects of survival strategies, especially grief. Of course, the intervention could not heal, but perhaps it set a model for subsequent cycles in the mourning process. Another case around acute bereavement is presented in Chapter 8 (Case 24).

SURVIVAL AND FULFILLMENT THERAPIES

The above cases indicate that wholist therapy does not only involve placing traumatic material in perspective, but, in addition, it explores adaptive alternatives which are added to the perspective. Furthermore, adaptive possibilities may be explored throughout the triaxial framework. Patients appreciate understanding their potentials for happiness as well as for unhappiness.

CASE 20: FULFILLMENT TREATMENT

A twenty-year-old, second generation of the Holocaust, university student presented with the feeling that she did not know who she was. She also saw the world as fearful for no apparent reason. She felt worst when she followed her inner artistic desires and "unusual" fun such as playing hockey. Further, she felt ungrateful and wrong for her resentments of her well-meaning loving parents. As a result of her predicaments she felt "depressed." All of her was "wrong." She would have fitted diagnoses of schizoid personality, anxiety, or depressive disorders.

It became clear that all her life her parents overrode her desires and thinking, and that the intensity of their love was based on extreme anxieties for their daughter's survival, in turn based on the parents' Holocaust experiences. In the parents' world, anything not directed to survival was dangerous. Hence studying humanities, artistic endeavors, or fun were seen as dangerous frivolities which the parents had to expunge from their daughter's mind.

In therapy the client had her fulfillment desires validated as normal. They were explored in detail, and thus she learned about her potentials over the triaxial framework; the adaptive alternatives to her parents' stress and trauma worlds.

Eventually the daughter became able to show gratitude to her parents for their survival concerns, but pointed out that after all they survived and had her in order for her to lead a normally fulfilled, not Holocaust-riddled life. Therefore, their purpose in survival was actually being fulfilled by her "different" ways.

From being a fear-filled robot repeating her parents' survival world, the daughter became alive, fulfilling her own life with zest (see also Case 44, p. 161).

Comment   The wholist perspective allowed a relatively fast appreciation of the contrasts between the patient's parents' survival modes imposed on the patient, and her own fulfillment desires. Survival modes are frequent philosophical bases for clients' lives. It can be a watershed to see that they can go beyond it to a new universe of fulfillment.

In summary, this chapter highlighted applications of key wholist concepts of survival strategies and triaxial framework through clinical examples. Issues of fulfillment as well as trauma therapy, treating defenses, and predictability of treatment outcomes, and prognosis were also addressed.

It was seen that both enthusiasm and pessimism need tempering, along with mindfulness of the potential to do harm. Perhaps in the golden mean of treatment one needs a hopeful, humble, astute, and diligent attitude as one applies oneself to symptoms across the triaxial framework, helping to replace maladaptive and traumatic responses with adaptive and fulfilling ones.

While highlighting different aspects of the wholist perspective, the different trauma treatment principles were implied. More detailed applications of the wholist perspective and trauma therapy principles in wholist treatment are described in the following chapters.

Chapter 8

Being There at the Trauma: Acute Treatment and Prevention

In this and the following chapters traumatic situations and their sequelae are examined in the light of wholist treatment, including the wholist perspective and trauma therapy principles. This chapter examines interventions in traumatic situations or immediately after their occurrence. The aim of such intervention is enhancement of adaptive responses and prevention of distorted ones which may evolve into later pathology (Foreman, 1994; Raphael et al., 1996). Later chapters examine ever-increasing gaps from traumatic situations to times of treatment.

In this chapter the first case is a simulated disaster exercise (Valent, Berah & Yuen, 1983), while the others are cases from the author's experience in emergency departments.

A JUMBO JET DISASTER EXERCISE

An unusual advantage of disaster exercises is the possibility to ethically observe what happens in traumatic situations and their immediate aftermaths, to be able to ask people why they behaved as they did, and to test acute preventive treatments.

Intuitive criticisms may state that exercises are different from real events, and pretend responses must differ from real ones. Nevertheless, army reports about well-prepared exercises (e.g., Sanner & Wolcott, 1983) note very realistic responses in them. The same was observed in this case. For instance, two subjects were treated for hyperventilation, one for asthma, another rang home to reassure her relatives that she survived the crash. Real anguish and anger were felt at perceived inadequacies of treatment. As a participant observer I noted responses in myself and others consistent with real situations. Nevertheless, the intensity of responses may have been relatively muted, as in a corner of one's mind most were aware of their safety.

Months of unsurpassed preparation went into this exercise. It simulated a belly flop of a jumbo jet carrying 420 passengers near an airport runway. Immediately after evacuation the plane burst into flames. Part of a real plane was ignited. Victims were painted by professionals with simulated wounds. Members of our mental health team participated as victims, helpers, and observers.

CASE 21: A DISASTER EXERCISE

Preimpact There was much denial (maladaptive flight) of the need for the exercise at all organizational levels, on the presumption that such a disaster would not occur. Resistance was overcome with patience, pointing out rewards, appeal to honor, common sense, and international regulations. Even so, some participation was half-hearted, and too little communication occurred between participating services.

Recognition of fears at all organizational levels of being overwhelmed by mass casualties (maladaptive adaptation) was countered by personal contact and confidence (*nonspecific treatment*), education and training (*symptomatic therapy*), and indication of likely achievements (adaptive rescue, assertiveness) (*specific therapy*).

Lack of recognition on the parameter axis led to lack of preparation for handling children, the bereaved, relatives, and the community. Such deficiencies are frequent in real disasters.

Approaching the airport, members of the medical team manifested anxiety by reluctance to read instructions and focusing on unimportant details such as a buckle on a helmet (maladaptive assertiveness, obsessional defenses). The mental health professional commented on and explained the anxiety, and instructed about other likely responses which would be encountered in victims and team members. Humor and leadership reestablished a workmanlike attitude (adaptive assertiveness).

Acknowledgment of fears, helped by therapist recognition of them in himself, provided a *"nonspecific"* example of handling performance anxiety. Coupled with providing understanding of current and expected survival strategy responses gave sufficient sense of control for high morale to reestablish itself (*symptomatic, specific treatment*).

Impact/Recoil Phase   The usual descriptions (e.g., Tyhurst, 1957) of lack of panic, and little inappropriate behavior in disasters was confirmed. Most victims were stunned and docile (adaptation), and were led to safety. Their nonthinking states lasted up to hours.

The minority who were judged by rescuers to exhibit inappropriate and uncooperative behavior, nevertheless, manifested adaptive survival strategies if judged from victims' perspectives. For instance, some wanted to return to the plane to save relatives (rescue). Others clung to rescuers because they were seen as saviors (attachment). Often, apparent victim confusion reflected being torn between competing survival strategies. Communication could have resolved most "inappropriate" behaviors. Instead victims were manhandled, coerced, and even slapped, causing great resentment.

Intense victim and rescuer survival strategies generally meshed well. Rescuers (rescue) did their best to move passengers to safe areas, and the stunned state of adaptation facilitated the passive movement of large numbers of people. *Recognition* of the great need of victims to know about and save their loved ones could preempt and treat much "inappropriate" behavior. Asking about the behavior could lead to clarification (symptomatic treatment). "Other rescuers are looking after those inside." Undue attachment responses could also be appeased, "If you cling less, I'll get you to a safe place quicker." Both impulses could be preempted by concurrent evacuation of families and friends.

Post Impact   The wounded and those in pain screamed for help (attachment). If their specific needs were unmet quickly, they felt totally alone and abandoned (maladaptive attachment), even with people milling around them. Most previously stunned victims continued to stand, sit, or lie silently, obediently and unobtrusively (adaptation). A few who seemed to act irrationally, again did so because they craved their absent loved ones (rescue, attachment). For the stunned time stood still, for the wounded it was inordinately long, for helpers it was inordinately short.

The rescuers felt thwarted by lack of equipment and were anguished by applying suboptimal treatment according to usual hospital standards (maladaptive rescue and assertiveness). Most stressful was having to prioritize treatment, which felt as if one was dispensing life and death (guilt of maladaptive rescue and competition).

The therapist reassured his colleagues that they were not "killing" victims, but actually saving as many as possible (*specific treatment* for maladaptive rescue and its meanings). The team was encouraged to stop for a cup of tea and review the situation (decompression; dual focus of attention seeing the circumstances, not the helpers as problems). Group morale was enhanced. For instance, one helper who obsessively tried to apply "good" treatment to one individual (maladaptive assertiveness) through being given space to see the situation, extended his therapeutic efficacy (adaptive assertiveness).

The therapist dealt with "difficult" people by helping to find relatives and friends, or at least information about them. Some relatives were united with their wounded folk, held their hands, and talked to them (adaptive attachment). The therapist encouraged Red Cross ladies who were just standing around to individually stay with those who felt isolated and abandoned. This was much appreciated by both parties, and assisted to dissolve stunned states.

Rescuers were too preoccupied to speak with victims about their feelings and experiences. The therapist did so *(recognition)*, held victims' hands, gave reassurance and information *(nonspecific treatment)*. Some victims spontaneously ventilated their emotions, judgments, and preliminary meanings, "This is what happens to me when I win a holiday!" (priority competition guilt). After a while the helper responded, "Maybe your winning did not cause the crash." The victim cried with relief. Maladaptive competition guilt and meaning were dissolved.

In retrospect the medical team should have been better prepared to modulate goal expectations and (assertiveness) judgments, and ethical ideals of best treatment for all, with prioritization of scarce resources in the service of the survival calculus (competition). The therapist was able to readjust appraisals to some extent, and to facilitate replacement of maladaptive assertiveness with adaptive assertiveness, competition, and rescue.

The value of facilitating physical and psychological connection with loved ones, and in their absence to helper substitutes was very clear. It provided a *specific* antidote to attachment trauma.

If not hospitalized, victims were taken for processing to a holding area where they were also given food, warmth, and comfort *(nonspecific)*. About 20 victims were hived off as "psychiatric," as their behavior was demanding, frightened, or clingy. The arbitrary division according to behavior belied the unrecognized commonality of both groups' anxieties about absent relatives and friends and numerous, sometimes intense, psychophysiological symptoms. Some victims in both groups developed psychosomatic illnesses which were ignored by attendant doctors.

Therapists again facilitated contact with and information about craved-for persons, and explained the nature and sense of biopsychosocial survival strategy responses *(symptomatic)*. Medical attention was drawn to psychosomatic illnesses. Two people had transient psychotic reactions—one thought the plane crashed specifically in order to kill her, the other thought that she had caused the crash. Both were reassured when they came to understand that they were searching for (flight and rescue) meanings of the crash *(specific therapy)*. Two victims were given Valium—one for hyperventilation, the other because her separation distress panicked those around her *(symptomatic)*.

Some who lost boundaries between the exercise and reality were "talked down" *(specific* reconciliation of trauma and current world).

The above was a demonstration of how overloaded and untrained physicians can ignore biological, psychological, and social stress symptoms and illnesses, and separate biological and psychosocial on the basis of behavior and inability to communicate with victims' distress. And yet most symptoms were, in fact, part of a biopsychosocial unit highly amenable to unified treatment.

Debrief (two days later) Victims and rescuers met to discuss their feelings and what could be learned for future disaster treatment *(recognition)*. The meeting was on "home ground" and all were encouraged to feel safe and free to say whatever they wanted (*nonspecific*). Victims expressed much anger for having been ignored, left alone, not listened to, manhandled, and for receiving wrong treatment (maladaptive attachment). Rescuers expressed their frustration and guilt (maladaptive rescue, assertiveness). In time both groups came to reconcile each other's concerns and perspectives in terms of their disparate various survival strategies at the time (*symptomatic and specific treatments*). Both groups were chastened and somewhat wiser about vulnerabilities and inabilities to overcome massive disasters. Creative views including logistics, training needs, and ethical guidelines were offered. Victims and helpers came to see that, in fact, they had participated in a successful exercise which had the potential to help victims. Its purpose, and theirs with it, was fulfilled (*specific treatment across the triaxial framework*).

The debriefing gave words and understanding to victim and rescuer experiences, provided a rich meaningful story of the event, and facilitated the purpose of the exercise.

Comment It may be seen that most interventions occurred at fluctuating triaxial pressure points. However, the salience and immediacy of the traumatic situation, and understanding of survival strategies and the triaxial framework, facilitated quick diagnoses and treatments. To ensure that trauma treatment would be applied at its maximum potential required checking and planning in quieter phases (see pp. 97–98).

In fact, as well as many technical logistical improvements, subsequent disaster plans made provisions for children, the bereaved, and relatives. The exercise also contributed to early centralized registration and distribution of victim information, promoting contact between victims and their relatives, friends, or substitute carers, availability to victims of mobile phones, distribution of information about expected responses, and routine inclusion of mental health helpers in outreach medical teams. The recommendation that mental health professionals be present at all hierarchical level disasters was implemented statewide after a major actual disaster the following year.

It was additionally interesting to note how quickly stress responses, judgments, and provisional meanings progressed into symptoms and illnesses, and how effectively they could be reversed with treatment. This adds weight to the possibility that earliest, but well-tailored interventions may alleviate traumas and mitigate their sequelae in nonsimulated situations.

Indeed, lessons learned in this exercise were implemented and confirmed in earliest interventions in emergency department traumas and in other disasters.

INTERVENTIONS IN TRAUMATIC SITUATIONS IN THE EMERGENCY DEPARTMENT

The context of the psychiatric liaison traumatology team in the emergency department needs to be mentioned, as without its acceptance within the wider goals of the department and personal trust, it could not have done its work. The trust took years to develop and was based on proven efficacy of work synergism, interest to help staff welfare, and personal friendships. The liaison team consisted of the director (the author) who also partook in senior management decisions in the department as a whole, two psychologists, a senior psychiatric (at times also psychology) trainee, two nurses, a social worker, and students.

The following cases were treated at increasing intervals from their traumatic situations.

Interventions During Traumatic Situations

The two men below who were resuscitated following severe heart attacks demonstrate the subjective differences between presence and absence of acute trauma treatment. The two men replicated in an intense way feelings the wounded in the disaster exercise felt when they were attended, and when not attended.

CASE 22: CONNECTION DURING TRAUMA

The first man said, "I knew I was in a bad way, but it all meant nothing to me. The only thing I remember of the whole event was the nurse who held my hand and talked to me. She was my angel, and I'll never forget her. I am so grateful to her. I knew that she was explaining things to me, but I didn't care. I just listened to her voice. I still don't know what they did to me or how long it took. I just concentrated on her, and she never left me."

CASE 23: LACK OF CONNECTION DURING TRAUMA

The second man said, "It was the most horrific experience of my life. I felt totally alone. I know there were people everywhere about me, but I felt totally alone floating in space with my limbs in the air with things jabbed into them. The instruments were like the jaws of a shark. The noise was chaotic, with shouts and commands making me think they did not know what they were doing; they were just experimenting on me. And it went on forever."

Comment It may be seen that treatment principles which provided for adaptive attachment (care and empathy from rescuers) and flight (safe sanctuary) countered attachment and flight traumas. In their absence, attachment and flight traumas occurred. In both cases primitive survival responses connected with atavistic and early spiritual meanings in terms of being hunted by monsters and being rescued by angels.

Treatment principles included *recognition* of the patient's terror, *nonspecific* provision of the nurse as a counter-trauma environment of safety and kindness, *symptomatic* sedation, relief of pain, explanation and reassurance, and *specific* counters to abandonment and feeling trapped.

It may be thought that such treatment principles occur intuitively and ubiquitously. However, stressed and uninformed helpers, as in the disaster exercise, may not have the necessary resources to empathize with trauma victims. Traumatology team members have often substituted for the "good nurse." However, to ensure that this became a routine part of treatment, staff discussion resulted in a protocol (Appendix 3), in which a specific nurse is designated to concentrate on psychosocial needs of severely physically ill patients and their families. This includes arranging as much contact and information between them as is possible and appropriate. Routine availability of mobile phones for patients to be able to contact relatives has been instituted throughout the department.

Immediately After Traumatic Situations

The following cases indicate the fast compounding of traumatic situations with judgments and meanings even of existential proportions, and the need to incorporate them in treatments.

CASE 24: RETRIEVING MOTHER'S SOUL

A Vietnamese woman wailed with loud continuous distress following her mother's death of a stroke in the emergency department. We met her in the relatives' distress room near where her mother lay. The woman told us spontaneously the details of her mother's illness and death.

The relentlessness of the woman's crying evoked a countertransference response that something was unexplained. This prompted the question what worried her most about her mother's death? With extreme anguish she stated that it was the perdition of her mother's soul. The daughter had converted to Catholicism, and her mother was in the process of doing so. Because she had not speeded up the process sufficiently, and so *because of her,* her mother's soul was lost forever (traumatic rescue at sacred spiritual depth).

Immersion into the daughter's religious views and further detailed history revealed that just prior to the mother losing consciousness, she and the daughter were singing Christian psalms, and the mother seemed to be steeped in their spirit. It was suggested that in her last conscious moments the mother's soul had been spiritually converted and saved (adaptive rescue alternative). The daughter hoped that this was possible, but wanted it confirmed by a priest. The hospital priest was appraised of the situation, and he confirmed the suggestion. The daughter's anguish visibly lightened. She was then helped with normal grieving.

It may be said that *specific therapy* of rescue trauma at the particular sacred triaxial point allowed an adaptive rescue view to supplant a maladaptive and traumatic one. This allowed adaptive grief to proceed, and potentially long-term unresolved grief and depression were averted. The next case demonstrates a similar wholist treatment approach extended over many triaxial points. The checklist summarized in Table 3 aided in tailoring treatment according to circumstances and available resources.

CASE 25: DEATH OF A YOUNG HUSBAND

Our team was informed that a 34-year-old man had died in the department, and the widow's distress was extreme and hard to bear. The two-year-younger widow was accompanied by her parents, but her two children, aged 4, and 18 months, were being minded.

We obtained as much history as possible about the family, and about the diagnosis, treatment, and mode of death of the deceased.

The team quickly *recognized* that this would be a heavy commitment requiring some time. It assessed its rationale and goals (to facilitate adaptation in the family), its own parameters such as available skills, emotional responses (such as horror that a person similar to us in age had died), and logistical resources. A sense of being over-whelmed was acknowledged as countertransference and eased when considered as probably similar to what the family felt. Approximate roles were assigned to avoid duplication. For instance, the social worker was to give information about social resources. Others were assigned to deal with expected waves of relatives. It was noted that the children, in particular, must not be forgotten.

A quiet area abutting the department was made available for as long as necessary. The body could be viewed in an adjacent room. Warm refreshments kept on being brought by sympathetic staff (*nonspecific treatment*).

Two team members approached the widow and her parents. Caroline detailed how her husband had suffered from a disease of the heart wall for a year. He had been short of breath a few days previously, but was quite well that morning. He collapsed suddenly while changing the baby. She tried to resuscitate him but couldn't. Within three minutes she had summoned a doctor neighbor, but his efforts failed too. Caroline was anguished whether she could have done anything to save her husband, and also how much he had suffered while dying (traumatic rescue anguish). All the details, medical evidence, and knowledge of the survival strategy rescue were examined and fed back, leading to the categorical conclusion, "You naturally feel you should have been able to save him, or his suffering, but you did all you could, and he did not suffer." (*symptomatic and specific treatment of* rescue trauma and guilt).

The mood changed to blaming the husband for not having taken enough care of himself, being a workaholic, not caring for her. Enraged, she said, "I could have killed him, the way he carried on." The humor of her statement was not lost on her. The parents followed their daughter's feelings themselves. They emphasized how pig-headed the husband had been. "You could kill the part of him that killed himself." (*specific treatment* of maladaptive fight—against the enemy part of the husband).

Caroline then sobbed bitterly clutching at her heart (grief) (*nonspecific* support). Her parents hugged her. After some minutes she said, "I cannot believe it. I seem to forget every now and then that it happened." "You need some relief from the pain so you can deal with it." (explanation of defenses.) And she burst into painful sobs again.

Caroline next wondered whether the illness was contagious (consideration of flight). She was reassured that they were all safe (adaptive flight).

Next she considered why her husband had died and not her, and who was better off. Eventually the helper said, "Neither you nor he had the power to decide who would live and who would die." (*symptomatic and specific* treatment of mal-adaptive competition and preemption of priority guilt).

She became bitter at the wrecked dreams of marriage. "You feel cheated." (giving words to maladaptive cooperation). "Yes, by him, by Fate." (beginning of meaning and spiritual levels). Caroline, followed by her parents, revisited each survival strategy at different triaxial points and from different angles.

Throughout, Caroline received new waves of relatives, and somewhat in the role of hostess (*nonspecific* accordance of dignity and collaborative role) took them to the body (assertiveness control). The treatment team had refreshments, and digested what happened (decompression, reinforcement of rescue, assertiveness).

Caroline asked about the children seeing the body. She was advised how children of different ages conceive of acute death. Scenarios of short- and long-term implications of seeing and not seeing the body were imagined (education, *symptomatic treatment*). Caroline decided (assertiveness) to have the children brought in, and she supported them (not unlike the way she had been supported a short time before), when she took them in to see their father (adaptive caretaking).

She asked how she might influence the meaning for the children of their father's death. She explored her own judgments, meanings, identity, and values (depth axis) and decided to pass them on to her children.

Caroline asked about transplantation of her husband's organs. When a heart transplant had been considered for her husband he expressed a desire to donate his own organs, should he die. Only the corneas could be harvested, but this gave Caroline much satisfaction. Her husband's death created some good, and so it had some purpose after all.

The waves of relatives were counseled in their own right. The deceased's mother was checked for her heart condition and encouraged not to forget her medication. Family members were given pamphlets explaining likely responses, and were warned to drive carefully. Social frameworks were set up by the social worker. Follow-up appointments were made (parameter axis treatment).

The debrief session (for a more detailed description see Case 41, p. 157) was a secondary cameo of what was described above. Staff were reassured that they had done everything possible to save the deceased. The anger at their impotence was channeled creatively to the establishment of a more suitable viewing room for the deceased. The department staff were grateful for the model of how to deal with bereaved relatives, and this made the traumatology team feel that their efforts bore long-term fruit. The man's death achieved meaning for helpers too.

Comment   It may be seen how bearing in mind the wholist perspective and treatment principles enabled *recognition* of individual and family traumas, provision of space and empathic therapeutic relationships in a counter-trauma environment to deal with them (*nonspecific* treatment), *symptomatic* clarification, education, warnings and medication, and *specific* trauma treatment. In the latter each maladaptive survival strategy (as in Case 19, Chapter 7), and its biological, psychological, and social aspects were recognized at all depth levels, processed, and then viewed concurrently with their adaptive counterparts. Treatment took note of current and future phases, included the widow, all members of the family (especially including children), and both victims and helpers.

To an outsider the team may have appeared to be doing very little, mostly listening, occasionally saying something, patting, or holding a hand. This resembles the apparent smooth measured pace of medical first aid when done well. Yet thinking and emotions were highly pressured, alternating from empathic immersion to understanding responses and treatment principles within a wholist framework. This resembles prioritizing first aid as emergencies present, while tailoring further treatment according to an overall medical framework.

In summary, it may be seen that the "black hole" of trauma is a focused event of high energy, yet with modes and means of observation of its dimensions, features and with rules of treatment which may influence its sequelae. It is as if the events of pebbles hitting ponds could be conceptualized, and thereby a range of ripple formations could be softened or smoothed. The wholist perspective ensures that this is done as accurately and widely as possible. And for the cases in this chapter, as early as possible.

Chapter 9

Early Stress and Trauma Treatments

In the last chapter responses were indissolubly part of an ongoing salient situation. In this chapter symptoms and illnesses are examined as evolving responses along the process axis. As such, they present point and line diagnoses with kennels for volume diagnoses (Chapter 5). It has already been suggested that acute stress responses may comprise acute stress disorder and adjustment disorders, and the end of the process axis comprises a variety of illnesses (Figure 2, Chapter 3, and Chapter 5). In this chapter, an expanded 6 categories of illnesses are presented along the process axis. They emphasize their origins from stressors, and their biopsychosocial associations.

It is suggested that this way of categorizing symptom and illness presentations is clinically extremely useful. It provides a heuristically encompassing means of categorizing clinical presentations of which, often a majority, do not fall into classical diagnoses. It provides, for instance, a way of looking at "functional" symptoms and overlays, and psychosocial contributions to physical illnesses.

The 6 categories of symptom and illness presentations examined are biological, psychological, and social stress response survival strategy fragments (see also Chapter 5); evolving and relived traumas; hysteria-type illnesses with emphasis on defenses and loss of memory; classical physical; and psychiatric illnesses; and also secondary symptoms derived from others (see Appendix 2, where the six categories are presented in a modified sequence for the sake of medical interns). Categories of illnesses can overlap as will be demonstrated by reexamining Case 2 (Chapter 1). It will be seen that in a general way time elapsed since traumatic events reflects the extent of disconnections and process axis ramifications and ramifications into the other axes, though the ramifications can also occur extremely quickly, as was seen in the previous chapter.

TREATMENT OF SURVIVAL STRATEGY STRESS RESPONSE FRAGMENTS PRESENTING AS SYMPTOMS AND ILLNESSES

Symptoms in this category are maladaptive biological, psychological, and social stress responses (Table 2) and their ramifications in the triaxial web. Their disconnections from their origins may be overcome through the wholist perspective and its language (Chapter 5), so that symptoms can be traced back to their survival strategy origins and contexts. Examples were Cases 1–6 and 10 (Chapters 1 and 5).

Stress symptoms may manifest as part of stress responses, of trauma, as refracted traumatic sequelae and as stress responses to new situations which threaten recurrence of stress or trauma. This is an example of how the disciplines of stress and trauma overlap and should not be separated. The following case is one of severe stress response which falls short of trauma.

CASE 26: STRESS HEADACHE

A 35-year-old Iraqi refugee from Sadam Hussein's regime was referred for severe tension and headaches not helped by medication *(symptomatic treatment)*. Asking about her greatest worries she told the story of hardships trekking through the desert and experiences in a Turkish refugee camp. She concluded saying that her mother had followed her and finished in the same camp.

With a little encouragement she added that her husband's relatives robbed and physically abused her mother in the camp. It was when she first heard reports of this that she became suffused with helpless rage (maladaptive fight), and developed the headaches. When the mother eventually joined her daughter, under promise of secrecy she confirmed the reports. Her fury generalized secretly to her husband, and her headaches worsened. When he pressured her to emigrate to join his abusive family in Germany, the headaches became intolerable. (On questioning, so did other tension pains in the chest, neck, and back.)

The pains were identified and understood as physiological manifestations of suppressed feelings of wanting to hurt and exact revenge (fight) on her mother's perpetrators. Suppression was motivated by fear of loss of her husband on whom she depended and to whom she was traditionally subservient (attachment), and not wanting to break her promise to her mother (cooperation).

Events were placed in context of past and present loyalties and values. Headaches developed in the session when the patient was angry with the therapist seemingly trapping her (transference).

After visualizing potential risks and hopes over a number of sessions, the patient expressed her rage to her husband against his family. The process of joining his family ceased, as did the headaches and other pains. Family readjustments followed.

Comment   The patient exemplifies common clinical presentations of autonomic (sympathetic and parasympathetic) nervous system arousal (Chapter 3) associated with different survival strategies. Because the autonomic system influences all bodily systems and organs, psychophysiological symptoms may be very wide-ranging. Though patients often emphasize only one or two manifestations, closer questioning often reveals a number of others.

Psychophysiological symptoms may become recurrent or entrenched. When a particular system or organ is chronically aroused or is vulnerable, specific psychosomatic illnesses such as angina (Case 2, Chapter 1), or asthma (Case 5, Chapter 5) may result (see also Chapter 4). The following case is another brief example.

CASE 27: STROKE AT RETIREMENT

An executive being forced to retire because of his age was stressed more than ever in his life as he believed that he was purposelessly handing over his life's work to an incompetent young man. He had to suppress his outrage as he felt all his values, goals, and identity crumble. In this state he developed a stroke some days before his retirement day. The man and his wife were relieved to be able to consider that at least the stroke might have some meaning. They started to consider their future options.

The following case highlights with psychological symptom fragments.

CASE 28: SEPARATION TRAUMA MASKING AS DEPRESSION

A 29-year-old woman presented to the emergency department with recurrent depression, suicidal ideas, and inappropriate aggression. Antidepressants (*symptomatic treatment*) in the past had questionable benefits. Asking about her greatest worries led to a puzzling new consideration that separation actually was her main problem. Asking her how she experienced separation, after further hesitation she described intense pain in the chest characteristic of yearning, and the emptiness, and craving of extreme need.

These feelings came on in the setting of her de facto boyfriend wanting to leave her. She complained that he was abusive and demanding, but without him she felt suicidal.

The patient impressed as a helpless child in interview, one who became aggressive when she felt her needs were unmet. History revealed an alcoholic father. She talked about him with gestures similar to those when she talked of her de facto. She was aggressive to the interviewer when she deemed him ungiving (transference).

Asked about when the patient first experienced the feelings she described, she remembered them from childhood when her father abused her, and mother did not help. She saw with a sense of revelation that what had been called depression were the above feelings which had recurred since childhood.

Her feelings were named, labeled, and explained in terms of maladaptive attachment, their roots surmised, and sense made of them. Her traumatic fears were imagined and verbalized, anchored in a consciously safe environment.

The patient realized that she was still seeing relationships as a child, but that she could learn alternatives. She accepted referral for psychotherapy.

Comment   These cases indicate how "everyday" stresses and conflicts can reach traumatic proportions, because to the subjects they mean threats to core aspects of survival and fulfillment. Which of the great variety of biological, psychological, and social symptom and illness fragments come to notice depends on which survival strategies are evoked, and a variety of triaxial, including cultural, influences.

In each of the above cases, wholist treatment combined the wholist perspective and tailored treatment principles to early, short interventions.

Recognition of underlying problems was facilitated by a wholist approach, reading different modes and means of communication (including transference and countertransference), locating on the triaxial framework survival strategy fragments, and tracing them back to their sources. *Nonspecific treatment* included the relationship, calm, hope, and simultaneous counter-trauma experience. *Symptomatic* treatment included clarification, translation of patient wholist language to common language, as well as relief from symptoms through human contact and drugs. *Specific treatment* included holding intense patient distress when traumatic situations surfaced even as current more hopeful alternatives were generated.

The wholist approach facilitated relatively fast diagnosis and expanded treatment opportunities. It can avert multiple tests, fragmentary treatment, and unconvincing reassurance. Specific treatment may be fast as in the first case when problems are new and solvable. When they combine with chronic problems, as in the last case, wholist diagnosis can facilitate effective referral.

LIVING AND RELIVING TRAUMATIC SITUATIONS

In this category of illnesses traumatic situations are experienced prospectively, or relived with variable awareness for their original contexts. As in the bushfires (Case 1, Chapter 1) and in the first case below, out of the traumatic event can be seen developing traumatic sequelae. In the second case below (e.g., Case 4, Chapter 5), symptoms are relived aspects of traumatic situations, but their significance is disconnected from awareness.

CASE 29: A SHOT MAN

A 32-year-old man was lying in shock, having been shot deliberately in the thigh by a gunman who was making his getaway after having robbed two security guards in a shopping center.

Two team members approached the man and his partner. One team member looked comfortingly and inquiringly at the patient. The latter said that his mind was blank and he felt cold. It was explained that the cold was physical shock and the blank was psychological shock. Both were common temporary protective processes (adaptation). A helper took his hand.

In contrast, the man's partner was hyperventilating, and had a great need to tell us all that had happened. As she recounted her panic (flight) for herself and especially her partner, her breathing eased. Comforting and empathy had now dissolved the patient's shock, and he too became keen to recount his story.

He described how he had witnessed, while hiding behind a column the gunman shoot two security guards in the legs and take their money bags. He followed the gunman at a distance, thinking he might identify the number of his getaway car. On the way he also spread warnings to passing shoppers, which led to most of them in the shopping center being secure out of the gunman's sight. Just short of the exit, the gunman discovered him, and shot him in the thigh. The man concluded his story somewhat surprisingly, "So it just proves again that I am a failure." He said that this was what he could not bear to think about when we first approached him.

This case illustrates once again how earliest judgments and meanings may combine with survival strategies and form a nucleus which is dissociated from awareness. Such a nucleus, together with the dissociation, can ramify across the triaxial framework (see also "Memories," Chapter 3).

While addressing later symptoms may have made treatment relatively difficult, the early wholist *recognition* of a trauma, and *nonspecific* counter-trauma environment of sympathy, empathy, and respect allowed the man to unfreeze his sense of failure (assertiveness trauma), and take control of his story (adaptive assertiveness) (see also Case 12, Chapter 6).

Together with the partner's opposite initial pressure to obtain relief by telling her story, one may have a sense of the delicate balance between telling and reliving, and avoiding and defending traumas. The balance is determined by fear of nonvalidation and retraumatization, as against receiving sympathy, understanding and tolerance, and hope of help.

Relatives arrived. The patient's mother was having an asthma attack, "I always get like this when I am upset. I rely on him, he is all I have." ("Attachment Illness," Chapter 4). She was successfully treated with drugs, some ventilation of her anxieties, and reassurance that her son would recover. Other family members were also facilitated by the helpers to ventilate their shock and dismay, and they too were given reassuring information.

The mother confirmed that her son had always thought poorly of himself as a result of his father's constant denigrations. As the relatives started to share their relief with the patient and bantered about his bravery, the father stayed surly in the background. However, over next week partner, newspapers, family, and ultimately the grudging father all hailed the patient as a hero. He was very touched by the demonstrations of relief, love, and admiration. He felt cherished and admired, perhaps for the first time.

All his responses at the time of the shooting were clarified from all survival strategy angles. So were judgments of them, concluding in the third session, "Whichever way we look at it, you were brave to follow the man and warn people at your risk." His self-image was changing.

During the next year in which the patient was followed up, he suffered no PTSD symptoms. He had been promoted at work, and his relationship with his partner was deepening. He was grateful for the initial intervention, which according to him, had led to him feeling better about himself than ever in his life.

Comments   This case is an example of a limited, tailored, volume intervention. For instance, the patient's relationships with his parents were not explored. Nevertheless, *symptomatic and specific* treatment elements were applied sufficiently for reprocessing of all survival strategies related to the event, and for negative judgments and meanings which compounded with past ones to be countered by their adaptive alternatives. The effects of outside influences such as public admiration, and *symptomatic treatment* of pain, relief, and surgery were also very important. At the same time, the partner and other relatives also benefited to some extent from the interventions (parameter axis). For instance, attention was drawn to the mother's asthma which, otherwise, would not have been treated.

CASE 30: HOT FLASHES IN THE NECK

A man presented many times to the emergency department with panic attacks associated with hot flushes in the left side of his neck. The symptom did not fit a medical condition. Normal tests and reassurance did not pacify him for long.

A wholist approach revealed that the first time the patient experienced the hot flush was as part of a recent coronary angiography. At the moment he had the experience he heard someone say, "Won't last long." In his heightened state of anxiety he took this to mean that he would die soon of heart disease (traumatic flight). While immersed in the telling of this experience, the patient relived the panic and hot flush of the first experience.

His need to constantly return to the department was understood now as being a sanctuary where a heart attack could be treated immediately. Investigation revealed that the comment did not relate to his condition. His fear of a heart attack could now be addressed realistically, resulting now in effective reassurance. Past threat and current reality were reconciled in a coherent story in which he had some control. His symptoms resolved enduringly within three sessions.

Comment   In both above cases the prevalent medical culture would have ignored the patients' psychosocial traumas, to the detriment of their biopsychosocial treatments. As it was, *recognition* and *nonspecific* treatment facilitated *specific* readjustments of traumatic meanings to more hopeful alternatives. As a result, symptoms were preempted in the first case, and resolved in the second.

The following cases demonstrate more intense and entrenched defensive disconnections and obfuscations.

"CHERISHED" SYMPTOMS AND ILLNESSES: HYSTERIA

In this category defenses are more pronounced, memories of initial traumatic situations are more inaccessible, and disconnected illnesses became the best available compromise solutions to the circumstances. The word cherished is used euphemistically to indicate that the person often does not seem to want to be cured of symptoms, but rather to have them confirmed.

Primary gain of symptoms is that they are instrumental in avoiding memories and recurrences of traumatic situations. Secondary gains include privileges of being ill including financial compensation, though the latter is often overstated. Symptoms may be both symbolic of traumatic situations, and be camouflaged in currently fashionable, even if passing diagnoses.

Treatment is elusive and doctors feel frustrated by many negative tests, recalcitrant and sometimes shifting symptoms. Anger is a hallmark countertransference response, masked by pejorative use of diagnoses such as hysteria, secondary gain, and finally malingering. The latter diagnosis, however, is seldom used because subjects seem to be genuinely unconscious of their motivations, even though on some level they may communicate a relative indifference to them (called *belle indifference*). Nevertheless, underlying the desire for illness status exist ambivalent desires for recognition of the primary fears, though with forlorn hope that anything can be done about them.

CASE 31: HYSTERICAL BACK PAIN RESOLVED

A hard-working migrant uncharacteristically took to bed with back pain. Investigations did not reveal sufficient damage for the degree of disability, and his wife and doctors became frustrated with him.

A wholist approach revealed that a month prior, while driving home late from work, the patient saw a boy sprawled on the road beside his bike. He was convinced the boy was his son, and that he had been killed. In fact, it was the son's friend, and he was severely injured. The man now believed that his son, who rode the same type of bike and was unattended during the parents' long working hours, would be killed. He developed a deep desire to stay at home to protect his son (rescue). However, to do so was too shameful and disloyal to his wife (maladaptive assertiveness, cooperation). His symptoms gave legitimacy to stay at home without shame. They also symbolized the injured boy's back injury.

In family therapy the fears were ventilated. The son, who was also frightened, promised to be careful, and greater supervision of him was worked out. The patient slowly returned to work and was pain free.

The following case of another back pain indicates how somatization hysterical patterns can become permanent.

CASE 32: UNRESOLVED HYSTERICAL BACK PAIN

A man from a strong patriarchal culture had been suffering back pain for 12 years, necessitating much care by his wife. The pain came on in the context of the wife refusing sex because she was told that a fifth child would kill her. However, the patient believed that she had a lover, and he became jealous and impotent (maladaptive competition, assertiveness). He was convinced that his status as a man, in fact his whole life, was crumbling around him. A fortuitous minor back injury gave the patient an honorable reason for his impotence as well as to stay at home and keep a vigil on his wife. He received care from his wife and compensation from work (secondary gain). When the care diminished, his symptoms increased. The system was too entrenched for treatment to be successful.

Comment   The last two cases are similar to classical hysterical conversion symptoms in soldiers whose paralyses and other physical symptoms allowed them to honorably avoid combat. They also resemble Freud's earliest cases of hysteria (e.g., Freud, 1886; 1888). Tracing symptoms back to their contexts is resisted because exposure is seen to ensure the happening of the very trauma that the symptoms hold at bay. As well, equilibria with secondary gains may be disturbed. However, as was seen in Case 30, if hope can be held that traumatic situations may not occur if symptoms are given up, deeper fulfillment desires may well up and lead to relinquishing the protective symptoms.

"CLASSICAL" ILLNESSES

It is suggested that all illnesses are best viewed as having different proportions of biological, psychological, and social stressor and stress response precedents. Then, even classical medical and psychiatric textbook illnesses may be seen to be influenced to some degree by psychosocial stressors, and this is consistent with the long-known increased incidence of all types of illnesses in proportion to severity of stressors (e.g., Holmes & Rahe, 1967). The following case of pneumonia illustrates this point to some extent.

CASE 33: DEPRESSION AND PNEUMONIA

A 99-year-old woman in a medical ward with pneumonia was approached by the author. Asking what worried her most, she related how everyone was saying "You only have three months to go!" that is, to her 100th birthday. But she came to see that her big birthday party was really seen by others as a farewell party, beyond which she was expendable, having done her job. She lost her enthusiasm, zest, and energy; indeed, she became depressed and withdrew to bed where she developed pneumonia.

She was treated with antibiotics and antidepressants (*symptomatic treatment*). *Specific treatment* involved family meetings in which the family was made aware of the patient's feelings. They realized that she would still be the same person after her 100th birthday as before. Instead of feeling cast out (maladaptive attachment) and as if preparing for her funeral (maladaptive adaptation), the patient came to look forward to her birthday and participated in it with relish (adaptive assertiveness).

CASE 34: CHRONIC SCHIZOPHRENIA

A young schizophrenic woman presented with exacerbation of voices calling her insulting sexual names. The initial question revealed that she had been sexually abused by her older brother for years. She had not mentioned this to previous psychiatrists. Current voices repeated her brother's insults. Further treatment for schizophrenia was able to include this new information. (See also Case 39b, Chapter 10.)

Comment   These two cases indicate the value of a wholist biopsychosocial approach even in cases with apparently clear medical or psychiatric diagnoses. The advantages are those of line and volume diagnoses over point ones (Chapter 5).

REVERBERATION WITH SYMPTOMS OF OTHERS: SECONDARY TRAUMATIC STRESS

In this category symptoms arise from identification with ill or deceased persons. This may arise from deep empathy, or a way to not feel guilt or grief. (Secondary symptoms in helpers are considered in Chapter 11.)

CASE 35: HUSBAND'S CHEST PAIN

A woman presented with atypical chest pain believing that she was having a heart attack. Physical examination was negative. Two weeks prior her husband had died of a heart attack, and she believed that he had experienced the same pain which she described. When she was enabled to describe how much she missed her husband and wished to be with him, her symptoms gave way to grief.

CASE 36: FATHER'S STROKE

A 59-year-old man had recurrent dizziness for which no organic cause was found. Touching his temple, the man expressed the belief that he had a brain tumor. However, x-rays and a brain scan were negative. Still, the man could not be reassured.

History revealed that the patient had been extremely close to his father who had died at the age of 59 of a stroke (the patient touched his temple the same way as above). Asking what symptoms the father had before he died revealed dizziness as the major complaint. He was now two weeks off the exact age at which his father had died. Noting the correspondence of the patient's age with his father's, the patient expressed a sense of guilt for surpassing his father's age of death (maladaptive competition, priority guilt). He also expressed sorrow that he had been overseas at the time his father died and had not helped him (maladaptive rescue, survivor guilt, maladaptive adaptation).

Examining his guilts in depth in terms of the present, it was suggested that perhaps his father would be delighted if the patient now lived beyond his age.

Attention was also drawn to the repeated gesture when the patient talked of his father's stroke and his own brain tumor. This led to the patient becoming able to verbalize his terror of a stroke, the brain tumor being a disguise for this terror. He was reexamined and was able to be properly reassured that he was not having a stroke. The man's arrested grief for his father thawed, his guilt abated, and his dizziness disappeared. He surpassed his father's age of death without mishap. His grief allowed him to separate from his father. (See also Case 16, Chapter 7.)

Comment   In both cases *recognition* involved seeing presenting symptoms as signifying a threat of being felled (maladaptive flight) like a near person had been. Such recognition was aided by the wholist approach to family history, and reading of nonverbal (body) language. The latter symoblized the dead person's fatal illness. The identification was associated with impacted grief (maladaptive adaptation), in part due to still prevailing guilt and in part to not letting go of a loved person (maladaptive attachment). Both were more intense at symbolically poignant times.

Nonspecific treatment provided safety, relationship, and a counter-trauma experience, such as a hospital environment in which the relatives had died but in which the patients were alive. *Symptomatic* treatment included normal medical diagnoses, but they were particularly ineffective here until the underlying fears and unresolved griefs were addressed. In *specific treatment,* merged views of past and present and the dead and living were disentangled through dual focus of attention to physical and psychological views of the dead person and of oneself. Differences between the live self and the dead other person became obvious. However, they became truly believable only when psychological paradoxes of guilt and reality of innocence, wanting to be with the person but not wanting to be dead, were put into new perspective. Then maladaptive survival strategies, especially attachment and adaptation, and their guilts gave way to adaptive grief.

SPANNING CATEGORIES OF ILLNESSES

In clinical practice categories of illnesses often overlap. For instance, reexamination of Case 2 (Chapter 1) indicates that the couple whose daughter was approaching the age at which a previous daughter had died suffered a range of symptoms and illnesses. Each partner suffered a wide range of categories of *stress response* symptoms. Some were similar to those experienced at the time of the *trauma,* others were *identifications* with what were thought to be symptoms suffered by the child at the time of death. Angina was consistent with *classical illness* ramification of stress responses.

In retrospect a wholist approach allowed *recognition* of the traumatic situation and diagnosis of maladaptive rescue, fight, assertiveness, and adaptation ramifications stemming from recent and past stressors. A volume diagnosis could be made. *Nonspecific* treatment included space to talk in a safe, trusting environment. *Symptomatic* treatment included treatment of angina. *Specific* treatment involved simultaneous contrasting in an aroused emotional state of past trauma and realistic hope of a number of survival strategies, subsumed in the hopeful meaning that the next child need not die. The dead child could be grieved, the new one enjoyed. This enhanced the beginning of a new and more fulfilling story.

TAILORING WHOLIST TREATMENT
TO EARLY TREATMENT SITUATIONS

Wholist treatment (wholist perspective and treatment principles) may be tailored to early treatment situations in particularly cost-effective ways.

In particular, a diligent wholist approach can diagnose crucial points in the triaxial web to which can be applied specific trauma and fulfillment treatments. Thus chances of crucial thrusts, as occurred in Case 12 (Chapter 7), can be increased and better controlled.

The lack of such an approach may lead to futile searches for diagnoses in many tests and referrals, and at best only partly effective nonspecific and symptomatic treatments, such as superficial reassurance about symptoms.

Wholist approaches can also lead to cost-effective wider social thrusts. For instance, pamphlets (Appendix 3) distributed on a wide scale to disaster victims and media is an efficient way to detail and explain common emotional, cognitive, physical and social responses. Similarly, a pamphlet (Appendix 2) was designed for medical students and interns detailing the categories of illnesses above.

Feedbacks and educative communications need to take into account the prevalent culture. For instance, because the medical culture concentrates on "classical" illnesses, rather than following symptoms as they evolve along the process axis, physical and psychiatric illness categories were detailed first in the pamphlet in Appendix 3. The remaining order (psychophysiological responses, traumatic states, secondary, hysterical-type symptoms) is listed according to gradual divergence from the medical model and frequency of presentations. Neither of the above pamphlets corresponds to an exposition of the wholist perspective but each is a practical application of it.

In summary, it may be seen again that the wholist perspective broadens views of patient symptoms, yet specifies them within heuristically sensible diagnostic categories. Such diagnoses facilitate well directed wholist treatments.

In this chapter the wholist perspective facilitated diagnostic categories along the process axis, particularly suitable to early treatment. However, it was seen that points on the process axis intersected with the other axes and ramified along them. This facilitated tailored volume (Chapter 5) treatments to be applied.

It may be seen that time of resolution of symptoms and their underlying problems ranged from a single session to only opening a path for further therapy. It may be that the extent of past and present problems and their capacity for solution are factors in determining speed of treatment. For instance, in the recent widow (Case 35) adaptive grief was facilitated in one session. The patient who needed to deal with an inner clinging child (Case 28) needed extended therapy.

Cases in the next chapter needed extensive therapy as adults, for childhood traumas that had ramified and entrenched themselves widely.

Chapter 10

Later Ramifications
of Traumatic Sequelae

This chapter examines treatment of later ramifications of traumatic events. Here the events and their sequelae become entrenched, and ramify triaxially into ever more symptoms and illnesses, personal meanings, character traits and social behavior. Although it is again difficult to predict in any one case how much treatment may be necessary (Chapter 7), relatively more treatment is required for sequelae of traumatic events which occurred earlier in life, over longer periods, which were more severe and less remembered. Conversely, single traumatic events occurring in adults not long before presentation may, if not compounded with other traumas, require relatively less arduous treatment.

The first case in this chapter falls into the latter category. It may be seen as a somewhat more entrenched equivalent of Case 28 (Chapter 9)—the man who was shot in the thigh. A number of cases in the intermediate range of entrenched sequelae has already been presented in other contexts (e.g., Cases 4, 11 in Chapter 5, Case 14 in Chapter 7).

The rest of the chapter will concentrate on treatment of adults who suffered severe childhood traumas. First, a session with one patient is described in some detail in order to give a feel for a cross section of what can occur over a long trauma therapy process. Then the therapies of Anne, a sexually abused child survivor of the Holocaust (Case 3, Chapter 1), and a survivor of neglect and sexual abuse in a nonwar family are presented concurrently in order to highlight similarities and differences in sequelae therapy, and issues such as memory. They are important as they illustrate "ultimate" yet not uncommon traumas. They also potentially reunify psychodynamic, psychoanalytic, and trauma therapy.

A CASE OF RELATIVELY RECENT UNCOMPLICATED TRAUMA

In this case a relatively healthy young male had been sexually assaulted 5 months prior to therapy.

CASE 37: SEXUALLY ASSAULTED ADULT MALE

A 19-year-old man presented because his family was at a loss to cope with his outbursts of rage and depressed withdrawal over the last few months.

The young man presented as self-consciously masculine, with leather jacket and boots. Nevertheless, his story belied this image. He said, "I cannot believe what happened to me." He described how he had been walking in a park in broad daylight, ". . . and this man came out from behind the bushes and he fondled my genitals. I brushed him away, and kept walking and he disappeared. I tried to just put it out of my mind, but it seems to upset me.

"I don't know why, but I feel like a volcano could explode out of me and I could run somebody down on my bike. This terrifies my family, and me too. So I make myself like granite and feel nothing, but my girlfriend left me because of this, and my parents get upset because I seem withdrawn."

Over eight sessions the event was examined from different angles. In the initial sessions different survival strategy responses were overviewed, not unlike with the recently bereaved mother (Case 18, Chapter 7). In the intermediate sessions the survival strategies and their ramifications were examined in more detail. The concluding sessions brought the event, its meaning, and new future together.

The first survival strategy which pressed for examination was fight, to which his rage and murderousness belonged. The latter came to be understood as a maladaptive retrospective desire to be rid of the man who took away his sense of control over his body and manhood. Feeling like granite was a way of numbing his feelings to keep him from murder as well as the sense of emasculation. Next, his walking away was examined in terms of flight, which also expressed itself in his desire to just get away from the whole event and forget it. The humiliation could be understood in terms of not contesting the event and humiliating the other man (maladaptive competition), but was explained in terms of shock (adaptation) at the time. In context, perhaps his physical survival was best served by his actual behavior, and was normal for the event.

The man expressed dismay at the return of his childhood asthma since the event. It was traced to suppressed sobbing (maladaptive adaptation) when he saw his friends with girlfriends. He had lost his, and had no one to confide in and reassure him (maladaptive attachment). He now cried for the loss of his girlfriend as well as his loss of masculine confidence (adaptation). His asthma resolved.

Throughout this process he absorbed my kindness and respect and confidence in him, including as a male. I gave him information about sexual molesters. He became reconciled and respectful of his own responses as he made sense of them. He came to see the assailant, not himself, as weak and sexually damaged.

He expressed his love for the flute which he had been studying, but which he had not played since the assault. Classical music seemed feminine, like the position he felt he was in when passively fondled. On the other hand, his father was a middling flautist, and he had always been afraid to surpass him. When he realized that his masculinity had not really been damaged and that his father wanted him to be a good flautist he returned to playing with zest. What's more, he overcame the responses to stress which he had learned from his father—aggression and withdrawal.

Three years later he was playing in a senior orchestra, had a girlfriend, and was grateful for me "having saved his life."

Comment   Wholist treatment of the young man included *recognition* of his trauma, its impact on him as a male adolescent, his survival strategy responses and ramifications, and defenses. *Nonspecific* treatment provided a countertrauma environment where an older male respected his sexuality and masculinity, plus where he had a different model to his father's responses to stress. *Symptomatic* treatment involved education about his responses, and advice about anger management and letting himself cry. *Specific* treatment allowed seeing himself in a positive light in relation to each aspect of his trauma and maladaptive survival strategy responses.

It may be said that therapy repaired the traumatic wound to this young man's developing sense of potency (assertiveness). In terms of fulfillment therapy, loving separation from father with confirmation of his own identity as a man and flautist were enhanced. The case also illustrates that crisis can lead to opportunity, not only to damage.

A SINGLE SESSION OF A COMPLEX
TRAUMA THERAPY: CROSS-SECTIONAL VIEW

Joanna has already been presented to illustrate defenses (Case 16, Chapter 7). In that summarized session she allowed herself to see herself beyond her defenses —as an abused child. By this session she had advanced further by putting her objective family relationships into more realistic perspective, and wanting more perspective on her abuse. It may be seen how her defenses had diminished.

It will be remembered that Joanna had suffered depressions and relationship problems. Nevertheless, during her therapy she built up a thriving business, a loving relationship, and rectified her relationships with her children. Concurrently she developed no memories of sexual abuse, nor appreciation of the relevance of her parents having been Holocaust survivors.

The context for the session was a visit from overseas of the father's brother. After years of silence the father rang Joanna, suggesting they show the visitors family solidarity. Instead, Joanna pleaded that they talk about the past. He refused, saying the past should be left in the past. For the first time she expressed her rage towards him as it became clear that he only cared for his image with his brother, and not her.

CASE 17/38: FACING WOUNDS

Joanna started, "I have cried a lot since the last session. I was scared how much crying I had in me. But I knew I could bring it here and I would not be flooded. . . . Actually the meeting with my cousins went well (warm smile). I brought them up-to-date. I told them that since my mother confronted my father with her remembering him coming out of my bedroom buttoning up his pajama trousers my father had stopped his denials. He concentrated on influencing her against me, saying I wanted to use her to put him in jail.

I started the party feeling, as usual, as a tenth-rate foreigner. But I was accepted warmly, and I remembered that Ella and Veronica (the cousins) believed me, because they had always felt uncomfortable with my father, and he was known as a sleazebag womanizer in the family. I was convinced that if my father had come, I would have gone up to him and told him he was not welcome—rapists were not welcome here. And he *had* told his brother that I was absent because of strange ideas since a brain infection some years ago! So we chatted about our children and ourselves, and a warm atmosphere developed between us."

Thus far I responded by acknowledging *(recognition)* that Joanna had done much brave work (Assertiveness) to have been able to express anger to her father, and I nodded agreement that I would support her in her grief (adaptation) *(nonspecific treatment)*.

Nevertheless, I was troubled by a sense of being conned. I saw this as countertransference, the feel of which was reminiscent of past attempts by Joanna to not be aware of her abuse. I speculated that perhaps the theme of the session was to be anger and grief (as aspects of her early abuse) and their avoidance, but in the bigger context of wanting to know and understand.

Joanna continued, "The others started to be critical of Uncle John (the visiting uncle). I decided to stick my neck out. I told them how he had looked strangely at me, so I asked him whether he was comparing me with his daughter, because we look very much alike. He said that I didn't look like anyone in the family, which is untrue. Later we sat near each other. I just put my hand over his, feeling for this old man visiting his family perhaps for the last time, but he was so rigid that I took it away.

"To my surprise my two cousins said together, 'Don't you see, your father got to him. He looked at you like a strange madwoman." And I knew it was true. And I cried, "What sort of father would so betray his daughter just so he could posture!?" And Ella and Veronica embraced me. And then they asked me, "Why does your mother still see him?" And I explained that to her mind he is still the hero who saved her life during the Holocaust, who supported her after she was raped by the Russians. She still believes that without him she would die. Only recently, when she saw that it is I who protect, and he who exploits her, that she has started to remember what he did to me.

"So my relatives did not think me crazy. But for me, I was hit in the guts, because this time I saw clearly that my father did not love me, and never had. I had always hoped that at the deepest level, somewhere, he loved me in his own distorted way. But he did not. The pain was too bad.

I felt that this could be the grief which Joanna had been avoiding, yet seeking to understand. I said, "Tell me about the pain."

My heart is so wounded (tears). How could a father ignore his child's pleas, just so he could look good? But my father was always concerned with his looks and himself. It is too much to bear, the wound is too great. When I compare this with how I love my children . . . , you know, Peter (her son) said to me how I was a model for him, how he respected me for achieving against odds. I just cried with gratitude that he saw me that way.

In the context of being accepted in the family and by me (attachment, cooperation) Joanne could grapple with her opposite experiences. The story with her uncle may well have symbolized the bigger one with her father, where the little girl wanted recognition of belonging, but was cast out instead. The cousins rallied around her, put into words her father's rejection, and, while acting as surrogate mothers, they wondered where her real mother was. Joanna explained how mother to this day arranged her mind according to her perceived survival needs. My role was to recognize and validate the story, which I did, with non-verbal nods and gestures. Also, I verbally clarified various adaptive and maladaptive attachment, cooperation, and adaptation feelings and their sources.

The story was cohering, but so was the pain of betrayal (maladaptive cooperation) by both parents. This needed to be assimilated before grief could have its way, but the pain could only be borne in the context of its opposite with her children and me. I felt I was experienced as a good father who was guiding her through difficult tasks, while she was experiencing herself as a good child and mother (transference, countertransference). The feeling of purposefulness of nurturance and trust across the generations (caretaking, attachment, cooperation) was serving as a foil to the experience of their perversion.

I formulated that Joanne was ready to start to assimilate these opposites which were sitting next to each other in the session. I braced myself for painful emotions such as sadness, but at the same time I was aware of their necessity for the triumph of trust, achievement, and beyond grief Joanna's new life (awareness of Joanna's and my own goal achievement, cooperation, and adaptation).

Joanna drifted off to describing everyday events. I was reminded of my previous countertransference response. Perhaps she was responding with avoidance of the forthcoming coherence. I tested the waters, encouraging in the process a view from the outside (*specific therapy*). I asked, "So what do you make of all this?"

She thought, "Well, that I am an adult who is not crazy, and people accept me for my good qualities." She drifted off again. I persisted, "So, how do you put it all together?" Reluctantly, (now we were really dealing with the countertransference reluctance) she added, "Well, after we talked about my father and mother, I took a whole lot of family photos. I was like the director of family constellations and memories." She stopped.

I took up the image. "So, if you were not just taking still photos but directing the film of your family memories, what would be the story?" Reluctantly but also with interest, puzzlement, and associated change in the state of consciousness, she said, "Well, I need to remember that in spite of all my sensations, flashbacks, worries about the past, I have a loving partner, children, I am capable at work, and my wider family accept me." I said, "Sure, but suppose you were selling the film, how would you sell the story to a producer?"

After a number of attempts, she said, "I don't know why it is so difficult to put the different parts together." We considered, and she said, "I suppose it is too painful to see it as a whole." Then she went on resolutely, "Well, it is about a sexually abused girl whose heart was broken." Joanne broke into sobs. "She is a woman who has achieved a lot, but she is also the little girl in pain." (sobs)

"How can she be both at the same time?" I asked. She considered through her tears, "Well, she carries the brokenhearted girl with her inside, all the time. The girl takes over at unexpected times, like now. It doesn't matter that she is an adult coper, the girl takes over." She sobbed.

"She *is* still a brokenhearted child? Is that the story of the film?" She broke down, "I cannot see the two at the same time! I know there are two opposite stories, but I cannot distinguish them. They take over whenever they want!"

"What distinguishes the two stories, how can you separate them?" "Well one belongs to a little girl, the other belongs to me now." She stopped. "So, from the director's point-of-view, what is the sequence of the story?" "Well, there was a little girl, then there was an adult woman." "And what separates them?" She could not separate the tenses, and I had to supply the final link, "Time. So what separates them and makes a story is time—there *was* an abused wounded girl in the past and there *is* a capable loving and loved adult woman now. That is how you expressed the story to your cousins."

"OK, so there was this little girl who was me whose heart was broken." She cried, but this time went on. "But she did not know this, because if she had known the meaning of it all, she would have died of her broken heart. So she put her wounded heart along with faith in deep freeze, hoping one day she would be loved. She struggled hard, went through many battles, and eventually she achieved her aim. She managed to make a meaningful life out of the rubble. She was still assailed by feelings from the past, but she was able to know they were from the past and not the present." She smiled wistfully, "It makes a compelling story. I have never been able to see it from outside like that."

We discussed its implications, for instance how the person deserved praise for her bravery.

She concluded, "It's like you made me write my CV. It takes 10 times to get it right, because you have to look at the whole of yourself from the outside and see who you are. But it is worth it." She went out satisfied with her CV.

Comment It may be noted how unremembered and disconnected aspects of the trauma story were recognized through wholist receptivity to different modes and means of communication (Chapter 5). For instance, the fragments of rejection and betrayal were played out almost at the same time in verbal communication, history, enactments, transference, and countertransference. All were received almost simultaneously in the crucible of therapy.

The session did not run smoothly with full understanding for the therapist. At times I was lost in countertransference responses; at other times I desperately made retrospective sense of what was going on. But on the whole, the framework gave me the kind of distance and understanding which I was able to impart by facilitating the translation from the wholist to ordinary language of cognitions and emotions in order for Joanna to integrate her story.

It may be that different empathic therapies could have covered the same ground. Yet the wholist treatment framework gave an additional means of understanding the patient's fragmented landscape and enhanced putting the fragments together within a meaningful journey.

To summarize, I *recognized* Joanna's readiness to embark on a deep awareness of her trauma, and provided the necessary *nonspecific* empathy and promise of support at the beginning of the session. Further recognition and explanations of her various fragments and their sources (*symptomatic*) provided some relief.

Specific treatment involved dual focus of attention in an altered state of consciousness on past traumatic and current fulfilling situations and corresponding survival strategy responses. Primary defenses of splitting, repression and dissociation were overcome, enabling past and present to be separated. This gave Joanna an unprecedented possibility to put past and present together in a new way, and to take control over her trauma story.

PROCESS IN COMPLEX TRAUMA
THERAPY: LONGITUDINAL VIEW

In contrast to the above cross-sectional view of complex therapy, the next two cases depict longitudinal processes of such therapies. (For complex therapy of transgenerational problems in a helper, see Case 44, Chapter 11.) The two current cases are presented jointly in order to highlight commonalties and differences among adults abused as children. For instance, marked differences result from having had good, even if murdered parents, as compared with living and present, yet neglectful and abusive ones. On the other hand, it will be seen that similarities in symptoms are found whether physical and sexual abuse is remembered or not. Further, remembering is relative, as even remembered traumas have some aspects of them out of awareness, while other traumas are not remembered at all. Treatment in both these cases was long, because of the multiplicity, severity, and extent of entrenched ramifications of survival strategies across the triaxial framework, and difficulty in full recovery of memories and their original contexts.

Anne is a sexually abused child survivor of the Holocaust described previously (Valent, 1994a, Case 3, Chapter 1). Bea presented as wanting to understand her schizophrenic illness. She also appeared in Case 8 (Chapter 5) illustrating countertransference. They are presented conjointly as Case 38a and 38b.

CASE 3/39a: LOVE SURVIVES BIGGEST TRAUMAS

Anne chose the furthest available seat, looked down, cried, and said "What do you want me to do?" Her desperate docility was telling. I said, "Tell me about yourself."

She heaved a sigh and said, "I am desperate. I am always having a bad time, I don't know why. Medication helps. For my friends I am vibrant, life of the party, that's how they see me. The Holocaust keeps coming back and I get depressed. I've done well. I have a husband and three children. But since I am not working I think more about the past.

CASE 8/39b: SCHIZOPHRENIA UNRAVELLED

Bea said, "I want to know about my schizophrenic breakdown. There must be reasons for it. Two previous therapists could not help me." Bea's discharge summary gave the diagnosis of schizophrenia. Symptoms included feeling controlled by the devil and UFO's, feeling television talked about her, not having control over her emotions, and auditory hallucinations. For some months prior she had made herself vomit to lose weight.

She said, "I must know what happened. When I got sick I had flashbacks to my childhood, like traveling back. I was falling into a pit. Life lost meaning and I became suicidal. So I was admitted."

Both women indicated that their problems stemmed back to their childhoods. Anne could remember the past, and did not wish to. In part she enacted it in her chair. Bea could not remember.

Anne said, "I was perhaps four when we went to Paris. I was the eldest of three children. One day I went down the street to play, I saw men in uniforms. I came back home; they were all gone. 'They'll be back.' I thought. The *concierge* took me to a family, and then I stayed with many different families, changing them each three months. They were not fond of me; they were paid to have me, they made sure I suffered. I had to kneel on wooden chairs to which they tied me, I had to have sex with men. They punished me because their lives were in danger. They threatened me with the wall oven. I knew Jewish children had been burnt in a synagogue. They threatened to turn me over to the Germans. That did not worry me. That was just another move. I just kept going because I was going to see my parents again. I suffered malnutrition, I was thin but with a big stomach, I had bronchitis a lot, always have had. I was in hospital. Then I was told that my parents would never come back by one of the women who took me from family to family. I tried to cut my wrists with secaturs. I am most upset because I feel sorry for myself. Why do these things come to me now, after all these years? I have many depressions; I have fears of fire and water, but I can't associate them with the Holocaust. It is because my children have left home. Maybe I associate them with my family having left me in the Holocaust."

Bea said, "My father was sexually over the limit. For instance, when I was 10 he showed us off to his friend when my sister and I were in the bath. His friend interfered with my sister; my parents knew about it. She is a recluse, still wets herself. Even the other day my father commented on his grandson's penis. He says his own is small, but it's not the size, it's how you handle it. And he gives an awful knowing wink. He makes me cringe when he hugs me and kisses me on the lips. He gives mother beer and says, 'Have a leg opener.' And she laughs. Then they go to bed. Wink, wink. I vomited the food he gave me; I vomited a lot before I went to hospital. I had many sexual dreams when I broke down. One terrible one was that I licked the genitals of a four-year-old girl. There were moments, I am terribly ashamed to admit, wanting my father sexually. But he revolts me.

I hated being a girl. It was a bad thing to be female in my family. I remember that at the age of eight I pulled on my clitoris trying to be a boy. And when I was admitted to hospital I did not know if I was male or female.

Bea described neglect, "They never came to school to see me perform. I was a smelly child with dirty dresses. For days my parents did not believe me when I had a broken hand."

My countertransference denial responses could have made me retrace the social history of nonrecognition of childhood abuse. It was tempting to interpret Bea's sexual attraction to her father as oedipal, her wanting a penis as envy, and her dream of abusing a four-year-old child as her masturbatory perversity. And surely Anne exaggerated, adding information from others into her story. Yet it was in the same French countryside where the first wave of child sexual abuse was discovered (Masson, 1984), and where Jews including children were burned in synagogues under the Nazis. And I remembered that those in power wanted to kill me when I was a child, just because I was Jewish. I overcame my horror, and recognized that both women were similarly genuine. To recognize the most heinous traumas, one needs to be open to, but in control of one's own traumas.

Both women needed *recognition* that what they said was valid, even when memories were clearly remembered. Anne started to tell her children of her childhood. To her surprise, they warmed to her rather than rejected her.

Over the years both women's initially condensed stories became ever more detailed, vivid and painful. Belief, validation, "holding," respect, collaboration within the therapeutic relationship, were in each case counter-traumatic foundations for hope (*nonspecific therapy*).

Anne returned to the first scene. "It is as if it were yesterday. While playing, the other children told me Germans shoot people like me. I ran back home in terror to see if my parents were shot." Anne found out the dates of her parents' deportation to Auschwitz, and their dates of death. Somehow the information was grounding.

"I always had colds, cold sores, and tonsillitis. When I was seven I had my tonsils out. There were other children there in white robes. I saw soldiers with machine guns and I dreamt that they shot off children's heads. I knew they were looking for me." The nightmares, cold and cold sores returned at this time. Anne started to describe episodes of sexual abuse more vividly. She also started to have nightmares about drowning in water, burning in fire.

"The man kept asking me to hop into his bed. He spoke with a soft lovely voice at first, and each time I thought that he liked me. I liked that, even though I knew what I would have to do. But there was no way out, so I did it. Obviously I did not respond well, because he became angry, angrier and more violent each time. I had bruises everywhere." She described pain, vaginal bleeding, being crushed, feeling suffocated, like a trapped animal being torn apart (traumatic flight).

What did Anne make of all this? "It was normal for me. I did not know all this was wrong, because a child has to be told something is wrong to know it is wrong. And when I mentioned to the lady of the house something of what was going on, she called me a liar, opened the wall oven, and said she would throw me in there if I lied again. The only other time I mentioned it was in my first school in the last home. The other children were horrified and ostracized me for some reason. The man put my head in a bucket of water full of snails. (Anne had good reasons to fear fire and water.) They said I was a liar, that I was disgusting, a slut. There was something too wrong about me. I attempted suicide with the secaturs."

One day she said that she was hearing voices. "Come to think of it, they were always there in a way. They belong to the men. They come at night and they are angry. They tell me that I swore to them never to tell, and now I have. They told me they would kill me if I ever told." Anne was terrified at nights that the men would come and kill her.

"When at last will you relieve me of all these sufferings?"

Bea returned to her breakdown. She recalled that it had been precipitated by a relative unexpectedly kissing her on the mouth and fondling her breast.

"When I broke down I dreamt that I was between two and four, and a man with a steel bar pressed against me below. I was hurting and burning inside and something like red ink spread around my genitals." She closed her legs firmly. "I remember my father's stubbled face and beery breath very close to me." (In a later session she remembered her father's wart imprinted in her vagina (see "Power of Words," Chapter 6). She made upward pelvic thrusts from deep in the chair. There was terror in her eyes. "I would give him the son he always wanted." As she looked for good things, she remembered her father's poetry. She clung to a savior image of me.

At home, she had induced her husband to be sexually aggressive to her. During intercourse she felt enraged, and she tightened her vagina to induce ejaculation as fast as possible to be rid of him. She fantasized happy sex with me, obsessively seeing me as the only hope of a good relationship. This alternated with accusations of my words physically and mentally intruding into her, yet she pleaded with me to save her and not abandon her. Without warning, in the next session she had a full blown schizophrenic recurrence. God and the devil were fighting within her. Voices called her a slut. She was readmitted to hospital. In contrast to her previous admission, she settled down quickly with little medication.

Her husband confronted the parents with father's sexual abuse. Even before he said what he came for, the mother said, "There is a lot of talk about incest these days." The father did not deny it, but he talked spontaneously about his own childhood abuse. Bea remembered how she had felt sorry for her father's desperation and waves of compassion made her go along with the things he needed so badly of her.

The spirals of memories became ever more vivid in an outside social context where some suggested that recovered sexual memories were implanted by therapists to cause a so-called false memory (*The New York Review,* Nov. 17, Dec. 1, 1994). So I asked myself whether when Bea said that my words felt like physical and mental intrusions, was this a symbolic sexual transference communication, or a coercion on my part to believe that she was abused? Similarly, were the guilt and shame of my clients evidence of their internal perverse fantasies, as Freud (1905b) came to suggest?

Yet I had no mission or reason to implant sexual abuse memories. I felt uncomfortable with the suggestion that sexual abuse could lead to schizophrenia, and hated the suffering associated with recounting the abuses. I had nothing to gain from the stories, but the prepetrators in them used extremes of coercion, to exact obedience and silence. It was voicing the abuse that evoked terror and psychosis. Emergence or accentuation of apparently senseless physical, mental, and social illnesses, which later turned out to be unconscious harbingers of trauma stories in which the illnesses had a coherent context, gave a sense of validity to the emerging jigsaw puzzle.

Similarly, guilt and shame for cooperating with their abuse seemed to be secondary false accusations by perpetrators of obedient victims who had no choice but to comply in order to survive, and self-accusations by victims in order to achieve a measure of coexistence, coherence, and hope. The patients hated their abuse stories and manifested terror, disgust, and postures of powerlessness and hopelessness consistent with the assaults which they were recounting. They were certainly not active agents seeking pleasure. The questions, I suggest, were countertransference responses to intimidation, terror, and horror.

Both patients had psychotic symptoms. One may speculate that Anne's degree of psychosis was the lesser because she maintained some awareness of connection between her hallucinations and her actual persecutors, while she also tenuously saw me represent safety from them in the present. Bea had not reached such a degree of synthesis, either because of lags in her capacities for laying down sufficient memories at the age her abuse occurred in order to make sense in their retrieval; and/or more intense coexistent defenses preventing knowledge that her source of security and purpose was also her threat and source of purposelessness. Thus integration held threats of survival for her. So Bea had no space to see me as a safe person separate to her father to whom she could communicate her sufferings. Finally, perhaps the schizophrenia had to be experienced in context of emergent memories of abuse to help achieve her goal of understanding it.

In terms of wholist treatment principles, *recognition* involved belief in the women's past traumas, full use of all modes and means of translating the wholist language, tracing current symptoms to childhood appraisals and survival strategies, and slowly naming aspects of traumas in which they arose. For instance, Bea's furious tightening of her vagina was speculated to be the child's only means of fight. Simultaneous *nonspecific* therapy included empathy, firm boundaries, routine, and other counter-trauma experiences. *Specific* therapy was a painful long process of many sessions such as the one with Joanna above. It was a potentially hazardous process, as seen when Bea experienced a relapse into her schizophrenia.

Anne became a central member of her child survivor group. Knowing that I was writing a book with child survivor stories, she asked if she could be one of the interviewees. She said it might help her and others if she told her story. So in the interview Anne brought the fragments of her story together for the first time. When she saw the video she was amazed to see that her life had a thread. However, when she read her story, she was involved emotionally in the thread—it was *her* story. She came to realize that it was to me and the world, not her parents, that she was telling her story.

"My parents were always with me at the time. That is what allowed me to keep going. They were the only ones I was going to tell. When I came out of the hospital, I was told my parents had died. Now I did not know which was worse— the sickness of dying with hunger or this mental sickness. I had such headaches suddenly, and I developed such mental blocks! So now I imagined them. I saw them in fantasy. I was off air for periods of time when I did not know what I was doing. But now I don't seem to have them in fantasy. You took their place. And when you were on holiday, it precipitated 50 years of loneliness." Anne sobbed with grief for the first time.

"With much trepidation Anne produced a photo of her father. "When I went back to the empty flat, before the *concierge* took me away, I saw this photo of my father and took it from the table. I kept it hidden all this time. It was what protected me. Now you are fighting the men and defeating them, they are going away. The sessions have become like meeting all my family. I have woken up like Sleeping Beauty after 50 years." She could trust and love now.

One day she said, "It is strange but it is as if I am giving up a child. I had always made my life into separate episodes, in which bad things were happening to another child. Now I see it, feel it, taste it. I feel ripped, I feel the blood. I thought I would die. But I see it whole now."

Bea appreciated passionately boundaries in therapy, such as her right to have her thoughts. She came to see exchange of thoughts as precious gifts which were food for the soul. Yet she became aware that whenever she dared to have a thought, her father's voice interposed, "Don't give me lip!," followed by a fist to the head, or "You stupid fuckin' slut! Get out of home, if you don't like it here!" Bea realized that she had learned to not think or feel. "One wrong thought and I get hit (like with a bolt of lightning) or thrown out." In her frightened states anything could be threatening—a noise, a footstep, the TV. Similarly, any impulse to a relationship (cooperation) evoked, "All females are seducers; you're not happy unless you have it rubbed!" Bea felt nauseous.

Bea severed external links with her family, and challenged them internally. She joined a group of adults who survived childhood sexual abuse. With increasing capacity to think, she progressed at work which became increasingly directed to awareness and treatment of traumatized and sexually abused children. "At least my experiences can be useful to others." She made friends and achieved respect. She grieved different aspects of her story, such as, "How cheaply my innocence went!" Another time, contemplating possibility of transgenerational love, she said, "I was torn from my innermost connections with the universe."

Increased hope was associated with each deepening and cohering fragments of experience which she could increasingly identify as memories. Palpitations, shortness of breath, pressure on the chest, genital feelings cohered as parts of similar experiences. She noted that one type of genital feeling started with an initially pleasant tingling in the vulva which woke her. This quickly turned into very unpleasant sensations which she could only rid through compulsive masturbation which revolted her as perverse. Accompanying images included fury at hateful animals which were clawing at her, and thoughts, "This is not my father. The devil is making him do this." Inside the fugue-like awareness of the cohering fragments was a black hole, madness. Inside that was an image of her father lapping at her 4-year-old vagina.

Both women slowly improved their external lives through gaining hope for worlds different to their traumatic pasts. Both joined peer groups and started to see purpose in their lives, and meanings in their sufferings, through helping others.

Both tackled the loss of their parents, Anne through death, Bea through becoming aware that her parents had not been parents. In both women, primitive defenses of dissociation and displacement became more apparent. In Bea's case, because of her younger age, they were tinged with atavistic images. Her defenses which replayed the social history of nonrecognition of childhood sexual abuse—being possessed by the devil, being immoral and perverse, and being mad, through recognition of traumatic memories gave way to sanity, morality, and the possibility to reconnect with a sacred universe.

The processes took years of many sessions, we see, for further reasons. For one thing, even to think about their abuse required extreme faith and courage, and led to a new crop of symptoms and defenses. Then it required all modes and means to trace all of them to their origins and to make sense of the many ramifications of the multiple facets of the many traumas.

For instance, exploration of various survival strategy ramifications of genital assault clarified a confusing range of initial genital responses. One was vaginal tightening, already seen to be part of a desire to be rid of the intrusion (fight). Another was panic due to perceived attack by a predator (flight). The pleasurable response was due to automatic cooperation, but it gave rise to a disgusted frenzied masturbation to bring it to an end. Desire to give poor father the son he always wanted included a caretaking response. Humiliation, feeling dirty, and desire to eliminate genitals may have been aspects of maladaptive competition and fight turned on unwanted parts of oneself. With each improvement, integration, and counter-trauma alternative, more vivid and more painful spirals of the traumatic experiences and their ramifications emerged.

Anne said, "I have realized that I have always lived in darkness, a terrible close envelope around me which did not let me breathe. When I realized that I was experiencing this, I remembered that after my tonsils operation I was put in a sack and thrown away. Perhaps there was a raid (the image of soldiers shooting children's heads off) and I was hidden this way. But the darkness, enclosure, feeling of being suffocated I remember clearly. My hand went toward the neck of the envelope but it was closed. I think I fainted. Then I suppose someone found the sack. I must have been near dead." The pervasive ramifications of this experience were explored with much pain.

"All my slides are out now. It is you I trust, you who can give me a sense of what it might be like to be touched and held without malice." She had a strong need to have one experience of being held this way. I hugged her at the end of the session. Next session she said, "It went to my depths; it was like infinite chocolate. Thank you."

Anne came to see me as an esteeming witness of her struggles. For the first time since earliest childhood she felt worthwhile and lovable, and could love too, without shame. She cried with aching agony of grief seeing her lost parents and me together in her mind for the first time.

"For the first time since childhood I am off drugs. And I can fight off the men at night on my own. I have always felt better for not thinking. But now I make connections in my mind. I remember now that the body aches, and cramps are the same as when I was kneeling tied to the chair; my lifelong constipation is connected with warnings that I must not soil myself while they were out. And I have realized that my depressions had always been there more or less since I knew my parents died." Anne now cried volumes of tears. "Oh, yes, I can see myself now. The little child all alone, frightened. I never told anyone any of this." The little girl and the courageous lady sobbed and wept as one united self-aware person.

Anne had publicly exposed her true identity in child survivor groups. "It is not right to hide who I am." Her claim for compensation was rejected as she had only been a child, and she could not prove the events she claimed had happened. To me she said two years after finishing therapy, "The struggle will always continue. But I cannot tell you how grateful I am to you for allowing me to feel alive and to experience love. I had given up on ever feeling them."

Bea came to see that her father's view of sex had pervaded everything in the family, and in her world it was the organizing principle of sense. She could see that I provided a different principle which included a nonexploitative, nonerotic, but rather a benevolent parent.

"I have realized that I have had vaginal sensations all my life. I kind of ignored them, thinking them to be just part of me (see also "Power of Words," Chapter 6). But they are not me, and I hate them! I feel something is forced to open up well before its time. A creature forced to open out. I have pain in the pelvis, in the tummy. I want to rub my back and groan. IT forced me to respond. I feel one part of me has had to mate with something of a different species. I've become locked with this animal and become part with it; I can't pry myself away. This part contaminates all my other parts."

Yet this alternated with new feelings, "It is as if my heart beat differently." This was seen to be associated with a new rhythm in her womb, connected with desires for companionship and intimacy. Bea developed some trusted friends who knew about her sexual abuse. She stood up for more recognition of traumatized and abused children, and both they and herself personally rose in the work hierarchy.

A friend lost her pregnancy. Bea experienced ovulation pain associated with a desire to replace the baby. She was struck with her capacity to give lovingly with her reproductive system. "Oh, it is so painful to hold in mind at the same time the way my father talked of sex and babies, and the way you say the word baby, showing that a man can cherish babies. Perhaps a man and I could cherish my baby." Two senior males asked her to join them in their most valued projects (their "babies").

Bea understood her schizophrenia now, and it had not recurred for a long time. "Now I need to understand my abuse exactly." From a safe distance she became aware of herself as a child in frozen terror, her head turned away in despair. A man intent on his penis rammed into the child. Bea said desperately, "That's men, they are animals only caring for their penises." She corrected herself, and separating past from present she said, "No, that's how my father was." She remembered the well-meaning men around her.

Bea's struggles continue. Her heart is softer, her resolve harder. She does not live in a paranoid world anymore, and sees herself as lovable and brave. She has cried bitterly at the huge amount that she had lost. Divorced now, she said, "I may have to grieve not having a family of my own too. But I am eternally grateful that I have learned of good in the world, and that I have a role in it. I would rather have the pain than be stuck in the worlds of compliance or schizophrenia."

Comment   Because in cases like Anne and Bea most severe traumas are experienced by the most vulnerable people, the wholist perspective and treatment principles, together with therapist requirements, are extended to the full (and so can be the satisfactions).

Recognition that severe traumas had occurred in the first place requires of therapists to imagine and reverberate with the most horrific victimizations and collapse of normal guidelines of morality, principles, and spirituality. Second, victims themselves avoid such recognition, plus it may be difficult for them due to lack of coherent memories, as well as initimidation against awareness.

Nevertheless, it was seen that clues to, say, childhood sexual problems may become available relatively quickly. Nonrecognition of their traumatic origins has led to the clues to be labeled as evil, demonic, sick, and mad. Currently they may be treated in a fragmented manner medically and psychiatrically, and psychoanalytically as perverse childhood fantasies. At worst nonrecognition can lead to unwitting countertransference reenactment of abuser-induced dulling of awareness, and blame and abuse of victims.

On the other hand, recognition requires full use of all the modes and means of gathering traumatic information, and transference and countertransference become very important. For instance, already in the first session, Anne's desperate docility reenacted an aspect of her victimization. One needs to be aware of countertransference impulses to avoid such clues, and of tendencies to feel that oneself is manufacturing them, for this may reflect victim fears of awareness and self-blame for it, reinforced by perpetrator intimidation and societal denial.

The two cases indicated how victims can arrange their memories according to perceived survival needs. For instance, both developed persecutory hallucinations at moments when they were about to disclose details of their persecutors, stopping the disclosures. (Sometimes such obfuscation may also serve to protect therapists from threatening perpetrators.) Threats of disclosure often arise from the past, but they may still reverberate objectively in the present.

Memories or awareness can thus be seen to be determined by a complex product of past and present survival needs, and fears of retraumatization and hope. Further, their coherence and content are influenced by the age at the time of the abuse. The younger the age, the more atavistic, ego-syntonic (e.g., eroticized world, sexual intrusions and grayness experienced as parts of oneself), fragmented, somatic, and action-related the memories. Similarly, the more dangerous and untenable in terms of life's purpose the awareness, the more intense are the defenses against it.

It is suggested that the cases in this chapter indicate that both sexual and nonsexual loss of awareness and memories can be replaced by symptoms, at all ages. This happened even in an adult following a single episode of relatively minor sexual abuse (Case 36). Similarly, though at first sight it may appear that Anne remembered her sexual abuse and Bea did not, it may be seen that both women had a range of memories and forgettings, and they were similar in sexual and nonsexual fields. Anne forgot that her parents had died, and being discarded in a sack. Bea had forgotten aspects of her neglect. Retrieval of all types of traumatic memories in the three cases followed similar processes. With recognition fully established, other treatment principles could now interact in healing.

Nonspecific Treatment   All counter-trauma components (Chapter 6) were utilized. In addition, at times one was challenged to be uniquely creative with them. For instance, my forming a group enabled child survivors like Anne to have a forum of peers. Writing her story in a book (Valent, 1994a) enhanced her being identified to herself and to others with pride. Responding to her request to be held physically required quick transference and countertransference diagnosis of the genuine need for this request, it not being tainted by either party with sexual abuse or malice, but its opposite. To have rejected the request at that unique poignant moment may have intimated such taint.

Symptomatic treatment included much education and explanation. Symptomatic treatments such as drugs in the past had little benefit, providing only partial or temporary relief.

Specific Treatment   Recognition and giving words to experiences such as pervading grayness or different vaginal sensations gave control over them and allowed their exploration. For instance, translating the latter allowed them to be understood to be associated with particular survival strategies in the context of specific aspects of abuse. Ramified judgments, and meanings stemming from such abuse also had to be similarly named. This was done in the context of hopeful alternatives; otherwise, threats of retraumatization obfuscated memories. Hopeful alternatives stemmed from nonspecific counter-trauma experiences and specific exploration of opposite survival strategies at particular triaxial points. So alternatives to specific traumatic vaginal sensations were specific positive vaginal sensations, and specific life-enveloping sensations (the hug) countered being enveloped in a sack. As confidence grew, not thinking and remembering in order to survive in the past gave way to thinking and remembering in the present in order to fulfill the future, and so awareness, memories, connections, and contexts filled the jigsaw puzzle of past traumas and current life.

This involved a long process during which at each triaxial point each survival strategy was experienced dually from past and present and its significance relearned in ever-increasing volumes of associations. The associations of awareness could then be forged into verbal memories subsuming traumatic engrams and current realities. Many such memories could eventually lead to a connected narrative. The narrative of both trauma and life became ever more coherent, and survival modes could be relinquished for their fulfillment alternatives in wider and deeper areas of life. Though grief had to fill much of what remained unfulfilled, both women used their new found wisdoms to enjoy and give to others within more purposeful lives.

It was confirmed that in order to involve oneself in the intense depths of human experience in a therapeutic relationship with those who experienced severe traumas, challenges therapists to reverberate with most basic instincts and, at the same time, to be theologians, jurists, and philosophers (Herman, 1992; Pearlman & Saakvitne, 1995). Indeed, therapists are challenged in every aspect of themselves, and they inevitably change in the process too. While the rewards can be immense, risks are also present. Therapist risks are explored in the next chapter.

In summary, while previous chapters described treatments at times when disconnections and forgettings of traumas were recent, this chapter takes up treatment when disconnection from memories is ever more entrenched, and symptoms and illnesses manifest in more fragmented ways.

The great horror of the original traumas, lack of verbal narrative memories and variable interests of all parties to not be aware, can lead to tyrannies of not knowing which may ramify from the individual, and the politics of the home, to wider social systems, ideologies and philosophies, all of which can be reflected in the helping professions (Chapter 11) and the consulting room. All these factors can contribute to the arduous task of recognition.

Sexual abuse victims were presented in this chapter because they have been both the material for the birth of traumatology and the most frequent and difficult targets for suppression of trauma and its therapy. Relatively recent sexual abuse in a male and the Holocaust's, as well as sexual abuse's, effects in a child were presented to compare gender, age and time of abuse, severity of traumatic situations, and documented against potentially contestable (Valent, 1995a) childhood traumas. It is suggested that once rationalizations that victims are bad, mad, or perverse are overcome and their traumas explored, they are consistent with each other and with the wholist view of the evolution of trauma sequelae. In other words, looking at traumatic events from their inception to years later indicates clinical and theoretical coherence of evolution of symptoms and their later recognition.

The cases in this chapter alert us especially to the need to admit traumatology as a possible contributor to symptoms and illnesses which have otherwise been dominated by genetic, biochemical, and internal instinctual paradigms. Adding the possibility of many symptoms and illnesses as ramifications of different facets of the same pebble in the pond, or as biopsychosocial sequelae of preceding traumas, enhances volume diagnoses and treatments (Chapter 5). For instance, it was useful to see palpitations, headaches, ear infection, genital sensations, phobias, depression, schizophrenia, alienation, relationship problems, shame, sense of injustice, and so on, as different points on different ripples emanating from similar sources.

Perhaps the above cases with the wholist perspective behind them can be part of a development containing more solid theory which will help to overcome the lags and fragmentations between medicine, psychiatry, psychology, psychoanalysis, and social and human sciences.

Perhaps, out of the personal holocausts of the most vulnerable, ignored, abused, blamed, perverted, and traumatized victims, we can learn the most about the nature of trauma, its healing, and the human spirit.

It is time to look at the other side of the victim-helper dyad. It will be seen that little may separate victims and their all too human helpers.

Chapter 11

Treating Helper Stresses and Illnesses

Impulses which help to save and take care of other people are considered noble, a relatively exalted depth axis judgment stemming from willingness to risk and suffer for the sake of others. At the seam where the pulse of life and trauma meet professional helpers, like noble warriors and philosophers of old, take up the cudgels of life to confront the worst human demons for the sake of the victims. If successful, they further their clients' and their own life purposes. If not, both are at risk. Hence, the same compassion and empathy which evoke noble impulses, also endanger.

Many workers have highlighted secondary stress and trauma illnesses in helpers (Chapter 2; Figley, 1995a; Valent, 1995a; Valent, 1994). Helper diagnoses have included "empathic strain" (Wilson et al., 1994), vicarious traumatization (Pearlman & Saakvitne, 1995), burnout, compassion fatigue, and secondary stress reactions and disorders (Figley, 1995b). The variety of symptoms in these diagnoses is very wide, ranging from physiological arousal to threats to existential meanings, paralleling in fact client symptoms.

In this chapter too, parallels are drawn between client and helper symptoms and illnesses, and their treatments. Though helpers may have symptoms anywhere on the triaxial framework, it is suggested that their secondary responses may initially be best conceptualized in parallel to process axis ramifications described for clients early after traumatic events (Chapter 9, Appendix 3).

DIAGNOSTIC CATEGORIES OF HELPER
STRESSES, TRAUMAS, AND ILLNESSES

As for clients, the categories of helper symptoms and illnesses will be examined according to survival strategy stress responses, living and reliving traumatic events, intensification of defenses leading to blind spots, and "classical" illnesses. Identification with others' illnesses is implied in the secondary nature of symptoms. However, it must be remembered that helpers also experience their own primary strains in helping situations, as well as bring external stresses and traumas and their sequelae into the situation. The following also lend themselves to point, line, and volume diagnosis (pp. 81–84).

Survival Strategy Stress Response Symptoms

Survival strategy stress responses (Table 2, Chapter 4) can be as varied and fluctuating for helpers as for victims (Chapters 4 and 5). This may be on the basis of empathic resonance with clients' triaxial frameworks, and their own primary responses in treatment situations. However, because rescue/caretaking and assertiveness/goal achievement are common survival strategies in helper roles, symptoms and illnesses pertaining to those two survival strategies are particularly common.

Stress symptoms of the former include feeling burdened and depleted, potentially leading to neglect and rejection of victims (Table 2). This is what may be called compassion stress (Figley, 1995b). Stress symptoms of the latter include frustration, tension (including various pains, arousal, and sleeplessness), willfulness, loss of control, impotence, and a sense of failure. Psychosocial ramifications include irritability, blame, absenteeism, and quitting. These symptoms correspond to demoralization, and the stress range of burn-out.

Empathic strain and secondary stress symptoms, on the other hand, may be said to comprise the whole variety of stressed survival strategies resulting from identification with and responding to client needs (Valent, 1995a; 1999).

Traumas and Traumatic Stress Disorders

Unsuccessful or maladaptive survival strategy stress responses may intensify to traumatic proportions. The feelings of compassion stress may then intensify and be called compassion fatigue, which is associated with intense anguish and survivor guilt for having let people down, and allowed them to suffer and even die (Table 2). Similarly, intense maladaptive assertiveness symptoms may reach traumatic dimensions of burn-out and exhaustion, and be associated with powerlessness and guilt and shame of personal failure and inadequacy (Table 2, Chapter 4).

Secondary Traumatic Stress Disorder   This may be said to involve traumatic intensity of any survival strategies. It is suggested that contents of secondary-like primary stress disorders are determined by survival strategies and their ramifications. However, it should be remembered that in this case, the primary traumatic stress disorder, e.g., PTSD, is in those helped.

Triggering of Past Traumas, Defenses, Blind Spots Current situations may compound with or unmask prior helper vulnerabilities. This may intensify defenses against reliving past traumas, and lead to therapeutic blind spots. For instance, helpers struggling to keep grief at bay may ignore, deny, or callously reject those suffering losses (see Case 40 below). Alternately, helpers may "decompensate" and suffer (re)lived traumatic events and their various sequelae. The trauma disorder in this case is primarily in the helper.

Psychosomatic and "Classical" Illnesses

Biological, psychological, and social stress responses may ramify into or precipitate a variety of illnesses. Their number and intensity is in proportion to number and intensity of stressors involved (e.g., Holmes & Rahe, 1967). Thus in our bush fire team, illnesses were minor and included flu and minor accidents (Berah, Jones, & Valent, 1984). In a more prolonged stress situation involving the closure of a hospital, the staff clinic was overfilled with a variety of illnesses including psychosomatic and "classical" ones. Examples were asthma, hyperthyroidism, acute pancreatitis on the basis of increased alcohol intake, and meningitis and stroke associated with losing jobs (Cases 2 and 27 are examples of work-related heart attack and stroke, respectively). Psychiatric illnesses included depressions, anxieties, and relationship problems. It should be noted that doctors (and perhaps other professional helpers) have higher mortality and morbidity rates than the general population in all of physical, psychological, and social illnesses. The same may apply to other professional rescuers.

MODES AND MEANS OF DIAGNOSING HELPER STRESSES AND ILLNESSES

Modes and means of helper diagnosis parallel and differ from those of primary victims. For instance, at the time of the trauma incidents, team leaders may call a break when they observe exhaustion to be setting in, or may institute routine debriefs after incidents to uncover and deal with inevitable symptoms. In later phases helpers may self-refer with a variety of symptoms. In each case it is important to recognize the possibility of symptoms being related to stresses of helping, and possibly compounding with prior stresses and traumas.

More difficult are situations of helper lags and, more so, defenses and blind spots. Both may present as individual and systemic problems in treating clients. Most common manifestations pertain to victim nonrecognition and include lack of communication, selective questioning, and direction to "passport diagnoses." Patient distress may manifest in acting out, premature terminations of treatment, intensification of symptoms and decompensations. Alternately, patients may become compliant and enmeshed with helpers and the system. Opposite to nonrecognition is overzealousness, such as in convergence phenomena in disasters. Both unwarranted avoidance and enthusiasm may reflect inner problems.

Helper lags may be rectified by education. Blind spots can be addressed gently in debriefs, but more so in supervision and therapy. However, defended helpers may resist, at times destructively, those who may read their minds and traumas. Their stresses and defenses may then go unrecognized. The following case demonstrates some of these points.

CASE 40: DOCTOR WITH BLIND SPOTS

A doctor who had lost three close family members in a plane crash tried to put the incident out of mind, including through overwork and self-medication. She specialized in psychiatry, unconsciously hoping that it would somehow resolve her stress. It did not. Her problems led to avoidance of talking in depth with patients, quickly diagnosing them as depressed or psychotic, and treating them with drugs. She also immersed herself in medical politics.

During a disaster her boss ordered the psychiatrist to take a team into the affected area. She and her inexperienced team members were initially excited and gratified at the unusual emotional outpourings and thanks they received for listening. They became caught up in the "post-disaster euphoria" belief that their efforts were normalizing people. As the honeymoon period passed, they became fatigued, demoralized, and suffered stress symptoms. They complained that people were talking of "irrelevant" problems, and were "not getting on with it." Reciprocally, victims complained that the helpers' insensitivity was worse than the disaster.

The psychiatrist in charge was unable to accept the losses in the disaster, or to support her team. She became highly stressed instead. After two weeks she directed the team to return to the hospital to treat "real" patients.

Comment   This case shows the lack of a wholist approach, together with lags, defenses and blind spots, leading to lack of recognition of victim and helper needs, and to helper stresses.

TREATMENT OF STRESSED AND TRAUMATIZED HELPERS

As for clients in previous chapters, helping helpers will be considered according to disaster phases and increasing entrenchment and complexity of the categories of symptoms and illnesses mentioned above.

During Traumatic Situations

Helping helpers in *a disaster exercise* has already been described (Chapter 8) to include overcoming authorities' denial, preparation of helpers for their responses, pointing them out when they occur, encouraging time out to "decompress" and regenerate, attending specific stress symptoms such as hyperventilation, and defuse. These interventions were seen to include all treatment principles at different times.

During the process of *a hospital closure* (see above), a stress team communicated with hospital staff individually, in units, in a public lecture, and through pamphlets (parameter axis–social levels), about their many intense responses. They were explained in terms of survival strategy responses and their ramifications (*recognition* and *symptomatic treatments*). Even most senior staff members were relieved to realize that they were not "cracking up" or "going mad," and were grateful to be empowered to communicate with and help their own staff (*nonspecific treatment*).

Postimpact Stress Responses and Ramifications: Debriefs

Crisis management of helpers during and soon after a traumatic situation includes decompression, deescalation, defusion, and debriefing (Chapter 2). (They have been described in the disaster exercise in Chapter 8.) The following describes in more detail helper interventions in Case 25 (Chapter 8), where a young widow was helped after her husband died in the emergency department.

During the time of the trauma, helping medical helpers in some ways paralleled treatment of victims. For instance, the primary team gave space to share feelings, "What a terrible event for the family!" and remarked about what it meant for the helpers (ventilation and becoming aware of own stress responses). The team provided a counter-trauma model as indicated, showing that much useful work could be done around a death (counteracted maladaptive goal achievement *nonspecific treatment*). Decompression included arranging for time out to obtain relief and take stock of the situation and oneself. After the intervention, the combined team had tea and coffee in the staff room and briefly expressed their feelings before going on with their work (demobilization), *nonspecific, some specific, treatment*. The next day a debriefing session was held.

Debriefing   The wholist treatment goal was to ensure that all maladaptive helper survival strategies were understood experientially and their adaptive counterparts and ramifications were facilitated. It is acknowledged that different team members had different needs which had to be catered to.

CASE 25 (continued)/41: DEATH OF A YOUNG HUSBAND—DEBRIEF

The emergency department doctor in charge of the deceased patient gave a clinical summary of the dead person's illness. A number of staff members expressed surprised relief to learn that the patient had been seriously ill and deteriorating over the last year.

The doctor then reviewed the man's collapse and treatment given. Some expressed disappointment and anger that certain treatments were omitted, while others expressed indirectly self-doubt at their own deficient interventions. The facilitator put rescue/caretaking anger and guilt tactfully into words. Discussion clarified that, in fact, all reasonable treatment had been given, and no significant mistakes had occurred.

Even in situations of compressed space and time helpers may not be cognizant of different angles of the whole picture. Clarification may relieve rescue anguish and sense of failure (maladaptive rescue, goal achievement). In fact team members came to feel proud of the professional skills and roles which they and their team had exercised (adaptive rescue, goal achievement).

Some expressed anger at the intensive care unit consultant who had quickly ordered an end to resuscitation efforts. He said, "Stop wasting more money. He is dead." and left. Discussion ensued. At the suggestion of the facilitator, the head of the emergency department invited the doctor to join the meeting. He came reluctantly and contemptuously confirmed that indeed staff had wasted their efforts on a dead man. When told he was insensitive, he rejoined, "If I felt for every dead patient, I could not do my job."

The discussion became stymied, until one member drew the consultant's attention to his attitude having hurt her. Others joined in with similar feelings. The hurt was clarified as deprivation of recognition that each staff member had done everything possible to save the patient (rescue), and to gradually let go (adaptation) of the patient to whom they had become quite attached. Instead they were humiliated for their feelings. They also felt denigrated, as if intensive care staff would have handled the resuscitation better (competition). The staff felt betrayed (cooperation), unappreciated for their genuine efforts. The facilitator tactfully helped to clarify these feelings in words, and indicated that their source was the death, not the consultant.

The doctor became disturbed, and indirectly expressed that he had difficulties with emotions. He agreed to follow the protocol where all treating personnel have to agree for resuscitation to be discontinued in the future. Emergency department staff's self-esteem was retrieved.

Though the confrontation was valuable, the facilitator made sure that the consultant was not scapegoated for helplessness to save the patient. It was sufficient to have his blind spot acknowledged, but so too were his skills and dilemmas. He left with his dignity intact.

Most survival strategies had been processed to some extent (*symptomatic, specific treatment*). The ground was now prepared for grief.

Some expressed the horror of a young person like themselves dying. They also put themselves in the widow's place. One member tearfully told how her brother had died and how she had felt. Others also shed tears. Grief for the patient, his family, and eventually for the helping staff who could not help was expressed.

Wider issues across the triaxial framework were now addressed. Dissatisfaction was expressed about the viewing room for the body (a better one came to be built).

The staff reviewed the story and their efforts as a whole. They were satisfied, though wistful, knowing that inevitably their efforts (not they) would fail at times. They were pleased that the patient's corneas were transplanted. They were grateful to have learned so much about care for the bereaved.

The staff's privileged role in the sacred nature of life and death, regeneration, and creation of knowledge was also put into words. The group's special bond was enhanced.

A nurse approached the facilitator soon after the meeting, saying that she could not work because she felt stressed and teary for some reason. It quickly became obvious that she identified the dead man with her fiancee. "I know it is silly, but I just want to touch him and see that he is alive." She was sent home. The next day she looked happy, "I just appreciate him that much more. It is so sad that the man died, and it can happen to anyone. But," she blushed, "I think we love each other, and we confirmed that we are together, alive, and we'll have a happy life."

Comment   Debrief protocols may belie the complex factors which need to be processed after traumatic events. Not all pebbles in the pond produce the same ripples, and each situation requires astute diagnosis and treatment. The wholist approach to treatment above allowed all survival strategies to be processed to adaptive conclusions, even as far as their ramifications to creativity, sacredness, shared wisdom and enhanced purpose.

The following case demonstrates how work stress may become compounded with other recent and current traumas.

CASE 42: A WEEPING NURSE

A nurse was referred by her superior because she was at times teary and could not concentrate on her work. The nurse said that she could not understand herself, as she had always been stable and competent. Her problems started after attending an older woman with breast cancer. In her history she stated that her mother was dying of breast cancer. The revealed conjunction brought tears to her eyes, but she quickly wiped them away. She said that she needed to work, and she became distracted. She reenacted with me the presenting problem (transference). I wondered what interfered with her rescue/caretaking of her mother, and what it meant that she was treating the wrong woman.

"Your mother has cancer, and you were treating this woman for cancer?"

"I keep thinking of my mother all the time. But we are short of money; I can't afford to travel overseas." She was protective of her husband's hard-earned savings, but she also deeply yearned for her mother, wanted to care for her and to say a proper good-bye to her (attachment, rescue, adaptation). I suggested that perhaps her husband had a right to know her feelings.

When he realized what ailed his wife, the husband said, "What did we save money for, if not a case like this? What is life about, if you cannot go to your dying mother?!" The nurse gratefully visited her mother and mourned her loss. She loved her husband more, and the two came to have a deeper understanding of each other and their marriage. She returned to work with added devotion.

Comment   Helpers have personal stresses, conflicts, and traumas like anyone else. As in the case of the Iraqi woman who could not express her feelings
with respect to her husband's family who harmed her mother (Case 26, Chapter
9), a wholist approach clarified crucial triaxial points, and enabled specific maladaptive survival strategies to be replaced by those in accordance with the nurse's
life's meanings. The next case illustrates evocation of longer term vulnerabilities and traumas.

Longer-Term Problems: Triggering of Past Traumas

Sometimes clinical stresses compound with more entrenched past traumas, and
require more help, akin to the bushfire victim (Case 14, Chapter 7).The following case required about a year of weekly therapy.

CASE 43: A VULNERABLE SURGEON

A young pediatric surgeon was very disturbed after a child under her care fell out
of bed. The child did not suffer ill effects, and the doctor knew that she could not
have prevented the incident. Nevertheless, she felt devastated and expected dire
repercussions and public humiliation.

The surgeon noted that she actually often expected humiliation by her superiors, and often felt devastated for insufficient reason. It became clear that more was
required than debrief-type treatment.

It took around 10 sessions to recognize that the initial event triggered the
reliving of aspects of childhood traumatic situations. The expected humiliation felt
exactly like the blame, denigration, and humiliation her father had meted out to her
throughout her childhood. She vividly recalled that no matter how painfully she
had followed his injunctions, she would always be shocked and pained by his
ridicule. (See also Paradigmatic case, Chapter 6.)

The devastation on the other hand belonged to a time when, as a child of similar
age to her patient, she had been physically abused by her father and neglected by
both parents. For instance, one night as she woke in pain and tried to go to the toilet
she fell out of her bunk bed and lost consciousness. She came to in the late morning,
no one having paid attention to her state. She could identify the feeling of devastation
now to contain a sense of being left to die. The meaning that she had been abused
and neglected clarified, and this was a key to many other childhood mysteries.

The surgeon confronted her father, hoping for some recognition and reconciliation. Instead, the father denigrated her more intensely and pushed her out of the
house, repeating his previous pattern. This confirmed her previous perceptions, and
she grieved for the father she never had and her deprivation and suffering.

At the same time, she stopped fearing humiliation at work, and as her confidence increased she was promoted. Her insights and example allowed her brother to
come out of his own abused cocoon with improvement in the sibling relationship
(parameter axis ramification).

Though pensive, the surgeon felt proud of herself as she realized that, rather
than becoming like her father, she chose a profession where she helped traumatized
children. And now she would never need to feel shame doing so.

Comment   This case reminds us that physical and emotional abuse is not the prerogative of lower socioeconomic strata, but can also occur in respectable middle class families. It also reminds us that helpers and helped are similarly vulnerable humans.

Wholist treatment in this case involved *recognition* that humiliation and devastation were symptom fragments of earlier traumatic situations triggered off by current events. Orientation of the symptoms in the triaxial framework and honing the diagnoses to shames of inadequacy (assertiveness), inability to please (attachment), inferiority (competition), and terror of abandonment and rejection (traumatic attachment), allowed tracing the symptoms to similar childhood feelings and their contexts. *Nonspecific* treatment included, respectively, a nurturing relationship, expectation of success, and respect from a father figure. *Symptomatic* treatment included clarification and learning skills in negotiating conflicts with superiors. *Specific* treatment included simultaneous experiential contrast of past terrors and other maladaptive responses with their current alternatives. Consolidating her sense of safety, belonging, sense of competence and victory over her father, on different depth and parameter axis levels, allowed the surgeon to remake her self-image and identity, and take up progress in her life in a fulfilling manner.

Long-Term Therapy for Helpers for Long-Term Problems

In this case work stress uncovered long-term vulnerabilities whose origins stretched back to the previous generation (compare with Case 20, Chapter 7). The helper's whole personality was affected, and this was reflected in her work and blind spots in it.

CASE 44: COMPLEX TRANSGENERATIONAL
PROBLEMS IN A HELPER

Evelyn was a psychologist who worked with a refugee organization many of whose clients were victims of political torture. She had been asked to debrief a large number of helpers who had been particularly busy during a recent flood of refugees. Evelyn sought help because she felt burnt out, complaining that nobody had debriefed her. She noted resentfully that this was typical of her role in the organization, that is, to help everyone without this being reciprocated. She also resented the paradox that in spite of deep reverberation with refugee clients, her deficiencies in treating them (highlighted in supervision), led to her having to assume ever higher organizational but non-clinical roles. Thus, she was asked to debrief counselors with whom she would have dearly like to be able to change places. She was at an age when she wanted more satisfaction out of work and of her life generally.

After a short debriefing-type intervention for her recent work stress, it became clear that the latter stated problems were much more important. I speculated that recent work stress possibly highlighted her counterfeit work achievement, for in reality she felt like a Cinderella. Provisionally, I formulated attachment, goal achievement, and rescue problems which had ramified into a dissatisfied sense of identity and existential meaning. The source of these problems was as yet unknown.

> Evelyn was a postwar child of Holocaust concentration camp survivors whose families had been wiped out. She only knew her parents as depressed, pessimistic, anxious, suspicious, and extremely needy.
>
> Using all modes and means of wholist communication (Chapter 5) allowed piecing together a picture in which Evelyn had never been recognized as a child in her own right. Rather, she was assigned different Holocaust-related roles, a prominent one being to replace the parents' parents and hence comfort her parents. Any claim for herself as a child, belonging to her parents, was at the cost of having to ferret herself into her parents' Holocaust world, in which children (like her parents in the past) were surrounded by danger of death.

Recognition dawned about two interweaving problems Evelyn shared with many second generation children. The first was stunting of her personal fulfillment needs (see also Case 20, Chapter 7) by devoting herself to help her parents (as they saw it) to survive. In the process Evelyn had to repress her own attachment terrors. The second problem was living in a quasi-Holocaust world which was the only one in which she could feel "at home." Evelyn came to see that she was continuing her learned childhood role at work; that is, occupying a false parent role comforting tortured people with her own needs being neglected.

> In the outside world Evelyn joined a second generation group in which she found to her surprise that others, including other helpers, shared similar problems to hers. At the same time by chance her father became seriously ill, and his intensified Holocaust relivings and overt demands on Evelyn confirmed clearly for her the world into which she had been inveigled and which had pervaded all her life.
>
> Slowly the problems encapsulated in her initial presentation could be viewed concurrently in a *trifocal* (as against the usual dual focus of attention) manner. The three foci were current, past, and transgenerational.
>
> For instance, her lack of ability to treat her tortured clients reflected her inability to care for her parents, and their own inabilities to save their parents. Similarly, not being recognized and cared for reflected her childhood Holocaust-tinged terrors imbued by her parents, and their own abandonments by their murdered parents.

Recognition was now extended, with the initially detected attachment, goal achievement, and rescue (as well as flight) problems being traced to their original contexts. *Nonspecific* therapy included attention on herself for herself with her own boundaries for the first time, and being able to validate her own needs. *Symptomatic* treatment involved explanation and mutual support with peers. *Specific therapy* involved a trifocal view of her symptoms, with specific hopeful alternatives.

> Evelyn said, "As I am emerging from the shadow of the Holocaust and I do not respond as if I was still there, does that mean the end of therapy?" We came to understand that such an ending would recreate parental hopes that survival till liberation was all that mattered (transference).

A long phase of (re)construction, or fulfillment therapy followed. Evelyn entered supervision and together with therapy she became aware of and corrected her wide ranging triaxial blind spots. This allowed her to at last treat patients, to her satisfaction. She also influenced her agency to have wider and deeper views of their clients.

In her personal life she dared to trust, feel secure, and find her naturally loving and lovable self. She reconciled that it was not her sacred duty to make up for the Holocaust, and she brought her newly-found self to her parents. Surprisingly, seeing their child happy led to the parents experiencing pleasure in her and themselves for the first time in more than 50 years, as they connected Evelyn with memories of their pre-Holocaust lives.

Comment It is not uncommon for children of traumatized parents to choose helping professions due to a learned diathesis to caretake. This may be a healthy direction and sublimation of loving rescue/caretaking impulses (Case 41), but it may be admixed as in the above case with secondary trauma blind spots.

This case demonstrates also the added difficulty with transgenerationally transmitted traumas. This is because traumatic stressors act on subjects from the start of their lives, and their pervasiveness may be accepted as part of oneself and the world. As well, the original trauma resides in the memories of others, and they may defend against sharing them. Then as one victim said, "I am full of scars, but I have no idea of the wounds." Treatment elements thus must be expanded to a triple focus of attention, which includes parental traumas.

In summary, it may be seen that helpers are vulnerable to stresses and traumas, suffer categories of illnesses, and require a range of treatments similar to their clients. However, being in positions of influence to help or harm their clients, it is incumbent on them to understand their potential influence on them, and in turn the influences on themselves as tools of healing. The injunction, "First know thyself," takes on special meaning, as it means knowing and understanding the life-trauma dialectic within one's own skin.

This chapter considered helper, cultural, and personal lags, defenses, and illnesses which are part of not knowing oneself or one's clients. Such lack of knowing can lead to triaxial blind spots, insufficient application of treatment principles, that is, clinical mismatches which may compound with the client's original stressors. On the other hand, it was shown that the wholist perspective can help to recognize, diagnose and treat helper stressors, lags, blind spots, and illnesses.

Like other acts of nobility, the intimate relationship where souls expose and risk themselves, must be governed by rules which minimize risks. In traumatology it is the ethics of helper professionalism. A code of ethics, adopted by the Australasian Society for Traumatic Stress Studies, is presented in Appendix 4.

The success of trauma therapy is reflected in a range of survival strategy fulfillments for both parties. For instance, in cooperation, both partners gain knowledge, wisdom, love, and creativity. The reward for the nobility of trauma therapy where two bodies and souls expose themselves to trauma in order to help one gain life, is that in fact both gain life in their different ways.

Chapter 12

Summary and Conclusion

This book started with the posing of the problem of how to conceptualize the wide variety of often fluctuating and contradictory traumatic stress and fulfill-ment phenomena and treatments applied to them, and how to rationalize both into a coherent framework. It was suggested that the wholist perspective was an anchoring framework which made sense of observations and treatments and enhanced the latter.

The wholist perspective was based on a broad and inclusive philosophy called the life-trauma dialectic and its tools were the triaxial framework and survival strategies. The life-trauma dialectic saw trauma disrupting the purposes of life which were to survive and fulfill and to help others do the same according to the life cycle. The disruptions had wide-ranging biological, psychological, and social sequelae in all aspects of life which contrasted with fulfillment potentials. The triaxial framework provided coordinate axes which served as the skeleton by which fulfillment and traumatic manifestations could be located, and survival strategies provided the flesh and blood which described what happened through-out the framework and at particular points and intersections and why.

The framework was particularly useful in supplying the missing circuitry for disconnected manifestations which could appear as symptom fragments or clusters forming illnesses. Such fragments in the past were rationalized to have appeared as punishment for sin, or possession by evil forces. Current scientific trends favor minute biological defects.

The wholist perspective enabled the development of a unified view with rational specifications of humans and their dysfunctions. It saw suffering and illnesses occurring in basically normal and moral humans, whose lives have been disrupted by trauma. The responses, including the disconnections developed as the best compromise solutions of maintaining as much life (survival and fulfillment) as possible under the circumstances.

The wholist philosophy overcomes the disadvantages of previous philosophical polarizations which have influenced views of suffering and their treatment. Thus the wholist perspective subsumes mind-body dualism in a triadic biopsychosocial view. This can overcome the fragmentation and incomplete treatments in somatic, psychological, and social disciplines and their subspecialties. The wholist view may see humans as butterflies whose bodies developed psychological and social wings. Disruptions usually affect all parts, but even if only one part is disrupted, the effects may ramify through the whole butterfly. The perspective spans whole-reductionist splits, seeing the importance of everything from life's purpose to smallest molecules. Linear-nonlinear polarizations are overcome by acknowledging that observations, processes, and treatments may be addressed at points, lines, and volumes of the triaxial framework and its contents. The philosophy also overcomes science-humanist splits, bringing emotions, morals, and other depth axis components within an overarching model. This helps to overcome the limitations of appreciating the core human experiences which trauma disrupts, which ". . . cannot be captured in (current) medical and scientific models . . ." (McFarlane & van der Kolk, 1996, p 573). The wholist perspective then overcomes the fragmentation of views and treatments which perhaps reflects the fragmentation which trauma can wreak.

The wholist perspective was next applied to principles of treatment which had been abstracted from treatments applied both over the history of traumatology and currently. Four ubiquitous treatment ingredients were noted to be recognition, and nonspecific, symptomatic, and specific therapies.

With respect to the first principle *recognition*, the wholist perspective recognizes the significance of fulfillment and trauma and their sequelae, and can orientate, define, hone, categorize, and make sense of them by tracing them to their sources. This can be done even if the connections between symptoms and sources are not in awareness. To do so required wholist receptivity, some appreciation of the wholist perspective, ability to read the modes and means of wholist language communications (such as transference and countertransference), and ability to translate them into common language. The wholist perspective could also recognize and provide a taxonomy of appraisals, traumas, disconnections, defenses, and a heuristically coherent classification of contradictory emotions, morals, values, and other components of the triaxial framework.

Last, the wholist perspective could help to recognize, define, and make sense of the great variety of diagnoses and treatments which have been applied in traumatology. They could be oriented and understood to deal with different sectors of the triaxial framework and different survival strategies. The perspective could thus provide for traumatology the kind of words and awareness which the wholist perspective provides to clients for their symptoms.

Applied to *nonspecific* trauma therapy the wholist perspective could hone and define its various aspects such as the therapeutic relationship, respect, holding, and empowerment, as providing specific counter-trauma experiences using specific survival strategies at specific triaxial points. Similarly, many *symptomatic* treatments could be defined as addressing specific maladaptive survival strategy symptoms and illnesses at specific triaxial points or clusters of such points.

The wholist perspective could be especially useful when applied to *specific* trauma and fulfillment therapy. As well as helping to trace symptoms back to sometimes unconscious sources, it could help to break the nexus between past and present by dual focus of attention at specific triaxial points on contrasts between specific traumatic survival strategy components of the past and their hopeful current alternatives. From this melting pot of thawed nodal constituents (sensations, cognitions, emotions, relationships, judgments, and meanings) new nodal experiences, their conglomerations, and significances could emerge. They in turn subsumed past and present realities both sequentially and coherently as part of a new narrative.

Again, processing this at many triaxial points and survival strategies allows integration of the complex jigsaw puzzle of people's lives and their disruptions. The puzzle is now in their conscious minds in verbal memory, under their ownership and control, available for use in their now resumed purposeful lives.

This achievement may be expressed from a cognitive view as changing normal reactions to abnormal circumstances to normal responses to current normal situations. Seeing emotions as central, it can be said that feelings from traumatic situations are replaced with positive feelings appropriate to present hopeful circumstances. On an identity level, this is expressed as victims becoming survivors. The wholist level subsumes these views, and adds that survival struggles are replaced by a path of fulfillment of life's purpose.

In summary, the wholist perspective applied to trauma and fulfillment therapy facilitates to orientate, decipher, and decouple past trauma responses from present reality and facilitates adaptive fulfilling responses to the latter. It utilizes all treatment principles, extending and enriching their use, as well as increasing control and ability to tailor them.

A FINAL PHILOSOPHICAL CONUNDRUM

It may be asked, what is the central reason for the irrationality or abnormality within traumatic stress wihch requires treatment? Janet and Freud described dissociation and splitting of consciousness as central disconnections both of the mind, and between trauma and symptoms. But we may also question, why live in two parallel states of consciousness (one aware and one not) whose interactions produce irrationality and illness? Why freeze traumatic conditions and live them as if they were still relevant, when they are not? This evolutionary "appendix of traumatology" which the discipline treats, may be seen as a part of long-term philosophical concerns about the reality of perceptions, knowl-edge, and being.

From within traumatology an example of a biological approach to the conundrum sees memory disturbances and dissociation as possibly originating in hippocampal disregulation or unintegrated hippocampal cognitive and amygdalar emotional pathways (Bremner, Vermetten, Southwick, Krystal, & Charney, 1998). A psychological approach harks back to Janet, and sees information node components becoming disassociated so that their components (biological, psychological, social, relationship, judgmental, and meaning information) are fragmented (Chapter 3). On an evolutionary level it may be said that ways of perceiving self needs (senses and feelings) and their sources (external observation) developed separately for different functions, and have a tendency to be unintegrated (Humphrey, 1993). Yet these descriptions of splits in the mind do not really answer the philosophical conundrum.

The wholist approach suggests that humans have capacities for arranging quantities and qualities of awareness in a sophisticated manner for the sake of survival and fulfillment. While fulfillment is associated with ever greater awareness, knowledge, and wisdom, trauma may require compromises in awareness if awareness leads to further trauma. For instance, grief for a buddy may be suppressed when a soldier has to keep fighting. An abused child may suppress awareness of being unloved and rejected in order to maintain vital social links and hope. Sophisticated means called defenses may thus influence a complex seesaw of awareness throughout the triaxial framework.

It may be that while, for fulfillment purposes, awareness and memories resemble reality but may be adjusted for minor inconsistencies, for survival purposes both memories and their obfuscations are engrammed more deeply. The conundrum of disconnections from the traumatic past which are frozen in a parallel unaware consciousness (sometimes simplistically called the unconscious or repressed memories), may then be a manifestation of a sophisticated step in evolution where humans both obfuscate dangerous awareness of peril, and yet communicate its contents through a very sophisticated code, here identified as the wholist language.

This facilitates both camouflage and communication to others who may arrange new circumstances of security. Not knowing is then not seen as a global unwanted defense or a perversion, but different and complex ways of avoiding retraumatization, while leaving the door open to change.

Yet this brings us back to the pathology of the evolutionary appendix in traumatology. This is to not be able to distinguish past and present and to be living past traumas in current secure circumstances. However, it is possible that, in their evolutionary past when humans occupied stable but harsh ecological niches, state dependent learning from single experiences (akin to imprinting) was essential to survive predators and natural disasters, and to be forever alert to them. In current flexible ecological niches such learning is frequently over-determined, even though defenses mitigate this. Hence the neuroses of civilization. The task of traumatology is to adjust the overlearning and to combine it with new learning appropriate to current hopeful realities.

In conclusion, this book provides a framework and language by which to understand and categorize the widespread, varied, fluctuating and contradictory both salient and also partly communicated sequelae of trauma and fulfillment. The wholist perspective also provides a framework for traumatology diagnoses and treatments, and helps to extend, enrich, as well as hone and tailor applications of comonly applied treatment principles.

It is hoped that the wholist perspective may enhance a confluence of treatment views along with increase in specialist skills. Such a confluence may diminish disparate treatments for trauma related fragments, and enhance unified strategic interventions at crucial points in the triaxial web which underlie the fragments. While forging and specifying a variety of treatments new, inclusive, creative treatments may emerge.

Perhaps quite new emphases may emerge, such as trauma prevention. Then it may be asked why pebbles are thrown into ponds in the first place, and how may this be prevented? Perhaps new parameter components, such as societies, will be foci for prevention.

Perhaps it is incumbent to finish on the note that neither theoretical nor clinical descriptions, however inclusive or detailed, can indicate the complex experiences in trauma and fulfillment therapy. This work provides a "feel" for the wealth of involvement and potential accomplishment. Because trauma affects the human core its therapy deals with essences of life. In the process both the helped and helpers become acquainted with their own essences. During their mutual struggles, if successful, both progress toward the fulfillment of their lives' purposes. It is hoped that this book contributes a little toward this goal.

Coping with a Major Personal Crisis

*Produced by the Australasian
Red Cross Society, Victorian Division*

Compiled by

    Dr. Paul Valent and Dr. Ellen Berah, Monash Medical Center, 246 Clayton Road, Clayton, Melbourne 3168
    Dr. Julie Jones and Ruth Wraith, Royal Children's Hospital, Flemigton Road, Melbourne 3052
    Rev. John Hill, Uniting Church Center.

Produced by the Australian Red Cross Society, Victorian Division, 171 City Road, South Melbourne, Victoria 3205.

What you have experienced is a unique and personal event. This booklet will help you to know how adults and children have reacted in similar situations. It will show how you can help *normal healing to occur* and how to *avoid some pitfalls.*

NORMAL FEELINGS AND EMOTIONS EXPERIENCED

Shock and Disbelief

- The event seems to be unreal, like a film or a dream.

Numbness

- Your emotions are cut off.

Fear

- Of death, injury, or harm to yourself and those you love.
- Of being left alone, of having to leave loved ones.
- Of "breaking down," or "losing control."
- Of a similar event happening again.

Helplessness

- Crises may reveal human frailty, as well as strength.

Euphoria

- Joy of survival, feeling high, excited, close to everyone.

Sadness

- For deaths, injuries, and losses of every kind.

Longing

- For all that has gone and will not be.

Guilt

- For not having helped or saved others.
- For being alive and uninjured.
- For being better off than others, having things.
- Regrets for things not done.

Shame

- For not having felt and reacted as you would have wished.
- For having been helpless, "emotional," and needing others.

Anger and Frustration

- At what happened, whoever caused it or allowed it to happen.
- At the injustice and the senselessness of it all.
- At the shame and indignities.
- At the lack of proper understanding by others, the red tape and ineffi-
ciencies.
- **Why me?   Why?!**

Let Down

- Disappointments, which alternate with . . .

Hope

- For the future, for better times.

These feelings are common and normal. Nature heals through allowing their expression. Expressing your emotions and feelings does not mean that you are out of control, or having a nervous breakdown. Even intense feelings occur for only limited periods. They can be dealt with, and you can put them on hold when necessary. You, or others, may block your feelings for fear that they are too painful. The most common ways of blocking are cutting off feelings and being overbusy.

Sometimes you may not be able to express or deal with your feelings immediately. Then your reactions may take some time, even months or years to be experienced. The earlier you are able to deal with these feelings, the sooner your healing begins. Prolonged blocking of feelings may lead to difficulties.

**Do remember that *abnormal* responses
are *normal* to *abnormal* situations.**

REMEMBERING AND MEMORIES

The events and feelings may return to you in your thoughts, daydreams, images, flashbacks, night dreams, and nightmares. You may remember past crises. These are normal ways to process the event and make meaning of it.

Suppression, pushing things out of your mind, may lead to loss of memory, concentration, and fuzziness of the mind.

Physical Reactions

Your body, as well as your mind, may be affected immediately or even many months later.

Common Reactions Include

- Tiredness, shakes, dizziness, palpitations.
- Difficulty in breathing, choking in the throat, and chest pains.
- Nausea, diarrhea, vomiting.
- Muscular tension, or pain, headaches, neck and back pain.
- Menstrual disorders, dragging in the womb. Miscarriages may occur.
- Increased or decreased sexual desire and activity. Pregnancies are more common after some crises.

Infections frequently occur when you are run down. Alcohol, coffee, and drug intake may increase due to extra tension. Accidents are more frequent after severe stress. Do take care.

FAMILY AND SOCIAL RELATIONSHIPS

You may form new friendships and groups. However, strains in relationships may also appear. As well as the good feelings of giving and receiving there may be conflict, anger, and jealousy. You may feel that too little or the wrong things are offered, or that you cannot give as much as expected. Changes may occur in the way families, friends, and the community relate to each other.

CHILDREN

Children also experience emotional and physical responses in crises. Their imaginings and nightmares add to the fear of the event. Children express themselves through talking, play, and drawing. Their distress may be shown by returning to earlier ways of behaving, such as clinging. Sometimes these behaviors may be a burden on already stressed parents and teachers. Yet children need the closeness and comforting of their families. They need to be understood, believed, and given honest explanations. They need reassurance about their own safety and that of the family and that they did not cause the event.

THE FOLLOWING MAKE THE EVENTS
AND THE FEELINGS ABOUT THEM EASIER TO BEAR

Doing Things

- To be active and useful may provide relief and a sense of control. *However, overactivity may be harmful if it stops feelings too much.*

Reality

- Facing reality will help you to come to terms with the event. For example, viewing the body, going to the funeral, returning to the scene, inspecting losses, and visiting the ill and injured.

Talking

- It will help you to talk about your experiences and how you feel about them, often many times. It also helps to listen to others who have been affected.

Support

- *Be open to receiving* support and comfort and *give* them when you can.

Privacy

- Make time and space for yourself to be alone with your own thoughts and feelings.

Exercise, Rest, and Recreation

- Are important to maintain your physical and mental health.

REACTIONS MAY BE MORE INTENSE OR TROUBLING FOR THE FOLLOWING PEOPLE

Bereaved

- Especially:
  - Where deaths were multiple, sudden, or violent.
  - When a child or young person died.
  - When the body was not found.
  - When the relationship with the person was difficult.

Elderly

- Readjustment may be harder because of reduced energy and time to rebuild.

Evacuated/Isolated

- Those who are hospitalized, evacuated, or alone may lose the support of friends and community. Isolation may also occur due to language or cultural differences.

Unwell and Disabled

- Anyone with illness or physical or mental disabilities needs special care and support.

Those With Other Crises

- People for whom the crisis is an addition to other painful experiences.
- People who are thrown back to the pain of a previous trauma or loss.

Emergency Workers/Volunteers/Helpers

- Especially people who:

- Have given deeply of themselves.
- Came into close contact with the injured, dying, or dead.
- Felt they failed to do their jobs properly.
- Experienced "burn-out."

SOME DO'S AND DON'TS

DON'T   Bottle up feelings.

DON'T   Avoid talking and thinking about what has happened.

DO   Allow yourself time to talk, grieve, be angry, cry, and laugh according to your needs.

DO   Allow your children to share in your grief and encourage them to express their own.

DO   Allow yourself to be part of a group of people who care about you and what you went through.

DO   Spend time alone when you need it.

DO   Recognize that everyone expresses things in their own way. Men generally find it harder to express emotion and weep. Children may need encouragement to express themselves.

DO   Take time out to sleep, rest, enjoy, and do routine things when possible.

DO   Allow your children to return to school and keep up with their activities as soon as they are ready.

DO   Express your needs clearly and honestly to family, friends, and officials.

WARNING
Accidents and Illnesses are More Common
After Severe Stresses, THEREFORE:

DO   Drive more carefully.

DO   Keep up usual safety standards.

DO   Continue your normal medical treatment.

DO   Watch your diet and physical health.

DO   Be more careful with coffee, cigarettes, alcohol, and drug intake.

SEEK PROFESSIONAL HELP IF

- Your **emotions or physical symptoms** are too intense or persistent.
- You feel too **numb, cut off,** or you have to keep active in order not to feel.
- You continue to have nightmares, poor sleep or **"flashbacks."**
- Your family, social, or work **relationships** suffer.
- **Sexual** problems develop.
- You experience loss of **memory** and **concentration**.
- Your **performance** suffers at school, work, or at home.
- You have **accidents** or **illnesses**.
- You increase **smoking, drinking,** or **drug** taking.
- You have **no one to talk to** about your experiences. You belong to **one of the special groups** mentioned above.
- You have **lost faith** in yourself or the world.

SEEKING SUPPORT IS A POSITIVE STEP

Deep reaching experiences may lead you
to have a sense of being different than before.

The inside, as well as the outside, changes.

In time you may develop a deeper understanding
of yourself and what it means to be a human being.

For further help please contact:

Biopsychosocial Approach to Patients (Incorporation of Biological, Psychological, & Social Aspects of Patients)

INTRODUCTION

1 Medical problems are almost always a conglomerate of somatic and psychosocial factors. Each aspect of this conglomerate needs elucidation and treatment.

2 Most psychosocial problems need to be attended to by the general medical staff, though the Psychiatric Liaison staff are very willing to help.

3 Emergency Department is the site of choice for effective intervention for somatic as well as psychosocial crises.

4 The total view of patients is both ancient and a recently evolving science.

The following is an introduction to the relatively recent BIOPSYCHOSOCIAL or triadic approach, which has been found to be useful in the Emergency Department. It may have more widespread application.

It is often said that there is no time for a full psychiatric history. The following should not take long, and may save much time and effort in the long run.

GENERAL HISTORY

This includes:
  (a) an open-ended introductory clinical question,
  (b) assessment of the person's background and personality, and
  (c) assessment of what stresses disturbed the equilibrium.

Opening Question

ASK   *"Of all the things that worry you, what worries you the most?"*
        Follow up the answer, even if at first it does not make sense.

Patient's Background and Personality

It is essential to know the person, and have a therapeutic alliance with him or
her, otherwise the patient may become one of the majority who do not comply
with prescribed treatment.

ASK
  • Age, occupation, where do you come from, marital status, who do you
live with?
  • What do you experience, do, when are you uptight?
  • Do you get anxious, depressed?
  • Can you relax?
  • How many hours a week do you work?
  • How do you see yourself?
  • How have you reacted to this problem in the past?

Stresses

The importance of physical stresses has long been known. Recently, much
literature indicates the importance of psychosocial stresses in all sorts of illnesses, such as accidents, psychosomatic illnesses, strokes, and even cancers.
The greater the stress, the more illnesses of all kinds

ASK
  • Have you had any major stresses recently?
  • Has anyone you know died recently, in the last year or so?
  • Have you separated from, or lost anyone recently, in any other way
(spouse, child, parents)?
  • Had trouble with police?
  • Trouble at work?
  • Anyone in your family ill?
  • Any other problems at all?

SPECIFIC HISTORY (CATEGORIES OF ILLNESSES) (See Table 4)

Table 4 indicates background and personality, and six categories of illnesses. Each category has its own "signature." Once a "signature" is noted, it needs to be fully explored. A "signature" implies an identifying feature of a type of illness, analogous to the way a person's signature identified him. A pain may have a somatic signature, e.g., a crushing retrosternal pain, or colicky RIF pain. If a symptom does not fit a somatic or another signature, it may fit one of the other five categories of illnesses.

The following refer to the six categories of illnesses in Table 4.

Table 4 Biopsychosocial Approach to Patients

Clinical Aspects	History	Treatment
General		
A. Patients' personalities are important	Assess personality. Who is this patient? His family? Culture?	Take personality into account in treatment
B. Stressful events precede illnesses	What stresses preceded the illnesses? Are they still operating?	Treat the stress
Specific Categories of Illnesses		
1. Many illnesses are typical, textbook-like, **somatic** illnesses	Does the illness have a somatic "signature"? Elicit typical history and preceding stresses	Treat somatic illness and preceding stress
2. Many illnesses, including those with somatic symptoms are typical **psychiatric** illnesses	Does the illness have a psychiatric "signature"? Elicit psychiatric history and preceding stresses	Treat psychiatric illness and preceding stress
3. **Autonomic nervous system arousal** produces diffuse symptoms	Does the illness have a physiological "signature"? Elicit physiological and psychosomatic history and stress	Treat physiological symptoms and preceding stress
4. Chronic, and even acute, **traumatic states** may be missed	Is the patient acutely anxious, depressed, confused because of recent trauma?	Give emergency supportive treatment
5. **Identification with another** produces symptoms	Does the illness have an idiosyncratic "signature"? Elicit identifications with others	Treat grief, guilt, anger
6. Symptoms may be **cherished** for psychosocial reasons	Does the illness have a hysteria-like "signature"? Elicit psychosocial history and stresses	Must treat the underlying conflicts

The following is in no way a substitute for a proper psychosocial history. The questions have been found to be useful in a screening procedure in a place like Emergency Department where fast screening is of importance. Once screening throws up something of importance, this must be explored more fully. A proper history must be taken soon after the screening.

Make a quick checklist of the categories of all illnesses with all patients by the end of your interview.

1 Textbook-like somatic illnesses

Many, though perhaps only a minority, of illnesses seen in the Emergency Department conform to the classical textbook-like illnesses.

ASK

• The classical somatic review questions which elicit classical somatic illnesses. All organ systems are systematically overviewed, and specific symptoms looked into more fully.

2 Textbook-like psychiatric illnesses

One should always keep in mind depression and schizophrenia, which are common illnesses, and may masquerade under physical symptoms, e.g., sleeplessness, constipation etc. Organic brain syndromes are also common, often not thought of, and missed.

Any patient who seems confused, should be given the **Cognitive Capacity Screening Examination**
(p. 5)

ASK

• Have you been depressed? Anxious? Worried? Uptight?
• Do you feel anyone is burdening you unduly?
• Trying to harm you?
• Talking about you behind your back?

3 Autonomic Nervous System Arousal

The physical accompaniments and psychological equivalents of emotions, and of sympathetic and parasympathetic activity, constitute a significant proportion of patient attendances. Symptoms themselves are very varied— palpitations, breathlessness, pains, feeling "off," tiredness sleeplessness, dry tongue constipation, diarrhea, etc. Psychosomatic illnesses occur when physiological activity concentrates on a target organ, e.g., asthma in lungs, colitis in bowels.

ASK

• Apart from this symptom, do you have any palpitations, sweating, hot and cold feelings, headaches, aches and pains, tiredness, lassitude, etc.?

- Do these symptoms come on when you are stressed? Uptight? Sad?
- Please breathe hard for 1 minute (Psychological symptoms are often reproduced by over breathing).

4 Traumatic states

Every physically traumatized patient is also psychologically traumatized. So is the family. Bereaved family members need special handling.

Assaulted, raped, or otherwise violated patients, and those shocked in accidents, need emergency psychosocial help. Extremes of emotion or defenses against them, e.g., denial, will be seen.

ASK

- What really happened? Have you experienced accidents, assaults, deaths, threat to life recently?
- What was the worst of your experience? Are you holding anything back?
- Are you shocked? Numb? Angry? Afraid? Are you holding back tears?

5 Identification with Another

Patients often assume the symptom of a lost or seriously ill family member or friend. Symptoms are as perceived by the patient, not necessarily as the dead person really suffered them. Thus a feared heart attack similar to a dead father's may present as sharp pains under the left nipple. Symptoms may arise at anniversaries of the deaths, at the age the other person died or took ill, and at other significant times.

ASK

- Have you known anyone else to have this illness? (Mother, father, sibling, spouse?)
- Has anyone died recently?
- What symptoms did your parents, spouse, have when they died?
- When did they become seriously ill?
- Is it the anniversary of a significant death?
- Were your parents (or near-ones) the age you are now when they died?

6 Cherished illnesses (Hysterias, Somatization)

Not all symptoms are presented for removal. Many are presented for confirmation, in order to serve certain aims outside the doctor-patient relationship. These patients are frustrating and evoke anger.

Many tests and much treatment lead nowhere.

Financial compensation claims are often implicated in this group, though more personal motivations to avoid anxiety and shame are much more common. These must be searched out.

ASK YOURSELF
• Am I angry, frustrated, powerless with this patient?
• Is the amount of complaining by the patient belied by the lack of distress actually manifested?
• What shame, anxiety, etc. may this symptom solve?

ASK THE PATIENT
• How long since you have been healthy?
• What happened around the time you first became ill?
• What stresses did you experience around that time?

COGNITIVE CAPACITY SCREENING EXAMINATION
FOR ORGANIC BRAIN SYNDROME

Instructions
Check items answered correctly. Write incorrect or unusual answers in the space provided. If necessary, urge patient once to complete task.

Introduction to patient
"I would like to ask you a few questions, some you will find very easy, and others may be very hard. Just do your best."

---

1. What day of the week is this?

   _____

2. What month?

   _____

3. What day of the month?

   _____

4. What year?

   _____

5. What place is this?

   _____

6. Repeat the numbers 8, 7, 2.

   _____

7. Say them backwards

   _____

8. Repeat these numbers 6, 3, 7, 1

   _____

9. Listen to these numbers 6, 9, 4. Count 1 through 10 out loud, then repeat 6, 9, 4.

   _____

10. Listen to these numbers 8, 1, 4, 3. Count 1 through 10 out loud, then repeat 8, 1, 4, 3.

    _____

11. Beginning with Sunday, say the days of the week backwards.

    _____

12. 9 divided by 3 is?

   _____

13. Add 5 (to the previous answer
    or 'to 12')

   _____

14. Take away 5 ('from 18')

   _____

   Repeat these words after me, and
   remember them. I will ask for
   them later

   HAT, CAR, TREE,
   TWENTY-SIX

15. The opposite of fast is slow.
    The opposite of up is

   _____

16. The opposite of large is?

   _____

17. The opposite of hard is?

   _____

18. An orange and a banana are both
    fruits.

   _____

   Red and blue are both:

   _____

19. A penny and a cent are both:

   _____

20. What were those words I asked
    you to remember? (HAT)

   _____

21. (CAR)

   _____

22. (TREE)

   _____

23. (TWENTY-SIX)

   _____

24. Take away 7 from 100, then take
    away 7 from what is left, and
    keep going

    100 minus 7 is?

   _____

25. Minus 7

   _____

26. Minus 7 (write down answers,
    check correct subtraction of 7)

   _____

27. Minus 7

   _____

28. Minus 7

   _____

29. Minus 7

   _____

30. Minus 7

   _____

TOTAL CORRECT _____
(Maximum score = 30)

Patient's occupation (previous if not employed): _____

    Education _____ Age _____

Estimated intelligence (based on education, occupation, and history, not on
    test score):   Below average _____   Average _____   Above average _____

Patient was: Cooperative _____   Uncooperative _____   Depressed _____
    Lethargic _____   Other _____

Medical Diagnosis _____

_____

_____

IF PATIENT'S SCORE IS LESS THAN 20, THE EXISTENCE OF DIMIN-
ISHED COGNITIVE CAPACITY IS PRESENT. THEREFORE, AN ORGANIC
MENTAL SYNDROME SHOULD BE SUSPECTED, AND THE FOLLOW-
ING INFORMATION OBTAINED.

Temp. _____   B.U.N. _____   Endocrine dysfunction? _____

B.P. _____   Glu _____   T2 _____   T4 _____   Ca. _____

P _____ etc. Hct _____   PO _____

Protocol for Psychosocial Support in Medical Emergencies

Because it is usually impossible to give full psychological and social support at the same time as medical support, one member of the team should be designated to deal with psychosocial problems.

The duties of that team member are the following.

THE PATIENT

1 **Physical comforting**—hold patient's hand, stroke brow.

2 **Verbal comforting**—explanation of what is going on, *"the doctor is going to put a needle in your arm which will help your circulation, breathing, pain, etc."*

3 **Reassurance**—find out what worries patient, and answer as truthfully and hopefully as possible, *"you will get extra care in the intensive care unit."* Do not give false hope if asked a direct question.

4 **Gather information and pass it on to the rest of the team**—assess quality of life of patient. In the elderly and terminally ill, determine the patient's and relatives' wishes about continuation of resuscitation.

THE FAMILY

5 **Liaise with family**—they also need 1–4. Give them factual information. Reassure them that everything possible is being done. Allay their guilt *"allowing him out into the chill, eating the hot curry, did not cause the trouble."* Let them ventilate their anger. If appropriate and desired, possibly facilitate them seeing, touching the patient.

THE TEAM

6 **Liaise with team**—keep them informed about patient's and relatives' feelings. Remind them, if necessary, that even unconscious patients may have a sense of what is said about them.

7 **Encourage the team**—encourage them to have a debrief on the patient. It is important that their anxieties and potential for guilt and feelings of inadequacy be dealt with. Their efforts should be rewarded with a sense of achievement.

YOURSELF

8 **Communicate**—you should also relate the difficult feelings which are inevitably evoked, in the debrief, and/or to someone experienced—your chief, senior nurse, Director of Casualty, Psychiatric Liaison Service.

Remember that even though in a medical emergency much effort is focused on physical procedures, there are concurrent psychological and social emergencies. How they are dealt with will affect the overall welfare of the patient, and of all concerned.

A Code of Ethics of the Australasian Society for Traumatic Stress Studies

The following is the Code of Ethics of the Australasian Society of Traumatic Stress Studies (ASTSS) as incorporated in its Bye-laws. Its purpose is to ensure maximal professional care for victims of traumatic stress. It is expected that members of the Society will abide by this code.

DEFINITION OF TERMS FOR THE PURPOSES OF THIS DOCUMENT

Society is the Australasian Society of Traumatic Stress Studies.

Severe stress, traumatic stress and trauma are states resulting from experiences or threats of experiences (stressors), which resulted or could result in any or all of physical, mental, social and spiritual annihilation of self or significant others.

Sequelae of such states can result in loss of previous life enhancing equilibria and result in biological, psychological and social symptoms and illnesses.

Traumatized people or victims have experienced such severe stress, traumatic stress or trauma.

Trauma therapy and trauma therapists. Trauma therapy is help administered by appropriately trained professionals (trauma therapists) to traumatized people in order to help them with the prevention, amelioration, healing and reduction of the consequences of severe stress, traumatic stress and trauma. Their prime obligation is to apply their expertise to the welfare of their clients or patients.

Clients and patients are traumatized people or victims who are receiving trauma therapy in a therapeutic relationship with trauma therapists.

ETHICAL PRINCIPLES

The following principles apply to behavior with clients and patients, in relation to therapists themselves, the community, and in research.

In Relation to Clients and Patients,

   1   **First do no harm.** This applies to physical, mental, social, cultural and spiritual well being.
   2   **Clients' or patients' welfare is the uppermost reason for intervention.** The welfare of clients is the prime reason to apply treatment, and their needs take precedence over the interests of therapists, other individuals, employers, third parties and institutions. The impetus to help should be assessed according to likely benefits and disadvantages to victims.
   3   **No discrimination.** Therapists must not discriminate against clients or patients on grounds of gender, sexual preference, age, race, ethnicity, religion, politics or ideology, nor should they try to impose their own ideological values on them.
   4   **No exploitation.** The particular vulnerability of traumatized people should be taken into account. Therapists must not exploit clients financially or sexually, nor advantage themselves through provided services and privileges provided by clients, nor exploit clients for academic or self-aggrandisement purposes. Therapists shall not receive or pay commission for referral of clients.
   5   **Consent and collaboration with clients or patients.** To the degree possible trauma therapy should be voluntarily consented to, be collaborative, patients and clients being empowered to have control over themselves and sharing power in the therapeutic process. The nature of treatment, its risks, side effects, and cost-benefit ratio such as short-term pain for long-term benefit should be explained. When patients or clients are not in control of their selves, and cannot give consent, it is their privilege to expect professional care on their behalf. However, a prime aim of treatment then is to facilitate their empowerment. When clients are approached as part of an outreach process, its rationale should be explained and permission be asked to continue. The rights and special needs of children, the elderly, the ill and ethnically unassimilated should be catered for.
   6   **Type of therapy and its length.** Practitioners should ensure that best available treatment resources and skills are applied to specific situations. The

type, frequency and duration of counseling and therapy should be tailored to clients' needs. Therapists should explain why a particular form of therapy is chosen and what alternatives exist. Overt or implied promises of safety, routine, time, punctuality, boundaries and care should be adhered to. To the extent possible, therapy should not be curtailed or extended for the benefit of therapists or third parties. Therapists should take into account hazards of terminating therapy.

7   **Confidentiality.** Whatever knowledge or information a professional derives during therapy remains confidential unless it involves threats to the lives of clients, others, or is subject to criminal law. Any audiovisual record of treatment (tape, video, etc.), material used for teaching or conferences where the person may be identified, must include informed, unpressured written consent. This includes agreement to the storage and use of the records. Students and conference viewers are bound by rules of confidentiality.

8   **Remuneration.** Remuneration for professional services are professional fees. These should be equitable, fair, and arrived at through mutual negotiation.

9   **Third parties.** The same ethical standards apply whether clients and patients themselves, or third parties pay professional fees. Any potential conflicts of interest which may impinge on therapy such as third party pressures, or influences of organizations and interested parties to whom therapists have obligations, should be declared and discussed with clients.

In Relation to Self,

1   **Recognition of skills required for trauma therapy.** Professionals recognise that trauma therapy requires special knowledge and skills which may not be fulfilled by having a mental health professional qualification. Practitioners should ensure that they acquire knowledge and skills pertinent to trauma therapy.

2   **Limitations of skills and referrals.** When professionals assess that their capacities to help are limited, they should declare to the degree appropriate their limitations, and alert authorities and clients to other options. Therapists should be willing to consult, ask for help and second opinions, and refer clients as appropriate.

3   **Maintaining professional skills and fitness.** It is incumbent on professionals to keep up with knowledge and skills in the field. They should ensure that they are physically and mentally fit, and that they deal with their own stresses, traumas and blind spots. To this effect professionals should partake of appropriate education, supervision, debriefing, and therapy. Institutions which employ trauma therapists should provide structures for support and prevention of secondary harm to therapists.

In Relation to Peers,

1   **Colleaguial respect.** Therapists must not adversely affect treatment offered by peers, but at the same time respect clients' rights for second opinions.

2 Respect for Service Networks. Practitioners need to know local government and nongovernment helper networks and cultures, and cooperate with and within them as much as possible.

3 Declaration of skills through professional network. Professionals should declare their skills through a professional trauma network, so that they may be asked to help in appropriate situations.

4 Advertising and competition. Practitioners have the right to let potential clients know of their skills, but these should not be exaggerated or advertised in a commercial manner. Others' skills should not be denigrated and territorial dominance over client populations should be avoided. Skills, training and knowledge should be shared and made open for critical assessment.

5 Limitations on unprofessional conduct. If it comes to the notice of practitioners that others are acting in unethical manner or one harmful to clients or the profession, education, personal approach and, as a last resort, legal avenues should be taken to protect clients and patients.

6 Supervisees and trainees. The same rules of confidentiality and protection against exploitation apply in teacher-student and supervisor-supervisee relationships as in the therapist-client one.

In Relation to the Community,

1 Trauma prevention. The Society and its members should provide education to the community about what makes it vulnerable to trauma, and how to prevent it.

2 Trauma consequences. The Society and its members should provide education to the community about how to prepare for trauma, what are its consequences, and what treatment skills and ethics are necessary to deal with them. Advice may be given about how to tap into available skills for specific needs. The Society should encourage and facilitate high level training of trauma therapists for the community.

3 Evolution of ethical principles. This code of ethics should be regularly reviewed. Consultation about ethical issues and dilemmas in the field of trauma and its treatment should occur within the Society, with other similar bodies and the community.

In Relation to Research,

1 First do no harm. Research should take into account the highly vulnerable state of traumatized subjects and the risk of retraumatization when asked to image their traumas. Welfare of victims must always precede the interests of professionals. Research should in no way prejudice healing.

2 Informed research goals. Because research always siphons some energy from patient welfare, its projected value for future generations of victims over current potential suffering must be assessed. To this end already available knowledge and previous similar research in the field, as well as established principles of research safety and ethics, must be heeded. For instance, subjects must be always free to discontinue research without guilt. The goal of research should not be partisan to a particular drug, type of therapy, person or group. Lack of benefits, side effects and negative effects should be reported as much as positive ones. Potential biases such as funding bodies, and institutional and relevant group attachment should be declared.

3   Informed subjects. The nature of the research, its goals, projected cost-benefit ratio, procedures, sponsorship, must be explained to subjects. Results of research should be freely available, including to the subjects.

4   Informed consent. Allowance should be made for subjects' suggestibility and reliance when asked to consent to research. Empowered client or patient consent should always be obtained.

5   Confidentiality. People's identities must be preserved from recognition. This is particularly important in high profile disasters involving high profile identities. Publication and research presentations should disguise identity of clients. Data bases must be kept confidential. Subjects should know and agree to the type of storage of data. Transfer or sale of identifying data should occur only with subjects' consent.

References

Abse, D.W. (1984). Brief historical overview of the concept of war neurosis and of associated treatment methods. In H.J. Schwartz (Ed.), *Psychotherapy of the Combat Veteran* (pp. 1–22). Lancaster, England: MTP Press.

Albeck, J.H. (1994). Intergenerational consequences of trauma: Reframing traps in treatment theory–A second-generation perspective. In M.B. Williams and J.F. Sommer, Jr. (Eds.), *Handbook of Post-Traumatic Therapy* (pp. 106–125). Westport, CT: Greenwood Press.

Alexander, F. (1950). *Psychosomatic Medicine.* New York: Norton.

Allen, J.G. (1995). *Coping with Trauma.* Washington DC: American Psychiatric Press.

American Psychiatric Association (1980/1994). *Diagnostic and Statistical Manual of Mental Disorders* (3rd and 4th eds). Washington DC: American Psychiatric Association.

Appels, A., & Mulder, P. (1989). Fatigue and heart disease. The association between "vital exhaustion" and past, present and future coronary heart disease. *Journal of Psychosomatic Research, 33*(6), 727–738.

Ardrey, R. (1967). *The Territorial Imperative. A Personal Inquiry into the Animal Origins of Property and Nations.* London: Collins.

Athens, L.H. (1989). *The Creation of Dangerous Violent Criminals.* London, New York: Routledge.

Barefoot, J.C., Dodge, K.A., Peterson, B.L., Dahlstrom, W.G., & Williams, X.B. (1989). The Cook-Medley hostility scale: Item content and ability to predict survival. *Psychosomatic Medicine, 51,* 46–57.

Barker, P. (1996). *The Regeneration Trilogy.* London: Viking.

Bartemeier, L.H., Kubie, L.S., Menninger, K.A., Romano, J., & Whitehorn, J.C. (1946). Combat exhaustion. *Journal of Nervous and Mental Disease, 104,* 358–389.

Bartrop, R.W., Lazarus, L., Luckhurst, E., Kiloh, I.G., & Penny, R. (1977). Depressed lymphocyte function after bereavement. *Lancet, 1,* 834–836.

Batson, C.D. (1978). Altruism and human kindness; Internal and external determinants of helping behavior. In L.A. Pervin and M. Lewis (Eds.), *Perspectives in Interactional Psychology.* New York: Plenum Press.

Bauer, M., Priebe, S., Häring, B., & Adamczak, K. (1993). Long-term sequelae of political imprisonment in East Germany. *Journal of Nervous and Mental Disease, 181*(4), 257–262.

Beck, A. T. (1976). *Cognitive Therapy and the Emotional Disorders.* New York: International Universities Press.

Becker, E. (1973). *The Denial of Death.* New York: The Free Press.

Benyakar, M., Kutz, I., Dasberg, H., & Stern, M.J. (1989). The collapse of a structure: A structural approach to trauma. *Journal of Traumatic Stress, 2*(4), 431–449.

Berah, E., Jones, H.J., & Valent, P. (1984). The experience of a mental health team involved in the early phase of a disaster. *Australian and New Zealand Journal of Psychiatry, 18,* 354–358.

Bergman, M.S. (1982). Recurrent problems in the treatment of survivors and their children. In M.S. Bergman and M.E. Jucovy (Eds.), *Generations of the Holocaust* (pp. 247–266). New York: Columbia University Press.

Bettelheim, B. (1943). Individual and mass behaviour in extreme situations. *The Journal of Abnormal and Social Psychology, 38*(4), 417–452.

Bettelheim, B. (1960). *The Informed Heart.* Illinois: The Free Press of Glencoe.

Blanchard, D.C., & Blanchard, R.J. (1988). Ethoexperimental approaches to the biology of emotion. *Annual Review of Psychology, 39,* 43–68.

Bloch, H.S. (1969). Army clinical psychiatry in the combat zone, 1967–1968. *American Journal of Psychiatry, 126*(3), 37–46.

Boman, B. (1982). The Vietnam veteran ten years on. *Australian and New Zealand Journal of Psychiatry, 16,* 107–127.

Booth, A., Shelley, G., & Mazur, A. (1990). Testosterone, and winning and losing in human competition. *Journal of Cell Biology, 110,* 43–52.

Bowlby, J. (1971). *Attachment and Loss: Vol. 1. Attachment.* Harmondsworth: Pelican.

Bowlby, J. (1975). *Attachment and Loss: Vol. 2. Separation.* Harmondsworth: Pelican.

Bowlby, J. (1981). *Attachment and Loss: Vol. 3. Loss: Sadness and Depression.* New York: Penguin.

Brainerd, C.J. (1978). *Piaget's theory of intelligence.* Englewood Cliffs, NJ: Prentice-Hall.

Brandon, S., Boakes, J., Glaser, D., & Green, R. (1998). Recovered memories of childhood sexual abuse. *British Journal of Psychiatry, 172,* 296–307.

Braun, B. G. (1993). Multiple personality disorder and posttraumatic stress disorder. In J. Wilson and B. Raphael (Eds.), *International Handbook of Traumatic Stress Syndromes* (pp. 35–48). New York: Plenum Press.

Bremner, J.D., Krystal, J.H., Southwick, S.M., & Charney, D.S. (1995). Functional neuroanatomical correlates of the effects of stress on memory. *Journal of Traumatic Stress, 8*(4), 527–554.

Bremner, J.D., & Marmar, C.R. (1998). *Trauma, Memory, and Dissociations.* Washington DC: American Psychiatric Press.

Bremner, J.D., Vermetten, E., Southwick, S.M., Krystal, J.H., & Charney, D.S. (1998). Trauma, memory, and dissociation: An integrative formulation. In J.D. Bremner and C.R. Marmar (Eds.), *Trauma, Memory, and Dissociation.* Washington: American Psychiatric Press.

Brende, J.O. (1993). A 12-step recovery progrm for victims of traumatic events. In J. Wilson and B. Rapael (Eds.), *International Handbook of Traumatic Stress Syndromes* (pp. 867–878). New York: Plenum Press.

Brett, E.A. (1996). The classification of posttraumatic stress disorder. In B.A. van der Kolk, A.C. McFarlane, and L. Weisath (Eds.), *Traumatic Stress: The Effects of Overwhelming Experience on Mind, Body, and Society* (pp. 117–128). New York: Guildford.

Breuer, J., & Freud, S. (1893). *Studies in hysteria.* In J. Strachey (Ed.) (1975), *The Standard Edition of the Complete Psychological Works of Sigmund Freud* (Vol. 2, pp. 1–251). London: The Hogarth Press.

Briere, J. (1992). *Abuse Trauma: Theory and Treatment of Lasting Effects.* Newbury Park, CA: Sage.

Briere, J. (1995). A self-trauma model for treating adult survivors of severe child abuse. In L. Berliner, J. Bulkley, C. Jenny, and T. Reid (Eds.), *The APSAC Handbook on Child Maltreatment.* Newbury Park, CA: Sage.

Browning, C.R. (1992). *Ordinary Men: Reserve Police Battalion 101 and the Final Solution in Poland.* New York: Harper Perennial.

Busuttil, W., & Busuttil, A. (1997). Debriefing and crisis intervention. In D. Black, M. Newman, J. Harris–Hendriks, and G. Mezey (Eds.), *Psychological Trauma* (pp. 238–249) London: Gaskell.

Calabrese, J.R., Kling, M.A., & Gold, P.W. (1987). Alterations in immunocompetence during stress, bereavement, and depression: Focus on neuroendocrine regulation. *American Journal of Psychiatry, 144*(9), 1123–1134.

Callahan, R. J. (1985). *Five Minute Phobia Cure.* Wilmington: Enterprise.

Callahan, R. J. (1993). *Why Do I Eat When I'm Not Hungry?* New York: Avon Books.

Callahan, R. J. (1996). A thought field (TFT) algorithm for trauma. *Traumatology (electronic journal), 1*(1).

Cameron-Bandler, L. (1978). *They Lived Happily Ever After.* Cupertino, CA: Meta Publications.

Canetti, E. (1973). *Crowds and Power.* New York: Penguin.

Cannon, W.B. (1939). *The Wisdom of the Body.* New York: Norton.

Cannon, W.B. (1963). *Bodily Change in Pain, Hunger, Fear, and Rage.* New York: Harper Torchbooks.

Carbonell, J.L., & Figley, C.R. (1996). A systematic clinical demonstration methodology: A collaboration between practitioners and clinical researchers. *Traumatology (electronic journal), 2*(1).

Chester, B. (1995). "That which does not destroy me": Treating survivors of political torture. In M.B. Williams and J.F. Sommer Jr. (Eds.), *Handbook of Post-Traumatic Therapy* (pp. 240–251). Westport, CT: Greenwood Press.

Coe, C.L., Wiener, S.G., Rosenberg, L.T., & Levine, S. (1985). Endocrine and immune responses to separation and maternal loss in nonhuman primates. In M. Reite and T. Field (Eds.), *The Psychobiology of Attachment and Separation* (pp. 163–200). New York: Academic Press.

Cohen, R.E., & Ahearn, F.L. (1980). *Handbook for Mental Health Care of Disaster Victims.* Maryland: John Hopkins University Press.

Collins, J.J., & Bailey, S.L. (1990). Traumatic stress disorder and violent behavior. *Journal of Traumatic Stress, 3*(2), 203–220.

Cummings, E.M., Hollenbeck, B., & Iannotti, R. (1986). Early organization of altruism and aggression: Developmental patterns and individual differences. In C. Zahn-Waxler, E.M. Cummings, and R. Iannotti (Eds.), *Altruism and Aggression (Biological and Social Origins)* (pp. 165–188). Cambridge: Cambridge University Press.

Cunningham, M., & Silove, D. (1993). Principles of treatment and service development for torture and trauma survivors. In J. Wilson and B. Raphael (Eds.), *International Handbook of Traumatic Stress Syndromes* (pp. 751–762). New York: Plenum Press.

Czikszentmihalyi, M., & Rathunde, K. (1993). The psychology of wisdom: An evolutionary interpretation. In R.J. Sternberg (Ed.), *Wisdom: Its Nature, Origins, and Development* (pp. 25–51). New York: Cambridge University Press.

Danieli, Y. (1980). Countertransference in the treatment and study of Nazi Holocaust survivors and their children. *Victimology: An International Journal, 5,* 355–367.

Danieli, Y. (1985). The treatment and prevention of long-term effects and intergenerational transmission of victimization: A lesson from Holocaust survivors and their children. In C.R. Figley (Ed.), *Trauma and Its Wake: The Study and Treatment of Post-Traumatic Stress Disorder* (pp. 295–313). New York: Brunner/Mazel.

Davidson, J.R.T., & van der Kolk, B.A. (1996). The psychopharmacological treatment of post-traumatic stress disorder. In B.A. Van der Kolk, A.C. McFarlane, and L. Weisath (Eds.), *Traumatic Stress: The Effects of Overwhelming Experience on Mind, Body, and Society* (pp. 510–524). New York: Guildford Press.

Davidson, L.M., Fleming, I., & Baum, A. (1986). Post-traumatic stress as a function of chronic stress and toxic exposure. In C.R. Figley (Ed.), *Trauma and Its Wake, Vol. II: Traumatic Stress Theory, Research, and Intervention* (p. 77). New York: Brunner/Mazel.

De Wind, E. (1971). Psychotherapy after traumatization caused by persecution. In H. Krystal and W.G. Niederland (Eds.), *Psychic Traumatization: Aftereffects in Individuals and Communities,* International Psychiatry Clinics (pp. 93–114). Boston: Little Brown.

Dimsdale, J.E. (1974). The coping behaviour of Nazi concentration camp survivors. *American Journal of Psychiatry, 131,* 792–797.

Donovan, D.M. (1991). Traumatology: A field whose time has come. *Journal of Traumatic Stress, 4,* 433–437.

Donovan, D.M. (1993). Traumatology: What's in a name? *Journal of Traumatic Stress, 6,* 409–412.

Dunn, W.H. (1942). Gastroinduodenal disorders: An important wartime medical problem. *War Medicine, 2,* 967–983.

Dutton, M.A. (1992). Assessment and treatment of post-traumatic stress disorder among battered women. In David W. Foy (Ed.), *Treating PTSD.* New York: Guildford Press.

Eisdorfer, C. (1985). The conceptualization of stress and a model for further study. In M.R. Zales (Ed.), *Stress in Health and Disease.* New York: Brunner/Mazel.

Ellis A., & Grieger, R. (Eds.). (1976). *Handbook of Rational-Emotive Therapy.* New York: Springer.

Engel, G.L. (1961). Is grief a disease? *Psychosomatic Medicine, 23,* 18–22.

Engel, G.L. (1977). The need for a new medical model: A challenge for biomedicine. *Science, 196,* 129–135.

Engel, G.L., & Schmale, A.H. (1972). *Conversation-withdrawal: A primary regulatory process for organismic homeostasis.* Ciba Foundation Symposium: Physiology of Emotion and Psychosomatic Illness. Elsevier, New York: Associated Scientific Publishers.

Field, T., & Reite, M. (1985). The psychobiology of attachment and separation: A summary. In M. Reite and T. Field (Eds.), *The Psychobiology of Attachment and Separation.* New York: Academic Press.

Figley, C.R. (1985). Introduction. In C.R. Figley (Ed.), *Trauma and Its Wake: The Study and Treatment of Post-traumatic Stress Disorder* (pp. xii–xxvi). New York: Brunner/Mazel.

Figley, C.R. (1988a). Post-traumatic family therapy. In F.M. Ochberg (Ed.), *Post-Traumatic Therapy and Victims of Violence* (pp. 83–109). New York: Brunner/Mazel

Figley, C.R. (1988b). Toward a field of traumatic stress. *Journal of Traumatic Stress, 1*(1), 3–16.

Figley, C.R., Carbonell, J.L. (1994). *The active ingredient project: Eliminating and preventing post-traumatic stress disorder.* Symp. Psychosocial Stress Research Program, Florida State University, Tallahassee, FL.

Figley, C.R. (1995a). Compassion fatigue as secondary traumatic stress disorder: An overview. In C.R. Figley, *Compassion Fatigue: Secondary Traumatic Stress Disorder in Helpers* (pp. 1–20). New York: Brunner/Mazel.

Figley, C.R. (1995b) (Ed.). *Compassion Fatigue: Secondary Traumatic Stress Disorder in Helpers.* New York: Brunner/Mazel.

Figley, C.R. (1996). The active ingredient hypothesis forum (electronic).

Figley, C.R. (1996a). Personal communication.

Figley, C.R. (1997). Personal communication.

Fleshner, M., Laudenslager, M.L., Simons, L., & Maier, S.F. (1989). Reduced serum antibodies associated with social defeat in rats. *Physiology and Behavior, 45,* 1183–1187.

Foa, E.B., Molnar, C., & Cashman, L. (1995). Change in rape narratives during exposure therapy for posttraumatic stress disorder. *Journal of Traumatic Stress, 8*(4), 675–690.

Foa, E.B., Steketee, G., & Rothbaum, B.O. (1989). Behavioral/cognitive conceptualizations of post-traumatic stress disorder. *Behavior Therapy, 20,* 155–176.

Fogelman, E. (1989). Group treatment as a therapeutic modality for generations of the Holocaust. In P. Marcus and A. Rosenberg (Eds.), *Healing Their Wounds: Psychotherapy with Holocaust Survivors and Their Families* (pp. 119–133). New York: Praeger.

Folks, D.G., & Kinney, F.C. (1995). Gastrointestinal conditions. In A. Stoudmire (Ed.), *Psychological Factors Affecting Medical Conditions.* Washington DC: American Psychiatric Press.

Foreman, C. (1994). Immediate post-disaster treatment of trauma. In M.B. Williams and J.F. Sommer Jr., *Handbook of Post-Traumatic Therapy* (pp. 267–282). Westport, CT: Greenwood Press.

Foy, D.W. (Ed.). (1992). *Treating PTSD: Cognitive-Behavioral Strategies.* New York: Guildford.

Frankl, V.E. (1959). *From Death-Camp to Existentialism.* Boston: International Universities Press, Beacon Press.

Frankl, V.E. (1967). *Psychotherapy and Existentialism.* New York: Washington Square Press.

Freud, S. (1886/1975). Report of my studies in Paris and Berlin. In J. Strachey (Ed.), *The Standard Edition of the Complete Psychological Works of Sigmund Freud* (Vol. 1, pp. 3–15). London: Hogarth Press.

Freud, S. (1888). Hysteria. *S.E., 1.*

Freud, S. (1894). The neuro-psychoses of defence. *S.E., 3.*

Freud, S. (1895). Studies on hysteria. *S.E., 2.*

Freud, S. (1905a) Fragment of an analysis of a case of hysteria. *S.E., 7,* pp. 3–122.

Freud, S. (1905b). Three essays on the theory of sexuality. *S.E., 7.*

Freud, S. (1914a) Remembering, repeating, and working-through. *S.E., 12,* pp. 147–156.

Freud, S. (1917). Mourning and melancholia. *S.E., 14.*

Freud, S. (1919) Introduction to psycho-analysis and the war neuroses. *S.E., 17,* 205–210.

Freud, S. (1920). Beyond the pleasure principle. *S.E., 18.*

Freud, S. (1921). Group psychology. *S.E., 18.*

Freud, S. (1926). Inhibitions, symptoms, and anxiety. *S.E., 20.*

Friedman, M.J. (1991). Biological approaches to the diagnosis and treatment of post-traumatic stress disorder. *Journal of Traumatic Stress, 4*(1), 67–91.

Friedman, M.J. (1993). Psychobiological and pharmacological approaches to treatment. In J. Wilson and B. Raphael (Eds.), *International Handbook of Traumatic Stress Syndromes* (pp. 785–794). New York: Plenum Press.

Gallo, F.P. (1996). Reflections on active ingredients in efficient treatments of PTSD. *Traumatology* (electronic), 2 (Parts 1, 2).

Gerbode, F. (1988). *Beyond Psychology: An Introduction to Metapsychology.* Palo Alto: IRM Press.

Gerbode, F. (1995). Traumatic incident reduction at the active ingredient project: A collaboration between practitioners and clinical researchers. Florida State University (unpublished), Tallahassee, FL.

Gibbs, M.S. (1989). Factors in the victim that mediate between disaster and psychopathology: A review. *Journal of Traumatic Stress, 2*(4), 489–514.

Glass, A.J. (1959). Psychological aspects of disaster. *Journal of American Medical Association, 171*(2), 222–225.

Goldstein, M.G., & Niaura, R. (1992). Psychological factors affecting physical condition. *Psychosomatics, 33*(2), 134–145.

Goldstein, M.G., & Niaura, R. (1995). Cardiovascular disease, part I: Coronary artery disease and sudden death. In A. Stoudemire (Ed.), *Psychological Factors Affecting Medical Conditions* (pp. 19–37). Washington DC: American Psychiatric Press.

Goodstein, R.K. (1984). Cerebrovascular accident: A multidimensional clinical problem. In D.W. Krueger (Ed.), *Emotional Rehabilitation of Physical Trauma and Disability* (pp. 157–170). Lancaster, England: MPH Press.

Grinker, R.R., & Spiegel, J.P. (1944). Brief psychotherapy in war neuroses. *Psychosomatic Medicine, 6,* 123–131.

Grinker, R.R., & Spiegel, J.P. (1945/1979). *Men Under Stress.* New York: Irvington.

Groen, J.J. (1976). Present status of the psychosomatic approach to bronchial asthma. In O.W. Hill (Ed.), *Modern Trends in Psychosomatic Medicine 3* (pp. 231–259). London, Boston: Butterworths.

Guntrip, H. (1973). *Psychoanalytic Theory, Therapy, and the Self.* New York: Basic Books.

Hammarberg, M., & Silver, S.M. (1994). Outcome of treatment for post-traumatic stress disorder in a primary care unit serving Vietnam veterans. *Journal of Traumatic Stress, 7*(2), 195–216.

Hartman, C.R., & Burgess, A.W. (1988). Rape trauma and treatment of the victim. In F.M. Ochberg (Ed.), *Post-Traumatic Therapy and Victims of Violence* (pp. 152–174). New York: Brunner/Mazel.

Harvey, J.H., Orbuch, T.L., Chwalisz, K.D., & Garwood, G. (1991). Coping with sexual assault: The roles of account-making and confiding. *Journal of Traumatic Stress, 4*(4), 515–532.

Hatfield, E., & Rapson, R. (1993). Love and attachment processes. In M. Lewis and J.M. Itaviland (Eds.), *Handbook of Emotions.* New York: Guildford.

Heath, R.G. (1992). Correlation of brain activity with emotion: A basis for developing treatment of violent-aggressive behavior. *Journal of the American Academy of Psychoanalysis, 20*(3), 335–346.

Heffron, E.F. (1977). Project outreach: Crisis intervention following natural disaster. *Journal of Community Psychiatry, 5*, 103–111.

Henry, J.P. (1986). Neuroendocrine patterns of emotional response. *Emotion: Theory, Research, and Experience, 3*, 37–60.

Henry, J.P. (1986a). Mechanisms by which stress can lead to coronary heart disease. *Postgraduate Medical Journal, 62*, 687–693.

Herman, J.L. (1981). *Father-Daughter Incest.* Cambridge, MA: Harvard University Press.

Herman, J.L. (1992). *Trauma and Recovery.* New York: Basic Books.

Herman, J., & Lawrence, L.R. (1995). Group therapy and self-help groups for adult survivors of childhood incest. In M.B. Williams and J.F. Sommer Jr. (Eds.), *Handbook of Post-Traumatic Therapy* (pp. 440–452). Westport, CT: Greenwood Press.

Hobbs, M., Mayon, R., Harrison, B., & Worlock, P. (1996). A randomized controlled trial of psychological debriefing for victims of road traffic accidents. *British Medical Journal, 313*, 1438–1439.

Hoch, F., Werle, E., & Weicker, H. (1988). Sympathoadrenergic regulation in elite fencers in training and competition. *International Journal of Sports Medicine, 9* (Supplement 2), 141–145.

Hocking, F.H. (1970). Psychiatric aspects of extreme environmental stress. *Diseases of the Nervous System, 31*, 542–545.

Holmes, T.H., & Rahe, R.H. (1967). The social readjustment rating scale. *Journal of Psychosomatic Research, 11*, 213–218.

Hoppe, K.D. (1968). Psychotherapy with concentration camp survivors. In H. Krystal (Ed.), *Massive Psychic Trauma* (pp. 204–219). New York: International Universities Press.

Horowitz, M. (1974). Stress response syndromes: Character style and dynamic psychotherapy. *Archives of General Psychiatry, 31*, 768–781.

Horowitz M. (1976/1992). *Stress Response Syndromes.* New York: Aronson.

Humphrey, N. (1993). *A History of the Mind.* London: Vintage.

Ingersoll, D.E., & Matthews, R.K. (1986). *The Philosophic Roots of Modern Ideology: Liberalism, Communism, Fascism.* Englewood, NJ: Prentice–Hall.

International Society of Traumatic Stress Studies. (1998). *Childhood Trauma Remembered: A Report on the Current Scientific Knowledge Base and Its Applications.*

Irwin, M., Daniels, M., & Weiner, H. (1987). Immune and neuroendocrine changes during bereavement. *Psychiatric Clinics of North America, 10*(3), 449–465.

Isaac, G.L. (1977). Traces of pleistocene hunters: An African example. In R.B. Lee and I. DeVore (Eds.), *Man the Hunter.* Chicago: Aldine.

Jemmott, J.B. (1987). Social motives and susceptibility to disease: Stalking individual differences in health risks. *Journal of Personality, 55*, 267–298.

Kardiner, A. (1941). *The Traumatic Neuroses of War.* New York: Paul B. Hoeber.

Kenardy, J.A., Webster, R.A., Lewin, T.J., Carr, V.J., Hazell, P.L., & Carter, G.L. (1996). Stress debriefing and patterns of recovery following a natural disaster. *Journal of Traumatic Stress, 9*, 37–49.

Kernberg, O. (1975). *Borderline Conditions and Pathological Narcissism.* New York: Science House.

Kestenberg, J. (1992). Children of survivors and child survivors. *Echoes of the Holocaust, 1*, 26–50.

Khan, M.M.R. (1964). Ego distortion, cumulative trauma, and the role of reconstruction in the analytic situation. *International Journal of Psychoanalysis, 45*, 272–279.

Kleber, R.J., & Brom, D. (1992). *Coping with Trauma: Theory, Prevention, and Treatment.* Amsterdam: Swets & Zeitlinger.

Klein, H. (1968). Problems in the psychotherapeutic treatment of Israeli survivors of the Holocaust. In H. Krystal (Ed.), *Massive Psychic Trauma* (pp. 233–244). New York: International Universities Press.

Klein, M. (1957/1975). Envy and gratutide. In M. Klein (Ed.), *Envy and Gratitude, and Other Works 1946–1963*. London: The Hogarth Press.

Kleiner, J. (1970). On nostalgia. *Bulletin of Philadelpia Association of Psychoanalysis, 20*, 11–30.

Knapp, P.H., Levy, E.M., Giorgi, R.G., Black, P.H., Fox, B.H., & Heeren, T.C. (1992). Short-term immunological effects of induced emotion. *Psychosomatic Medicine, 54*, 133–148.

Knol, B.W., & Egbering-Alink, S.T. (1989). Androgens, progestatens and agonistic behaviour: A review. *The Veterinary Quarterly, 11*(2), 94–101.

Koestler, A. (1974). *The Urge to Self-Destruction. The Heel of Achilles Essays.* Hutchinson: London.

Koestler, A. (1983). *Janus: A Summing Up.* London: Picador.

Kohlberg, L. (1981). *The meaning and measurement of moral development.* Heinz Warner Lecture Series. Worcester, MA: Clark University Press.

Kohlberg, L. (1985). A current statement on some theoretical issues. In J. Modgil and C. Modgil (Eds.), *Consensus and Controversy.* Philadelphia, PA: The Falmer Press.

Kohut, H. (1971). The Analysis of the Self. *Psychoanalytic Study of the Child* (monograph). New York: International Universities Press.

Kraemer, G.W. (1985). Effects of differences in early social experience on primate neurobiological-behavioral development. In M. Reite and T. Field (Eds.), *The Psychobiology of Attachment and Separation* (pp. 135–161). New York: Academic Press.

Krell, R. (1989). Alternative therapeutic approaches to Holocaust survivors. In P. Marcus and A. Rosenberg (Eds.), *Healing Their Wounds: Psychotherapy with Holocaust Survivors and Their Families* (pp. 215–226). New York: Praeger.

Krystal, H. (1971). Trauma: Considerations of its intensity and chronicity. In H. Krystal and W.G. Niederland (Eds.), *Psychic Traumatization: Aftereffects in Individuals and Communities* (pp 11–28). International Psychiatry Clinics. Boston: Little Brown.

Kubanyi, E.S., Gino, A., Denny, N.R., & Torigoe, R.Y. (1994). Relationship of cynical hostility and PTSD among Vietnam combat veterans. *Journal of Traumatic Stress, 7*(1), 21–32.

Kübler-Ross, E. (1969). *On Death and Dying.* New York: Macmillan.

Lane, R.D., & Schwartz, G.E. (1987). Levels of emotional awareness: A cognitive-developmental theory and its application to psychopathology. *American Journal of Psychiatry, 144*(2), 133–143.

Laub, D., & Auerhahn, N.C. (1993). Knowing and not knowing massive psychic trauma: Forms of traumatic memory. *International Journal of Psychoanalysis, 74*, 287–302.

Laughlin, W.S. (1977). An integrating biobehavior system and its evolutionary importance. In R.B. Lee and I. DeVore (Eds.), *Man the Hunter.* Chicago, IL: Aldine.

Lazarus, R.S., & Folkman, S. (1984). *Stress, Appraisal, and Coping.* New York: Springer.

Leavitt, F. (1997). False attribution of suggestibility to explain recovered memory of childhood sexual abuse following extended amnesia. *Child Abuse and Neglect, 21*, 265–272.

Lee, R.B. (1977). What hunters do for a living, or how to make out on scarce resources. In R.B. Lee and I. DeVore (Eds.), *Man the Hunter.* Chicago, IL: Aldine.

Levenson, J.L., & Bemis, C. (1995). Cancer onset and progression. In A. Stoudemire (Ed.), *Psychological Factors Affecting Medical Conditions* (pp. 81–98). Washington DC: American Psychiatric Press.

Lewis, M. (1995). Memory and psychoanalysis: A new look at infantile amnesia and transference. *Journal of the American Academy of Child and Adolescent Psychiatry, 34*, 405–417.

Lidz, T. (1946). Psychiatric casualties from Guadacanal. *Psychiatry, 9*, 193–213.

Liebowitz, M.R. (1983). *The Chemistry of Love.* Boston: Little Brown.

Lifton, R.J. (1967). *Death in Life.* New York: Touchstone, Simon and Schuster.

Lifton, R.J. (1973). *Home from the War.* New York: Touchstone, Simon and Schuster.

Lifton, R.J. (1978). Advocacy and corruption in the healing profession. In Charles R. Figley (Ed.), *Stress Disorders Among Vietnam Veterans* (pp. 209–230). New York: Brunner/Mazel.

Lifton, R.J. (1980). *The Broken Connection.* New York: Touchstone.

Lifton, R.J. (1986). *The Nazi Doctors*. London: Papermac.

Lilar, S. (1965). *Aspects of Love in Western Society*. London: Thames and Hudson.

Lindy, J.D. (Ed.) (1988). *Vietnam: A Casebook*. New York: Brunner/Mazel.

Loftus, E.F. (1993). The reality of repressed memories. *American Psychologist, 48*(5), 518–537.

Lum, L.C. (1975). Hyperventilation: The tip and the iceberg. *Journal of Psychosomatic Research, 19*, 375–383.

MacLean, P.D. (1973). *A triune concept of the brain and behaviour*. Toronto: Toronto University Press.

MacLean, P.D. (1985). Brain evolution relating to family, play, and the separation call. *Archives of General Psychiatry, 42*, 405–417.

Maier, S.F., & Seligman, M.E.P. (1976). Learned helplessness: theory and evidence. *Journal of Experimental Psychology, 105*, 3–46.

Manton, M., & Talbot, A. (1990). Crisis intervention after an armed hold-up: Guidelines for counselors. *Journal of Traumatic Stress, 3*(4), 507–522.

Marmar, C.R., Weiss, D.S., Schlenger, W.E., Fairbank, J.A., Kulka, R.A., & Hough, R.L. (1994). Peritraumatic dissociation and posttraumatic stress in male Vietnam theater veterans. *American Journal of Psychiatry, 151*, 902–907.

Maslow, A.H. (1970). *Motivation and Personality*. New York: Harper and Row.

Mason, J.W. (1968). The scope of psychoendocrine research. *Psychosomatic Medicine, 30*, 5(2), 565–574.

Masson, J.M. (1984). *The Assault on Truth: Freud's Suppression of the Seduction Theory*. New York: Penguin.

McClelland, D.C. (1975). *Power: The Inner Experience*. New York: Irvington Publishers.

McFarlane, A.C. (1988). The longitudinal course of posttraumatic morbidity: The range of outcomes and their predictors. *Journal of Nervous and Mental Disease, 176*(1), 30–39.

McFarlane, A.C., & de Girolamo, G. (1996) The nature of traumatic stressors and the epidemiology of posttraumatic reactions. In A.C. McFarlane and L. Weisath (Eds.), *Traumatic Stress: The Effects of Overwhelming Experience on Mind, Body, and Society* (pp. 129–154). New York: Guildford Press.

McFarlane, A.C., & van der Kolk, B.A. (1996). Conclusions and future directions. In B.A. Van der Kolk, A.C. McFarlane, and L. Weisath (Eds.), *Traumatic Stress: The Effects of Overwhelming Experience on Mind, Body, and Society*. New York: Guildford Press.

McFarlane, A.C., & Yehuda, R. (1995). Conflict between current knowledge about post-traumatic stress disorder and its original conceptual basis. *American Journal of Psychiatry, 152*, 1705–1713.

Meichenbaum, D., & Cameron, R. (1983). Stress inoculation training. Toward a general paradigm for training coping skills. In D. Meichenbaum and M.E. Jaremko (Eds.), *Stress Reduction and Prevention*. New York: Plenum.

Merwin, M.R., & Smith-Kurtz, B. (1988). Healing of the whole person. In F.M. Ochberg (Ed.), *Post-Traumatic Therapy and Victims of Violence* (pp. 57–82). New York: Brunner/Mazel.

Mitchell, J.T., & Dyregrov, A. (1993). Traumatic stress in disaster workers and emergency personnel: Prevention and intervention. In J. Wilson and B. Raphael (Eds.), *International Handbook of Traumatic Stress Syndromes* (pp. 905–914). New York: Plenum.

Mitchell, J.T., & Everly, G.S. (1995). Critical incident stress debriefing (CISD) and the prevention of work-related traumatic stress among high risk occupational groups. In G.S. Everly and J.M. Lating (Eds.), *Psychotraumatology: Key Papers and Core Concepts in Post-Traumatic Stress* (pp. 267–280). New York: Plenum.

Moran, M.G. (1995). Pulmonary and rheumatologic diseases. In A. Stoudemire (Ed.), *Psychological Factors Affecting Medical Conditions* (pp. 141–158). Washington DC: American Psychiatric Press.

Needles, W. (1946). The regression of psychiatry in the army. *Psychiatry, 9*, 167–185.

Niaura, R., & Goldstein, M.G. (1992). Psychological factors affecting physical condition: Cardiovascular disease literature review. *Psychosomatics, 33*(2), 146–153.

Niaura, R., & Goldstein, M.G. (1995). Cardiovascular disease, part II: Coronary artery disease and sudden death and hypertension. In A. Stoudemire (Ed.), *Psychological Factors Affecting Medical Conditions* (pp. 39–56). Washington DC: American Psychiatric Press.

Ochberg, F.M. (Ed.) (1988). *Post-Traumatic Therapy and Victims of Violence.* New York: Brunner/ Mazel.

Ochberg, F.M. (1993). Post-traumatic therapy. In J. Wilson and B. Raphael (Eds.), *International Handbook of Traumatic Stress Syndromes.* New York: Plenum.

Öhman, A. (1993). Fear and anxiety as emotional phenomena: Clinical phenomenology, evolutionary perspectives, and information-processing mechanisms. In M. Lewis and J.M. Haviland (Eds.), *Handbook of Emotions* (pp. 511–536). New York: Guildford Press.

Olweus, D., Mattsson, A., Schalling, D., & Low, H. (1988). Circulating testosterone levels and aggression in adolescent males: A causal analysis. *Psychosomatic Medicine, 50*(3), 261–272.

Panksepp, J. (1986). The neurochemistry of behavior. *Annual Review of Psychology, 37,* 77–107.

Panksepp, J. (1986a). The anatomy of emotions. In R. Plutchnik and H. Kellerman (Eds.), *Emotion: Theory, Research and Experience,* Vol. III. New York: Academic Press.

Panksepp, J. (1989b). The neurobiology of emotions: Of animal brains and human feelings. In H. Wagner and A. Manstead (Eds.), *Handbook of Social Psychophysiology.* New York: John Wiley and Sons.

Panksepp, J. (1993). Neurochemical control of moods and emotions: Amino acids to neuropeptides. In M. Lewis and J.M. Haviland (Eds.), *Handbook of Emotion* (pp. 87–107). New York: Guildford Press.

Panksepp, J., Siviy, S.M., & Normansell, L.A. (1985). Brain opioids and social emotions. In M. Reite and T. Field (Eds.), *The Psychobiology of Attachment and Separation* (pp. 3–50). New York: Academic Press.

Parad, H.J., Resnik, H.L.P., & Parad, L.G. (Eds.). (1976). *Emergency and Disaster Management.* Bowie, Maryland: Charles Press.

Parkes, C.M. (1972). *Bereavement: Studies of Grief in Adult Life.* London: Tavistock.

Parkes, C.M., & Weiss, R.S. (1983). *Recovery from Bereavement.* New York: Basic Books.

Pearlman, L.A., & Saakvitne, K.W. (1995). *Trauma and the Therapist.* New York: Norton.

Pearlman, L.A., & McCann, I.L. (1994). Integrating structured and unstructured approaches to taking a trauma history. In M.B. Williams and J.F. Sommer Jr., *Handbook of Post-Traumatic Therapy* (pp. 38–48). Westport, CT: Greenwood Press.

Pettera, R.L., Johnson, B.M., & Zimmer, R. (1969). Psychiatric management of combat reactions with emphasis on a reaction unique to Vietnam. *Military Medicine, 134*(9), 673–678.

Pynoos, R.S., & Eth, S. (1985). Developmental perspective on psychic trauma in childhood. In C.R. Figley (Ed.), *Trauma and Its Wake.* (pp. 36–52). New York: Brunner/Mazel.

Pynoos, R.S., & Nader, K. (1988). Psychological first aid and treatment approach to children exposed to community violence: Research implications. *Journal of Traumatic Stress. 4,* 445–473.

Pynoos, R.S., & Nader, K. (1989). *Prevention of Psychiatric Morbidity in Children After Disaster.* In D. Shaffer, I. Philips, N.B. Enzer, and N.B. (Eds.), OSAP Prevention Monograph 2. Prevention of Mental Disorders, Alcohol and Other Drug Use in Children and Adolescents. DHHS Publication (ADM) 89–1646 (pp. 225–271). Washington DC: U.S. Government Printing Office.

Pynoos, R.S., & Nader, K. (1991). Play and drawing techniques as tools for interviewing traumatised children. In C.E. Schaefer, K. Gitlin, and A. Sandgrund (Eds.), *Play, Diagnosis, and Assessment.* New York: John Wiley & Sons.

Pynoos, R.S., Steinberg, A.M., & Goenjian, A. (1996). Traumatic stress in childhood and adolescence: Recent developments and current controversies. In B.A. van der Kolk, A.C. McFarlane, and L. Weisath (Eds.), *Traumatic Stress: The Effects of Overwhelming Experience on Mind, Body, and Society* (pp. 331–358). New York: Guildford Press.

Quarantelli, E.L. (1954). The nature and conditions of panic. *American Journal of Sociology, 60,* 267–275.

Rando, T.A. (1993). *Treatment of Complicated Mourning.* Champaign, IL: Research Press.

Raphael, B. (1984). *The Anatomy of Bereavement.* London: Hutchinson.

Raphael, B. (1986). *When Disaster Strikes.* London: Hutchinson.

Raphael, B., Wilson, J., Meldrum, L., & McFarlane, A.C. (1996). Acute preventive interventions. In B.A. van der Kolk, A.C. McFarlane, and L. Weisath (Eds.), *Traumatic Stress: The Effects of Overwhelming Experience on Mind, Body, and Society* (pp. 463–479). New York: Guildford Press.

Raphael, B. (1997). The interaction of trauma and grief. In D. Black, M. Newman, J. Harris-Hendriks, and G. Mezey (Eds.), *Psychological Trauma* (pp. 31–43) London: Gaskell.

Rees, W.D., & Lutkins, S. (1967). Mortality of bereavement. *British Medical Journal, 4,* 13–16.

Resnick, H. S., & Newton, T. (1992). Assessment and treatment of post-traumatic stress disorder in adult survivors of sexual assault. In David W. Foy (Ed), *Treating PTSD.* New York: Guildford Press.

Robertson, J., & Robertson, J. (1967–1973). *Young Children in Brief Separation.* Film Series. London: Tavistock Child Development Research Unit. New York: New York University Film Library.

Robinson, D.M. (1993). Wisdom through the ages. In R.J. Sternberg (Ed.), *Wisdom: Its Nature, Origins and Development* (pp. 13–24). New York: Cambridge University Press.

Robinson, R.C., & Mitchell, J.T. (1993). Evaluation of psychological debriefings. *Journal of Traumatic Stress, 6*(3), 367–383.

Rosenblatt, J.S. (1989). The physiological and evolutionary background of maternal responsiveness. *New Directions for Child Development, 43,* 15–30.

Rothbaum, B.O., & Foa, E.B. (1993). Subtypes of post-traumatic stress disorder and duration of symptoms. In J.R.T. Davidson and E.B. Foa (Eds.), *Post-Traumatic Stress Disorder: DSM-IV and Beyond* (pp. 23–35).Washington DC: American Psychiatric Press.

Rozin, P., Haidt, J., & McCauley, C.R. (1993). Disgust. In M. Lewis and J.M. Haviland (Eds.), *Handbook of Emotions* (pp. 575–594). New York: Guildford Press.

Salasin, S.E., & Rich, R.F. (1993). Mental health policy for victims of violence: The case against women. In J. Wilson and B. Raphael (Eds.), *International Handbook of Traumatic Stress Syndromes* (pp. 947–956). New York: Plenum Press.

Salmon, T. (1919). The war neuroses and their lesson. *New York State Journal of Medicine, 59,* 933–934.

Sanner, P.H., & Wolcott, B.W. (1983). Stress reactions among participants in mass casualty simulations. *Annals of Emergency Medicine, 12,* 426–428.

Schmale, A.H. (1972). Giving up as a final common pathway to changes in health. *Advances in Psychosomatic Medicine, 8,* 20–40.

Scott, J.P. (1989). *The Evolution of Social Systems.* New York: Gordon and Breach Science Publishers.

Segal, H. (1975). *Introduction to the Work of Melanie Klein.* London: Hogarth.

Selye, H. (1936). A syndrome produced by various nocuous agents. *Nature (London), 148,* 84–85.

Selye, H. (1973). The evolution of the stress concept. *American Scientist, 61*(6), 692–699.

Shaikh, M.B., Brutus, M., Siegel, H.E., & Siegel, A. (1985). Topographically organized midbrain modulation of predatory and defensive aggression in the cat. *Brain Research, 336,* 308–12.

Shalev, A.Y. (1996). Stress versus traumatic stress: From acute homeostatic reactions to chronic psychopathology. In B.A. van der Kolk, A.C. McFarlane, and L. Weisath (Eds.), *Traumatic Stress: The Effects of Overwhelming Experience on Mind, Body, and Society* (pp. 77–101). New York: Guildford Press.

Shalev, A.Y., Orr, S.P., & Pitman, R.K. (1993). Psychophysiologic assessment of traumatic imagery in Israeli civilian patients with post-traumatic stress disorder. *American Journal of Psychiatry, 150,* 620–624.

Shalit, E. (1994). The relation between aggression and fear of annihilation in Israel. *Political Psychology, 15*(3), 415–434.

Shapiro, F. (1993). Eye movement desensitization and reprocessing (EMDR) in 1992. *Journal of Traumatic Stress, 6*(3), 417–422.

Shapiro, F. (1995). *Eye Movement Desensitization and Reprocessing: Basic Principles, Protocols, and Procedures.* New York: Guildford Press.

Sherman, J.S. (1998). Effects of psychotheraputic treatments for PTSD: A meta-analysis of controlled clinical trials. *Journal of Traumatic Stress, 11,* 413–435.

Silver, J.M., Sandberg, D.P., & Hales, R.E. (1990). New approaches in the pharmacotherapy of post-traumatic stress disorder. *Journal of Clinical Psychiatry, 51*(10) (Supplement), 33–38.

Silver, S.M., & Iacono, C. (1986). Symptom groups and family patterns of Vietnam veterans with post-traumatic stress disorders. In C.R. Figley (Ed.), *Trauma and Its Wake, Vol. II: Traumatic Stress Theory, Research, and Intervention* (pp. 78–96). New York: Brunner/Mazel.

Simpson, M.A. (1993). Traumatic stress and the bruising of the soul: The effects of torture and coercive interrogation. In J. Wilson and B. Raphael (Eds.), *International Handbook of Traumatic Stress Syndromes* (pp. 667–684). New York: Plenum Press.

Singh, B.S., & Raphael, B. (1981). Post-disaster morbidity of the bereaved. *Journal of Nervous and Mental Disease, 169*(4), 208–212.

Siporin, M. (1976) Altruism, disaster, and crisis intervention. In H. Parad, H.L.P. Resnik, and L.G. Parad (Eds.), *Emergency and Disaster Management* (pp. 213–229). Maryland: Charles Press.

Sipprelle, R.C. (1992). A vet center experience: Multievent trauma, delayed treatment type. In David W. Foy (Ed.). *Treating PTSD.* New York: Guildford Press.

Smith, G.C. (1991). The brain and higher mental function. *Australian and New Zealand Journal of Psychiatry, 25,* 215–230.

Smyth, L.D. (1994). *Clinician's Manual for the Cognitive-Behavioral Treatment of Post Traumatic Stress Disorder.* Havre de Grace: RTR Publishing.

Solomon, S.D., Gerritty, E.T., & Muff, A.M. (1992). Efficacy of treatments for post-traumatic stress disorder. *Journal of the American Medical Association, 268,* 633–638.

Solomon, Z. (1993) *Combat Stress Reaction: The Enduring Toll of War.* New York, Plenum Press.

Solomon, Z., Laor, N., & McFarlane, A.C. (1996). Acute posttraumatic reactions in soldiers and civilians. In B.A. van der Kolk, A.C. McFarlane, and L. Weisath (Eds.), *Traumatic Stress: The Effects of Overwhelming Experience on Mind, Body, and Society* (pp. 102–114). New York: Guildford.

Southwick, S.M., Bremner, D., Krystal, J.H., & Charney, D.S. (1994). Psychobiologic research in post-traumatic stress disorder. *Psychiatric Clinics of North America, 17*(2), 251–264.

Spitz, R.A. (1965). *The First Year of Life. A Psychoanalytic Study of Normal and Deviant Development of Object Relations.* New York: International Universities Press.

Stearns, C.Z. (1993). Sadness. In M. Lewis and J.M. Haviland (Eds.), *Handbook of Emotions,* (pp 547–561). New York: Guildford Press.

Steinberg, A. (1989). Holocaust survivors and their children: A review of the clinical literature. In P. Marcus and A. Rosenberg, (Eds.), *Healing Their Wounds: Psychotherapy with Holocaust Survivors and Their Families* (pp. 23–48). New York: Praeger.

Steklis, H.D., & Kling, A. (1985). Topographically organized midbrain modulation of predatory and defensive aggression in the cat. *Brain Research, 336,* 308–312.

Steptoe, A. (1981). *Psychological Factors in Cardiovascular Disorders.* London: Academic Press.

Stern, D.N. (1984). *The Interpersonal World of the Infant.* New York: Basic Books.

Sternberg, R.J. (Ed.). (1990/1993). *Wisdom: Its Nature, Origins, and Development.* New York: Cambridge University Press.

Sutherland, S.M., & Davidson, J.R.T. (1994). Pharmacotherapy for post-traumatic stress disorder, *Psychiatric Clinics of North America, 17*(2), 409–423.

Sutker, P.B., Uddo, M., Brailey, K., Allain, A.N., & Errera, P. (1994). Psychological symptoms and psychiatric diagnoses in Operation Desert Storm troops serving graves registration duty. *Journal of Traumatic Stress, 7*(2), 159–172.

Tanay, E. (1968). Initiation of psychotherapy with survivors of Nazi persecution. In H. Krystal, (Ed.), *Massive Psychic Trauma* (pp. 219–233). New York: International Universities Press.

Taylor, G.J. (1987). *Psychosomatic Medicine and Contemporary Psychoanalysis.* Madison, CT: International Universities Press.

Terr, L.C. (1987). Childhood psychic trauma. In J.D. Noshpitz (Ed.), *Basic Handbook of Child Psychiatry.* New York: Basic Books.

Terr, L. (1990). *Too Scared to Cry.* New York: Harper and Row.

The New York Review, Crews, F. (1994). The revenge of the repressed. November 17, December 1.

Threlkeld, M.E., & Thyer, B.A. (1992). Sexual and physical abuse histories among child and adolescent psychiatric outpatients. *Journal of Traumatic Stress, 5*(3), 491–496.

Tiger, L., & Fox, R. (1971). *The Imperial Animal.* New York: Holt, Rinehart and Winston.

Tinnin, L. (1994). The double-mindedness of human memory. *ISTSS Stress Points,* Fall, 3.

Toubiana, Y., Milgram, N., & Falach, H. (1986). The stress and coping of uprooted settlers: The Yamit experience. In N.A. Milgram (Ed.), *Stress and Coping in Time of War: Generalizations from the Israeli Experience* (pp. 275–293). New York: Brunner/Mazel.

Trimble, M.R. (1985). Post-traumatic stress disorder: History of a concept. In C. Figley (Ed.), *Trauma and Its Wake: The Study and Treatment of Post-Traumatic Stress Disorder* (pp. 5–14). New York: Brunner/Mazel.

Trivers, R.L. (1971). The evolution of reciprocal altruism. *Quarterly Review of Biology, 46,* 35–57.

Tuchman, B. (1983). *Practising History.* London: Papermac.

Turner, S.W., McFarlane A.C., & van der Kolk, B.A. (1996). The therapeutic environment and new explorations in the treatment of post-traumatic stress disorder. In B.A. van der Kolk, A.C. McFarlane, and L. Weisath (Eds.), *Traumatic Stress: The Effects of Overwhelming Experience on Mind, Body, and Society* (pp. 537–558). New York: Guildford Press.

Tyhurst, J.S. (1957). Psychological and social aspects of civilian disaster. *Canadian Medical Association Journal, 76,* 385–393.

Ursin, H., Baade, E., & Levine, S. (Eds.). (1978). *Psychobiology of Stress. A Study of Coping Men.* New York: Academic Press.

Vaillant, G.E. (1992). *Ego Mechanisms of Defense: A Guide for Clinicians and Researchers.* Washington DC: American Psychiatric Press.

Vaillant, G.E. (1993). *The Wisdom of the Ego.* Cambridge, MA: Harvard University Press.

Valent, P. (1978). Issues with dying patients. *Medical Journal of Australia, 1,* 433–437.

Valent, P. (1979). Management of the dying patient. *Patient Management, March,* 7–9.

Valent, P. (1994a). *Child Survivors: Adults Living with Childhood Trauma.* Melbourne: Heinemann/ Reed Books.

Valent, P. (1994b). A child survivor's appraisal of his own interview. In J.S. Kestenberg and E. Fogelman (Eds.), *Children During the Nazi Reign: Psychological Perspective on the Interview Process* (pp. 12–135). Westport: Praeger.

Valent, P. (1995a). Survival strategies: A framework for understanding secondary traumatic stress and coping in helpers. In C.R. Figley (Ed.), *Compassion Fatigue: Secondary Traumatic Stress Disorder in Helpers* (pp. 21–50). New York: Brunner/Mazel.

Valent, P. (1995b). Documented childhood trauma (Holocaust): Its sequelae and applications to other traumas. *Psychiatry, Psychology, and Law, 2,* 81–89.

Valent, P. (1998a). *From Survival to Fulfillment: A Framework for the Life-Trauma Dialectic.* Washington DC: Taylor & Francis.

Valent, P. (1998b). Child survivors: A review. In J. Kestenberg and C. Kahn (Eds.), *Children Surviving Persecution: An International Study of Trauma and Healing.* New York: Praeger (in press).

Valent, P. (1999). A wholist perspective of compassion fatigue. In C.R. Figley (Ed.), *Treating Compassion Fatigue.* Philadelphia: Brunner/Mazel.

Valent, P., Berah, E., Jones, J., Wraith, R., & Hill, J. (1995). Coping with a major personal crisis. *Australian Red Cross* (pamphlet).

Valent P., Berah E., & Yuen A. (1983). Tullamarine Disaster Exercise (Melbourne: Video).

Valent, P. (1988). Clinical Aspects of Motor Vehicle "Accidents" (Melbourne: unpublished).

van der Hart, O., & Horst, R. (1989). The dissociation theory of Pierre Janet. *Journal of Traumatic Stress, 2*(4), 397–412.

van der Kolk, B.A. (1987). The separation cry and the trauma response: Developmental issues in the psychobiology of attachment and separation. In B.A. van der Kolk (Ed.), *Psychological Trauma* (pp. 31–62). Washington DC: American Psychiatric Press.

van der Kolk, B.A. (1994). The body keeps the score: Memory and the evolving psychobiology of post-traumatic stress. *Harvard Review of Psychiatry, 1,* 253–265.

van der Kolk, B.A. (1996a). The body keeps the score: Approaches to the psychobiology of posttraumatic stress disorder. In B.A. van der Kolk, A.C. McFarlane, and L. Weisath (Eds.), *Traumatic Stress: The Effects of Overwhelming Experience on Mind, Body, and Society.* New York: Guildford Press.

van der Kolk, B.A. (1996b). Trauma and memory. In B.A. van der Kolk, A.C. McFarlane, and L. Weisath (Eds.), *Traumatic Stress: The Effects of Overwhelming Experience on Mind, Body, and Society* (pp. 279–302). New York: Guildford Press.

van der Kolk, B.A., Boyd, H., Krystal, J., & Greenberg, M. (1984). Post-traumatic stress disorder as a biologically based disorder: Implications of the animal model of inescapable shock. In B.A. van der Kolk (Ed.), *Post-Traumatic Stress Disorder: Psychological and Biological Sequelae* (pp. 123–134). Washington DC: American Psychiatric Press.

van der Kolk, B.A., Brown, P., & van der Hart, O. (1989). Pierre Janet on post-traumatic stress. *Journal of Traumatic Stress, 2*(4), 365–378.

van der Kolk, B.A., & Fisler, R. (1995). Dissociation and the fragmentary nature of traumatic memories: Overview and exploratory study. *Journal of Traumatic Stress, 8*(4), 505–526.

van der Kolk, B.A., & Greenberg, M.S. (1987). The psychobiology of the trauma response: Hyperarousal, constriction, and addiction to traumatic reexposure. In B.A. van der Kolk (Ed.), *Psychological Trauma* (pp. 63–88). Washington DC: American Psychiatric Press.

van der Kolk, B.A., & McFarlane, A.C. (1996). The black hole of trauma. In B.A. van der Kolk, A.C. McFarlane, and L. Weisath (Eds.), *Traumatic Stress: The Effects of Overwhelming Experience on Mind, Body, and Society* (pp. 3–23). New York: Guildford Press.

van der Kolk, B.A., McFarlane, A.C., & van der Hart, O. (1996). A general approach to treatment of posttraumatic stress disorder. In B.A. van der Kolk, A.C. McFarlane, and L. Weisath (Eds.), *Traumatic Stress: The Effects of Overwhelming Experience on Mind, Body, and Society* (pp. 417–440). New York: Guildford Press.

Vargas, L.A., Loya, F., & Hodde-Vargas, J. (1989). Exploring the multidimensional aspects of grief reactions. *American Journal of Psychiatry, 146*(11), 1484–1488.

Wallace, A.F.C. (1957). Mazeway disintegration: The individual's perception of socio-cultural disorganization. *Human Organization, 16,* 23–27.

Walsh, A. (1991). *Intellectual Imbalance, Love Deprivation, and Violent Delinquency.* Springfield, IL: Charles Thomas.

Weiner, H. (1977). Psychobiological contributions to human disease. Summary and conclusions. In *Psychobiology and Human Disease* (pp. 82–85). New York: Elsevier, North–Holland.

Weisaeth, L., & Eitinger, L. (1993). Post-traumatic stress phenomena: Common themes across wars, disasters, and traumatic events. In J. Wilson and B. Raphael (Eds.), *International Handbook of Traumatic Stress Syndromes* (pp. 69–78). New York: Plenum.

Williams, M.B. (1995). Establishing safety in survivors of severe sexual abuse. In M.B. Williams and J.F. Sommer Jr. (Eds.), *Handbook of Post-Traumatic Therapy* (pp. 162–178). Westport, CT: Greenwood Press.

Wilson, E.O. (1975). *Sociobiology.* Cambridge, MA: The Belknap Press of Harvard University Press.

Wilson, J.P. (1989). Culture and trauma: The sacred pipe revisited. In J.P. Wilson (Ed.), *Trauma, Transformation and Healing: An Integrative Approach to Theory, Research, and Post-Traumatic Therapy* (pp. 38–71). New York: Brunner/Mazel.

Wilson, J.P., & Lindy, J.D. (1994). Empathic strain and countertransference. In J.P. Wilson and J.D. Lindy (Eds.), *Countertransference in the Treatment of PTSD.* New York, London: Guildford Press.

Wilson J. P., Lindy, J.D., & Raphael, B. (1994). Empathic strain and therapist defense: Type I and II countertransference reactions. In J.P. Wilson and J.D. Lindy (Eds.), *Countertransference in the Treatment of PTSD.* New York, London: The Guildford Press.

Winnicott, D.W. (1960a). The theory of the parent-infant relationship. *International Journal of Psychoanalysis, 41,* 585–595.

Winnicott, D.W. (1960b/1982). Ego distortion in terms of true and false self. In J.S. Sutherland (Ed.), *The Maturational Processes and the Facilitating Environment* (pp. 140–152). London: Hogarth Press and the Institute of Psychoanalysis.

Wolpe, J. (1958). *Psychotherapy by Reciprocal Inhibition.* Stanford: Stanford University Press.

Yahr, P. (1983). Hormonal influences on shock-induced fighting. In B.B. Svare (Ed.), *Hormones and Aggressive Behavior.* New York: Plenum Press.

Yahr, P. (1983). Hormonal influences on shock-induced fighting. In B.B. Svare (Ed.), *Hormones and Aggressive Behavior.* New York: Plenum Press.

Yehuda, R., & McFarlane, A.C. (1995). Conflict between current knowledge about PTSD and its original conceptual basis. *American Journal of Psychiatry, 152,* 1705–1713.

Yehuda, R., Southwick, S.M., Mason, J.W., & Giller, F.M. (1990). Interactions of the hypothalamic-pituitary-adrenal axis and the catecholaminergic system of the stress disorder. In E.L. Giller (Ed.), *Biological Assessment and Treatment of PTSD* (pp. 115–134). Washington DC: American Psychiatric Press.

Young, B., & Black, D. (1997). Bereavement counselling. In D. Black, M. Newman, J. Harris-Hendriks, and G. Mezey (Eds.), *Psychological Trauma* (pp. 250–263) London: Gaskell.

Young, M.A. (1988). Support services for victims. In F.M. Ochberg (Ed.), *Post-Traumatic Therapy and Victims of Violence* (pp. 330–351). New York: Brunner/Mazel.

Youniss, J. (1986). Development in reciprocity through friendship. In C. Zahn-Waxler, E.M. Cummings, and R. Iannotti (Eds.), *Altruism and Aggression (Biological and Social Origins)* (pp. 88–106). Cambridge: Cambridge University Press.

Zahn-Waxler, C., Cummings, E.M., & Iannotti, R. (1986). Introduction. In C. Zahn-Waxler, E.M. Cummings and R. Iannotti (Eds.), *Altruism and Aggression (Biological and Social Origins)* (pp. 1–18). Cambridge: Cambridge University Press.

Zaidi, L.Y., & Foy, D.W. (1994). Childhood abuse experiences and combat-related PTSD. *Journal of Traumatic Stress, 7*(1), 33–42.

Subject Index

substitution, 98, 129
as symbols, 129
Symptoms, psychophysiological, 5, 6, 30,
116, 124, 127. *See also* Physiological
responses
in adaptation, 53
in assertiveness, 51
in attachment, 48
in cooperation, 64
in fight, 57, 124–125
in flight, 58, 59
hyperventilation, 114, 127
Synthesis, 39

Territoriality, 50, 56
Terror, 44, 58, 59
frozen, 58, 104, 149
Terrorization, 44, 61. *See also* Intimidation
Therapy, *see* Treatment
Thinking, 89
Thought field therapy (TFT), 19–20
Threats, 44, 56
Time relativity, 115
Torture, 15
Training, 32
Transference, 10, 21, **73,** 89, 98, 124, 125,
139, 143–144, 162, 166
Transference cures, 10, 19, 90, 99
Transgenerational. *See also* Second
generation
grief symptoms, 54
history taking, 72
transfer of symptoms, 109
stressors, 29
vulnerabilities, 31, 141, 161
Trauma, **32,** 122
in adaptation, 53
anxieties, categorization, 77
in assertiveness, 51
in attachment, 48, 74, 110, 116, 118
as collapse of the self, 32
in competition, 61
component of process axis, 28, 29
in cooperation, 64
cosmology, 38–39
definition, 4, 32
depth axis, 47, 49, 52, 55, 58, 60, 63
in flight, 59, 110
history of, 72
in human function levels, 37–40
as human nightmares, 37
and judgments, *see* Judgments

in life-trauma dialectic, 3
and meaning 32, 127. *See also* Meaning
ramifications, 135–152
recognition, 69–85. *See also* Recognition
reliving, *see* Reliving
remembering *See* Memories
in rescue, 46, 119, 120
specific treatment of, 91–95. *See also*
Treatment, specific
story, *see* Narrative
and stress, 30, 124, 126
Trauma Survivors Anonymous, 14
Traumatic incident reduction (TIR), 19
Traumatic situations, 11–16, 32, 118–122,
142
component of parameter axis, 28, 36
factors in, 28
phases of, 28, 36
challenges and cultures in, 36
treatments in different, 11–16
Traumatic state, 32
Traumatic stress
categorization of manifestations, 77
definition, 28
honing of manifestations, 76–77
introduction, 1
sense of manifestations, 75–76
Traumatization, 32
vicarious, 22
Traumatology:
"appendix" in, 91, 168
definition, ix
irrationality in, 91, 168–169
primary task of, 34
team in emergency department, 117–118
and trauma, 32
and wholist perspective, 167
Treatment, therapy. *See also* Treatment,
according to traumatic situations,
Treatment methods, Treatment,
nonspecific, Treatment principles,
Treatment, specific, Treatment,
symptomatic
acute, 113–117, 118–119
of defenses, 107–108
fulfillment, 93–94, 111–112, 163
along depth axis, 108–110, 121
drugs, *see* Drug treatment
of helpers, 156–163
insight, 91
of judgments, 84, 128, 131
line, 82–83, 97–98, 166
of meanings, 84, 128

Name Index

Abse, D.W., 9, 11
Adam (biblical), xii
Adamczak, K., 61
Ahearn, F.L., 14
Albeck, J.H., 13
Alexander, F., 49
Allain, A.N., 54
Allen, J.G., 48
American Psychiatric Association, 4, 28, 34, 35
Appels, A., 51, 62
Ardrey, R., 55
Aristotle, 37
Athens, L.H., 57, 58
Auerhahn, N.C., 33, 35

Baade, E., 50
Bailey, S.L., 57
Barefoot, J.C., 57
Barker, P., 11
Bartemeier, L.H., 11, 51
Bartrop, R.W., 30, 53
Batson, C.D., 45, 47
Bauer, M., 61
Baum, A., 28
Becker, E., 3
Bemis, C. 54
Benyakar, M., 32
Berah, E., 5, 113, 155
Bergman, M.S., 13
Bettelheim, B., 53
Black, D., 16
Black, P.H., 59
Blanchard, D.C., 61
Blanchard, R.J., 61

Bloch, H.S., 12
Boakes, J., 34
Boman, B., 51
Booth, A., 61
Bowlby, J., 47, 49, 52, 55
Boyd, H., 59
Brailey, K., 54
Brainerd, C.J., 36
Brandon, S., 34
Braun, B.G., 33, 35
Bremner, J. D., 17, 30, 34, 168
Brende, J.O., 14
Brett, E.A., 34
Breuer, J., 10, 33, 60
Briere, J., 21
Brom, D., 10, 19, 20, 21, 22
Brown, P., 32
Browning, C.R., 56, 57
Brutus, M., 50
Burgess, A.W., 14
Busuttil, A., 14
Busuttil, W., 14

Calabrese, J.R., 30, 53
Callahan, R.J., 19
Cameron-Bandler, L., 19
Canetti, E., 58
Cannon, W.B., 30
Carbonell, J.L., 19
Carr, V.J., 18
Carter, G.L., 18
Cashman, L., 20
Charcot, J.M., 9
Charney, D.S., 30, 168
Chester, B., 15

225

Cases Index

Index of Figures and Tables